Ian R N

CW00872152

Pan' e Pomodor
My Passage To Puglia

Pan' e Pomodor - My Passage to Puglia

ISBN 978-1-4303-2583-3

Second edition

Copyright © Ian R McEwan 2011

The right of Ian R McEwan to be identified as the author of this work has been asserted in accordance with sections 77 and 78 of the Copyright Designs and Patents Act 1988.

Some of the names in this book are fictional.

This book is sold subject to the condition that it shall not by way of trade or otherwise, be lent, re-sold, hired out or otherwise circulated in any form of binding or cover other than that in which it is published and without a similar condition including this condition being imposed on the subsequent purchaser.

Cover artwork and photography by Margherita McEwan

ianrmcewan@gmail.com

For Margherita

Preface

The text includes words in Italian and in the dialect of Vico del Gargano. I spell the Italian words true to the language whereas I write the dialect words in a form to make them intelligible by English speakers who should be able to pronounce the words.

The locals write the dialect using Italian spelling and phonetics - a form that would be rather difficult to pronounce.

For the *appassionati* the dialect should be pronounced with passion, almost sung à la *fortepiano*.

Contents

Part I - Pan' e Pomodor

Pan' e Pomodor

The old man, warned by his barking dog, turned to face us. His weathered features were as gnarled as the olive trees we had seen along the route. Considering the conditions he looked rather odd dressed in a jacket, buttoned up to the collar, his head protected by a snug fitting beret.

We were just entering the outskirts of Vico del Gargano in the gathering dusk when our car was forced to a crawl by the shadowy figures ahead.

He was sitting side-saddle on a donkey, his weight counter-balanced by a swaying load of wood on which a mongrel terrier was perilously perched. A small herd of goats trailed behind him.

He growled something at the goats then waved us on with a broad smile. His mouth was almost devoid of teeth; those that remained seemed in more risk of spilling out than the dog did of tumbling from its perch.

Where on Earth was she taking me?

~~~

The year was 1981, shortly after Margaret and I were married. Like myself, Margaret was born in Scotland but her roots are in Italy. Her father came from this small town in the Gargano, the spur of Italy's heel. She had taken her first steps and spoken her first words here.

When Margaret was born, her parents, who hardly spoke a word of English, gave her name as Margherita. The Scottish registrar produced a birth certificate bearing the name Margaret. So, until she married, she bore an Italian surname with a very non-Italian, diminutive laden forename.

Outside the family, friends referred to her as Margaret or Maggie

1

- her former flatmates managed to derive other unflattering forms that I won't repeat here. Within the family, she is Margherita, Rita or even simply "Ree". Spoilt for choice and not wishing to add to her identity crisis, I call her "*M*".

In the months leading up to our marriage *M* took me to visit her family in the UK on a number of occasions and invariably, as is the Italian way, food played a major role. The meals were always excellent, as *M*'s mother Emilia is an accomplished cook. The accompanying wine was a new experience for me. *M*'s father Vincenzo made his own wine from Italian grapes. *Vino Naturale* he called it.

However, the meals were more memorable for the conversations. Unless they were talking to me, Vincenzo and Emilia always spoke Italian and generally, their three daughters replied in English. I tried to keep up with this multi-channel conversation by asking *M* what they had said, but if the explanation ever came things had moved on. So, much of my time at these family meals was spent in a state of semi-comprehension only relieved by a refilled glass of red, no black, *Vino Naturale*.

How could it be? In the seventies, I had spent some time consulting to the computer manufacturer Olivetti at their headquarters in Ivrea near Turin, and to make things easier (especially in the restaurants) I had learnt some basic Italian. It was puzzling that I never understood any Italian words that Vincenzo and Emilia uttered.

~~~

It was mid-afternoon on a hot June day. We had just left Bologna after visiting *M*'s grandparents and other relatives. In the city the atmosphere was stifling, they called it *afa*, and all we wanted to do was get into the car to move some air.

We headed down the A14 motorway towards the south east of Italy. A little over an hour later we passed Rimini where we left the steaming Po valley. By this time the car was an oven and the *autostrada* a cauldron. We hoped that the coast road would bring some relief.

M had made this journey nearly every year of her life with her family. Like so many other Italian migrants, they returned to their natural home each summer. Luckily, *M* assured me, the traffic was light compared to the August stampede and we were making good time.

After the straights of Emilia Romagna the motorway twists its way down the Adriatic coast, shooting through tunnels and flying over deep valleys – at times an awesome feat of engineering. However, we saw little of the scenery. The heat haze obscured much from our view; we could barely make out hilltop villages unless they were literally on top of the motorway.

The traffic eased as we progressed through the Marche, Abruzzo, Molise and by the time we entered the plains of Puglia it was virtually non-existent. As the motorway straightened the intense heat resurfaced from the tarmac but despite the high temperature the motorway was a pleasure to drive, made even pleasanter by the tidy central reservation lined with Oleanders in full bloom - much easier on the eye than debris, litter and weeds found on the UK motorways.

Soon after joining the plain we reached the exit at Poggio Imperiale, some 300 miles south of Bologna - a four-hour drive with a short stop for petrol. There was nothing at the imperiously named Poggio, just a tollbooth whose shelter gave very little relief from the heat. My eyes were smarting, my clothes sticking to my skin. I felt uncomfortable and so far south, a little exposed. The surly service of the attendant in the booth didn't help.

We headed east along a superstrada, sandwiched between the Adriatic, hidden by the haze somewhere to our north, and white slag heaps of stone quarries to our south. As we sped across the plain, passing field after field of tomatoes, melons and salad crops, the pickers were just finishing their day's labour and trucks were departing with the produce for the next day's markets.

The road began to roller coaster leaving the productive monotony of the flat behind and as the haze lifted with the onset of cooler air, a mountainous landscape emerged ahead of us. The terrain changed; it was uncultivated, desolate, stony and most of it overgrown with gorse and fenced only by impenetrable *fichi d'India* - prickly pear plants.

Nobody seemed to live in this inhospitable terrain anymore - it seemed that people had long abandoned the few buildings we saw and now most of these were derelict.

With the changing landscape, the free-flowing *superstrada* began to clog and progress slowed as we encountered clusters of trucks, vans and campervans. Occasionally the pace would wither even further as the convoy attempted to pass one of the many *treruote* (a

3

three wheeler motorbike with a cab and a pickup rear) weighed down with wood or some other commodity heading home at a snail's pace after a day's enterprise.

Impatient car drivers woke us from a motion-induced state of security. They showed no fear jockeying for position to overtake the slow moving traffic as close to bends as they possibly could. Oncoming drivers performed similar feats as they turned a two-lane road into a three-lane death trap. At intervals battered and twisted sections of roadside barrier bore testimony to some very eccentric driving.

After negotiating a headland we began a long descent, hugging the steep rocky foothills to our south. Far below, towards the Adriatic, we could make out Lago di Varano, one of two salt-water lakes, each separated from the sea by narrow spits. We saw the first signs of habitation. The map, which did not show the new *superstrada*, revealed three villages ahead - Cagnano Varano, Carpino, and Ischitella.

M pointed to the highest village. "That's Ischitella; we have to head for there."

We flashed through a tunnel under the suburbs of Cagnano and when we emerged the barren landscape gave way to olive plantations as far as the eye could see. Straight ahead and below, was Carpino, seemingly carved from the hillside, its houses smouldering in the fading light. Beyond lay the improbable Ischitella, a jigsaw of white buildings clinging to the hillside still bathed in sunshine.

A few minutes after passing Carpino the *superstrada* came to an abrupt end and we started a steep, twisty ascent to Ischitella some 300 metres above. As we passed through the village the light was fading but the streets were alive. It was still very hot and the inhabitants had abandoned their houses to take advantage of whatever evening cool they could find.

From Ischitella we continued the ascent for another 15 minutes, or so, and then the silhouette of the historic quarter of Vico del Gargano came into view dominated by the dome of the Chiesa Madre (Mother Church) and the square tower of the fairy-tale castle of the Della Bella family. The sun was setting behind us and, at last, cool air was breezing into the car.

~~~

The first sign of life was the old man, cautiously dressed against the evening cool of the open countryside at 500 metres. His goats didn't seem at all phased by our hot engine pursuing them or his gruff commands - it was their road and we had to squeeze by as best we could.

We passed a sign welcoming us to Vico del Gargano in four languages: Italian, German, English and French. The sign, as weathered as the old man's face, was a European Community initiative that seemingly served as a target for local youths toting pellet guns.

Tall blocks of flats flanked the road instantly eliminating the memory of the first sighting of the picturesque old town. Vico now seemed dark and ominous; there was little street lighting and the buildings had blocked out the setting sun's rays. We ground to a halt on the approach to a roundabout. The community was out in force on foot, on donkey, riding 2, 3 or 4-wheeled vehicles.

"Does that man need a licence to drive a rotavator?" I mused.

The cool air evaporated as we sat motionless, absorbing the heat of the day trapped in the street by the apartment blocks as if they were giant night storage heaters.

Unwittingly, we had managed to get ourselves caught up in the queue for a petrol station, bizarrely situated on the roundabout. We signalled to extract ourselves, but no one was going to let us out. Horns were blasting and whistles blowing as the police tried to disengage the traffic. The old man on the donkey overtook us riding boldly into the mayhem, his horned goats neatly threading their way through the motorised obstacles, his dog watching their every move.

Taking advantage of their wake we nudged out and negotiated our way on to the roundabout, where we became another log in the jam as vehicles vied for position on the grid and pedestrians weaved in and out of the gaps. All were taking advantage of my lack of local knowledge. This was a roundabout with only one rule - give way to those entering it.

I had hesitated as *M* urged me on. "It's your right of way."

The police whistled at me and gesticulated that I should move on, but where to? Eventually they physically intervened, dispersed the unruly rabble ahead of us and we edged sheepishly off the roundabout.

The street we entered worked little better than the roundabout as a river of people flowed along the course where cars ought to have been.

"*Lo Striscio* - the shuffle," explained *M*. The local population was out for a walk, arms linked, their defensive walls spanned the road, and the traffic could go to hell! We carefully navigated through the masses and as familiar landmarks refreshed *M*'s memory she directed me to take a tight right hand turn. We plunged down a hill for ten metres, turned sharp left, nearly demolished a public water fountain, and then continued the descent until we reached a fork in the road.

M directed me left, it was dark and the heat seemed to intensify along with the smell of the drains. We passed into a narrow street with steps of all sizes protruding at every conceivable angle preventing direct passage. After 50 metres we reached an impasse. The road became a staircase. This journey's end.

~~~

Travel-weary and slightly unnerved by our downtown Vico experience we eased our sticky stiff bodies out of the car. The street was deserted but our arrival stirred a household; the beaded fly-screen in a doorway near the car rattled and split open. In the backlight from the house I could make out the face of an old woman, dressed in black, her hands securing a hastily donned headscarf. All that was missing were the dangling hooped earrings and a crystal ball.

I thought she was about to tell us the obvious - that we'd taken the wrong street - when *M* called out, "Antonietta, *ciao*." The old woman's face beamed, once again revealing that a dentist would do well in Vico.

Antonietta called to someone in the house as she made her way down the steps to give *M* a long affectionate hug, showering her with kisses. A man's disembodied face appeared through the fly-screen, "What's up?" or something to that effect he inquired. The old woman said, "*Y'eh Margherit'.*" He too descended into the street, dressed in working boots, trousers and vest and gave *M* a warm welcome.

These two old people then turned their attention to me. "Who was I?" I assumed they were asking. *M* introduced Antonietta and her husband Tittino; they in turn gave me a kind of a bear hug and kisses on both cheeks followed by what I took as a look of approval. Then they turned their attention back to *M*, Antonietta grasping her hand.

"*Trash, trash,*" I heard as they beckoned to us making signs that we should enter the house. "*Trash, trash?*" I pondered. What on earth are they saying?

M was resisting. "*No, no, non vogliamo disturbare.*"

"*Tenet' fam'? Trash, trash ama man'yah,*" Tittino insisted. *M* translated. They'd asked if we were hungry, insisted that we go in and eat. *M* said that we didn't want to disturb them especially as they were still eating, but they wouldn't take no for an answer. With little resistance we relented and entered the house.

"So what's this 'trash, trash'?" I asked, but there was too much bustle for me to get an answer.

Tittino led me up the steps into a vaulted room about 5 metres square. I cricked my neck to admire a fresco high above in the centre of the ceiling then my gaze dropped to absorb the unusual layout of the room.

We had entered through the front door in the corner of the room. Directly in front of me sideboards lined the wall. To their right, a rectangular table with six chairs crammed up against some armchairs, which in turn lined up against the foot of a large curtained bed. The whole giving the semblance of an orderly queue from left to right: storage, table, armchairs and bed - lay the table, eat, sit and sleep.

Tittino ushered me to a place at the table, whilst pulling his braces over wide lean shoulders. He sat at the head with his back to a cast iron stove, with me at his right hand. Antonietta cleared a little debris from their meal to make space and laid plates and glasses. Tittino poured the wine from a 2-litre bottle - it was black.

"*Salout*!" he toasted our health.

We chinked glasses and drank. It was *Vino Naturale* he insisted, "*y'eh bo'ohn?*" It was indeed *buono*, but it was a lot harsher than the wine I had drunk with Vincenzo.

Antonietta was quizzing *M*. From her actions I assumed she was asking her if we wanted something to eat or drink. Then she launched an avalanche of catch-up-on-family-news questions as she scuttled round the room tidying. My gaze followed her and fell on the massive expanse of mahogany wardrobe that flanked the bed just as she was pulling a vast curtain across the room, screening off the bedroom area.

I submitted to a familiar incomprehension as the conversation went far beyond simple enquiry about *M*'s family. The only sure thing was that the language they spoke resembled that spoken by *M*'s parents and it wasn't Italian.

Antonietta simultaneously busied herself stocking the table from the sideboards; scurrying in and out of the tiniest kitchen behind me and emerging with all sorts of jars and bottles until there was very little room left on the table.

There were olives, sun-dried tomatoes in oil, green things in oil (which had to be chillies), ripe plum tomatoes, anchovies and a big bottle of olive oil. Tittino pointed at everything and made a gesture that I should eat. He took a half-moon of bread out of a plastic bag hooked on the back of his chair and placed it so that one point on the circumference was tight to his vest and, with a large carving knife, began sawing towards his body. He deftly took off a slice the length of my forearm and placed it in front of me.

I took another sip of wine, as it seemed the easiest thing to do - wash away the journey. Meanwhile Tittino took a great ball of cheese from the table and holding it in the palm of his hand he sliced off a round and handed it to me. This was more familiar territory, although I was still hesitant. The cheese had a pungent smell; in fact all sorts of unfamiliar odours were beginning to have an effect as Antonietta continued to load the table.

Tittino urged me to try the cheese. He made a gesture, pressing and twisting his index finger into his cheek while saying '*buono, buono*'.

"At last some Italian," I thought.

My relief was to be short-lived. He downed his glass and re-filled it as I tried the cheese. It tingled on the tongue, it was strong, it had an animal smell - it was good; it was *piccante*; it softened the wine; it made me drink!

"*Che formaggio e?*" I boldly practiced my scant Italian on Tittino, as *M* continued to answer Antonietta's myriad of questions.

"*Cash'e-cavadd,*" he replied cutting off another chunk.

I continued to eat the cheese, non-the wiser. As I pondered what he had said, I bit off a piece that was completely different in texture, sort of gritty and stale. I wanted to spit it out, but I managed to swallow it with a gulp of wine. *M* noticed my discomfort - I had eaten the rind, the skin of the cheese that all and sundry handle.

Antonietta now turned her attention to me. "Why was Eeeaann not eating?" She motioned to the slice of bread on the table in front of me and handed me the tomatoes. "*Mahnj', mahnj',*" she urged. I gestured that I was fine, but she wouldn't hear of it. She took the bread in one hand, sliced some tomatoes in half and rubbed the pulp into the bread on both sides, applied a little salt and then drizzled olive oil liberally over the top and handed it to me.

"What, soggy bread? No I can't eat that! I've never eaten soggy bread!" I pleaded with *M* for help.

"Try it," *M* urged.

Antonietta and Tittino seemed instinctively to sense my plight. "Hadn't I ever eaten *Pan' e Pomodor*?"

I succumbed. Using both hands to level the long slice of bread, I tentatively bit off a chunk. Olive oil dribbled down my fingers and fell on to the table. The crust was not so soggy; it wasn't that bad. I took another bite as they all watched me. The centre was much soggier, but yes, I could confirm to them that it was indeed '*buono*'. They seemed satisfied. Tittino busied himself slicing the whole loaf while Antonietta ladled olives and peppers onto a plate.

I made my way slowly through the *pan' e pomodor* and was surprised how the combination of the cheese, the preserves and the oily tomato soaked bread worked.

In the thick of this banquet children began to appear. They buzzed around the table picking off food as they went. *M* was re-familiarizing herself with who they all were, while also trying to sneak a little to eat.

The children must have spread the news of our arrival, as other adults began to visit - by this time Eeeaann had become Gianni, as they all seemed to struggle with my name (they'd heard of English John for Giovanni, but never Scottish Ian so we settled for Gianni). Each was introduced to me and, in that very British way, I stumbled around not knowing whether to embrace these strangers or just shake hands - I let them lead. As for their names, I simply couldn't keep track.

As the evening drew on I found myself sitting at a men-only table with a women and children audience on the boundaries. One of the women was breast-feeding a child - our unfamiliarity not, apparently, making the slightest bit of difference.

I had eaten my share, but with the flow of wine it was still difficult to refuse olives in brine, olives in vinegar, olives in oil with all kinds of herbs. Everything was homemade, home grown, or both - except for the bread. However Tittino's son-in-law, Franco, was by now sitting next to me. He was the baker, just having a coffee before he went off to work.

"*Confusione, confusione*," Tittino kept on apologising to me in Italian with an air of inevitability and a broad smile on his face. Well there was no misunderstanding there. Every now and again he would show his authority and cuff one of the kids or bark some order at them in the local dialect, but the *confusione* carried on despite his clout.

After the long journey, the wine and the food, I felt the call of nature. Eventually I plucked up courage and asked the whereabouts of the toilet. Antonietta led me out into the street to a door directly opposite their front door. She turned on the light and I found myself in her storeroom, full of bottles of preserves, containers, baskets, bottles of wine and all manner of bric-a-brac. The toilet was in the corner. She fussed about a little and then left me to it.

When I emerged, Antonietta was sitting on her steps opposite talking to one of the little urchins. She beckoned me back into the house - obviously she had kept guard on the unlocked door.

Tittino welcomed me back with another glass. He was running the show, his whole family (at least I thought it was) gathered in the room that formed his house; there were sons and daughters, grandchildren, nephews and nieces. He held his full head of hair high; his thick-rimmed bi-focal glasses perched on the end of a large Roman nose supported by a thick moustache. This was his domain; his table and he wanted to share it with two special guests.

One by one he took the photographs off the wall. There was one of him and Antonietta when they were young; in their kind old faces the youthful resemblance was good, but what sort of life had weathered these two old people who were once so handsome? He showed me a picture of his donkey Rosina. The implication, as I understood it, was that a man here without a donkey was nobody. As I admired the picture of a broad-smiling Tittino standing with his donkey next to an immaculate dry-stone wall, he disappeared outside and in little time reappeared at the door with the beast as if to prove that she really existed. It was time to go!

We tried to extract ourselves, but it became obvious that signalling our attention to leave was only a token offer that our hosts met with a further bombardment of refreshment. Antonietta swamped the table with bottles: grappa, brandy, whisky, and cool *limoncino*. Of course, Antonietta had made the lemon liqueur herself so we had to try it. We toasted each other, toasted the *limoncino*, toasted Rosina ... it seemed we would never leave, but eventually, with embraces and promises to return, we departed.

~~~

Before we left Vico that evening, we went to visit *M*'s great uncle and aunt, Zio Tommaso and Zia Masuccia. We left the car outside Antonietta's and walked far enough up the street for *M* to explain that Tittino and Antonietta were not relatives, just old friends of the family.

We turned up some steps, which paradoxically were wider than the street we had driven down earlier.

"That's where the loo used to be!" *M* pointed out a tiny door under some external stairs and went on to enlighten me. "It was once the only one in the street and one of the first in Vico. No running water or light though. We had to take a candle and flush with a jug from a large bucket of water."

As we climbed the steep staircase that arched the loo, I felt fortunate to have used Antonietta's mod cons.

Her great uncle and aunt's house was again a single room with kitchen, dining and bedroom space tightly fitted in. The ceiling was timber-beamed with whitewashed boards contrasting the splendour of Tittino and Antonietta's impeccably plastered and frescoed stone arched vault. The scene here with this gentle elderly couple was very much calmer, although other relations had heard of our arrival and popped in to say hello.

With these duties over, we embraced and departed. Sadly, it was the last time that we would see Zio Tommaso.

~~~

We managed to navigate out of nighttime Vico, now quieter and enjoying much cooler evening air, and descended the 500 metres to the seaside village of Rodi Garganico where it was still very warm. We had arranged to stay at a villa in an orange grove belonging to *M*'s Zio Franco and Zia Rosa and had picked up the keys from her uncle and aunt in Bologna.

In the days that followed, we soaked up the sunshine at the villa or went down to the beach. We picked peaches, cherries and loquats from the trees surrounding the villa. There were abundant lemons and although the orange season was officially over there was still plenty of ripe fruit for juicing. We went to market and tried out the local restaurants freshly opened for the summer season. It was very quiet considering the warm summer weather. There were very few Italian visitors and we only encountered one or two Dutch or German camper vans on the roads.

It was a time of reflection. With the visit to Vico, I had experienced Vincenzo's dialect, Vicaiolo, first hand. I imagined it must be like going to Newcastle after marrying into a Geordie family.

11

I had enjoyed the unreserved welcome from its generous people, although the *confusione* was a bit much to handle.

Vico had also come as a complete surprise. In all the months leading up to our visit, *M* had never revealed a detail about it.

In the evenings, we drove up to Vico, walked around the Centro Storico and visited other relatives. I was fascinated. It was like stepping back in time. If there hadn't been any cars, and the ones that were there would have long been consigned to the scrap heap anywhere else in Europe, it could have been another century. There was no doubt that its people were poor in this material world, but it was abundantly clear they were rich in many other ways.

Apart from historic villages, the Gargano had forested mountains, mile upon mile of rugged but beautiful coastline. It had its own enigmatic language. The food was refreshingly simple, but truly flavourful. The wine was harsh, peasant-like but honest. It was a secret paradise.

Vico and Rodi were captivating - both a fusion of ancient houses, narrow streets, alleys, stairways and rainwater gullies. Their centres filled with bakers, butchers, delicatessens, *pasticcerie*, tailors, shoemakers, barbers and bars. Each day we could buy fruit, vegetables and locally caught fish at the market. It was refreshing in a supermarket age.

I loved it - *M* always had.

We considered that it would be a wonderful place to live - charming people, authentic food, natural wine and, of course, sunshine. But could we just abandon the UK?

Yes, on the one hand, property was cheap - according to Vincenzo, they couldn't give it away. The cost of living was incomparable even if expressed in millions. Surely it would be easy?

On the other hand, no, we were too realistic. There was no living to be made from olives, oranges and lemons. How would we pay the bills without income? And anyway, it was just too remote and for me the strange language seemed an insurmountable barrier.

We departed for Rome with the seed of a dream quietly germinating in our hearts.

Vicaiolo - The Dialect

In those first few hours at Vico, I had been thoroughly immersed in Vicaiolo, the local dialect, literally thrown in at the deep end. Unlike being at Vincenzo's house, where they at least spoke some English with only a modicum of *confusione*, this was the real thing. But it wasn't so much what they said but how they talked – it was the tone of the dialect that struck me the most.

For a start, their voices boomed; they didn't have a conversation - they contested it. The synchronized hand motions and emotional delivery were very Italian but the sound was far harsher, though it had a melodious rhythm, for they seemed to sing the words with combined joy, lamentation and anger.

But why Vicaiolo? Why not Garganese? *M* explained that every village had its own dialect. The people from Rodi and Ischitella speak their own dialects and apparently, they are significantly different from Vicaiolo. This I found difficult to believe for villages only a few kilometres apart - we have dialects in the UK but it's hard to imagine that the folks in Newcastle speak a different dialect to their neighbours across the river Tyne in Gateshead!

The first dialect word I learnt was *cash'e-cavadd*. The Italian name for this tongue-tickling cheese is *caciocavallo*; literally horse cheese, but it's made from cow's milk. Makers form the cheese by hand into a ball and hang it with a piece of string - the hanging process leaves a knob on top. The cheese got the name, supposedly, because people used to carry them into the countryside with two or more roped together at the knob straddling the saddle on the back of a horse, mule or donkey.

Then there was *mahnj'* which means eat, derived from the Italian verb *mangiare*. It seemed to me that most words in the dialect were, in some way, curtailed or the endings were emphasised, but I was failing to pick out any rules. *Mahnj* would be pronounced "*mahnj'uh*" by some and "*mahn'yuh*" by others.

During our visit with Tittino and Antonietta I was invited time and time again to have "*na tzek d'uh voyn - un po' di vino* - a little wine." I had this expression off pat by the end of the evening; but there would be variations that I would have to cope with as the various visitors jostled to teach me their language: "*n'ah gotch d'uh voyn - una goccia di vino* - a drop of wine"; "*noo boo'kweer d'uh voyn - un bichiere di vino* - a glass of wine."

This only added to the *confusione* at the table; the assembled, adults and children alike were undoubtedly enjoying my predicament as I tried to parrot the phrases. I struggled, I couldn't help feeling that there simply were no rules; everyone seemed to pronounce the same phrase differently. It was subtle, but definitely different. How many ways were there to say 'have some more wine?'

In fact there seemed to be widespread divergence and even disagreement on pronunciation, which may account for the phrase "*ah capoyt? - hai capito?* - understood?" which was used constantly. They would say something like "Today, I went to the beach - *ah capoyt?*" as if there could be some doubt in what they had said. But, instead of pronouncing "*ah capoyt?*" some would pronounce it "*ah capout?*"

When I challenged *M* to clarify this contradiction I was in for a surprise. Vicaiolo had a dialect within the dialect - there was high Vicaiolo and low Vicaiolo - a class distinction that not only permeated through the language but also surfaced in the Vichesi attitudes to each other.

Low Vicaiolo was spoken in poorer areas of the Centro Storico and was considered coarser - they would say "*ah capout?*" or "*man-yuh*". Whereas Vichesi, who considered themselves well-to-do spoke a more refined dialect "*ah capoyt?*" or "*manj*", which *M* suggested was closer to the pronunciation in Italian.

She went on to explain that the discrimination manifested itself in many ways, but none more obvious than the hand of marriage. Perhaps not these days, but not so long ago a high Vichese would not even consider marrying a low Vichese.

Despite these undertones, I found the language charming and lyrical and I just wanted to know more. I dismissed the discrimination as a legacy of the past - surely these people, who while seemingly poor but so generous, couldn't treat each other with such disdain.

~~~

I continued to pick up phrases here and there. My favourite on that first visit was "*ya muh chu'nuh*". As visitors left the house or, more likely, were arranging with others that they were going to leave, they would use this expression in response to "*chu na ma yoh?*" My elementary Italian already possessed the simple expressions *andiamo* (let's go) or *andiamo?* (shall we go?), but the Vicaiolo versions were both baffling and intriguing.

One thing that was for certain - the dialect would be a challenge. Its resemblance, in the low or high form, to Italian could be described as sketchy to say the least and there were no books to learn from. I had learnt French and German at school to some proficiency and taught myself rudimentary Italian later on, but I am not a natural linguist - I need to see things written down to have any real chance of learning a language well.

~~~

It seemed odd to me that I had never picked up any of these phrases on visits with *M*'s parents; but on our return to the UK I was about to learn that speaking Vicaiolo was considered taboo. It was fine for them to speak it, but definitely not for me.

"No, no, no," they exclaimed at the casual comment that I would like to learn a little more of the dialect. "You must learn Italian. Vicaiolo is bad for you. People will look down on you."

I was to learn that Italians in the North look down their Roman noses at people speaking southern dialects.

"Yes, but if we went there to live," I ventured - for even though it was a remote idea, we thought a holiday home might be an option - "Italian would be almost useless".

"What? Live in Vico? Are you out of your minds? No, you couldn't live there! Why would you want to leave us? We spent a lifetime escaping from there. Do you realise that there are no hospitals? You've got a good job. What would you do there? Nothing works there! They're always on strike!" came the tirade.

We were clearly insane. Clearly drunk!

"No, no you don't understand," I protested. "We won't live in Vico; we'll buy an old house in the country and do it up."

"In the country? You are mad! No one lives in the country.

Every house has been broken into and plundered - you can't leave anything unguarded. If you sleep there, they'll come in the night and slit your throats!" was Vincenzo's immediate retort.

"Well it was jus'a thought ... anymore wine?" I chose the path of least resistance and once again lapsed into a state of semi-comprehension as the others chatted round the table. Obviously, it would not be tactful to bring the subject up again; after all, the chances that we would ever go there to live were slim.

~~~

So it was that for years the prospect of me learning any dialect was nil. It was not only *M*'s parents who resisted helping me but the rest of our Italian family too. Nearly all of them had long since moved to Bologna and were now Bolognese. In fact, those relatives that had learnt Italian spoke the Bologna dialect - apparently no disgrace in that. "No Eeeannn," they all said, "you must learn Italian - Vicaiolo's bad for you."

I repeatedly tried to make clear that I didn't want to speak the dialect. Imagine going to Newcastle and trying to speak Geordie, even sound Geordie. Natural linguists, Peter Ustinov comes to mind, might just make it but me without the help of a book and my pathetic capacity to parrot, definitely not. No, I simply wanted to understand the dialect - but my rationale fell on to deaf ears.

As the years passed, I had to satisfy myself with picking up a few choice phrases on holiday. Here the people from Vico were trying to help me. After all, it was the only way they could communicate with me. Of course, I made an ass of myself trying to pronounce the words. It seems that most people know how to distort their tongues into excruciating positions to say words such as "*Ee' vretyuh*" - the dialect for ears.

They would twirl their tongue to a point and thrust it to the roof of the mouth behind the front teeth to deliver the final "*tyuh*" then expect me to do the same.

But my efforts in tongue and mouth gymnastics were doomed to fail amid roars of laughter. It would be unfair to say that they were doing it for fun, but they were well entertained watching me contort my tongue, mouth and face only to blurt out something phonetically ridiculous.

No, no, Vicaiolo was a language strictly for the locals.

The Gargano

For some 20 years, we set off from the UK in the trusty Volvo Estate to spend a good part of August in Vico. We would usually drive straight there completing the journey within 24 hours with a short stop for sleep.

The journeys were always hazardous especially on the arterial routes around Paris and Dijon packed with French holidaymakers literally headed in all directions. If we were spared summer storms though, the journey across France for the most part was comfortable, but there was nothing quite like passing under Monte Bianco and arriving in Italy.

If we thought French drivers were unpredictable, the Italians were undeniably reckless and very intimate. There we would be, shooting down the *autostrada* at a legal 90mph overtaking the slower traffic when I would see lights flashing on the horizon behind. Within seconds some maniac would draw up behind. If we couldn't find a way into the inside lane he would hog our tail, or more accurately become our tail.

Then there were the slow drivers who seemed to have no concept of lanes. They would be driving some clapped-out Fiat, five up with a lounge suite haphazardly tied to the roof rack. The boot would be scraping along the tarmac and the driver nonchalantly gesticulating away to his passengers as he straddled two lanes.

"Toot him, flash him. Do it the Italian way!" *M* would say. I would, in a non-aggressive way, but to no effect. The only way to pass him would be by using a narrower strip of the carriageway and praying that one of his gestures wouldn't cause his car to swerve violently into our path.

The motorway from Turin to Milan and then on past Bologna to

Rimini provided some 5 or 6 hours of sizzling, perilous and occasionally entertaining driving. If our timing was bad and the Italians were just starting their August break then the meandering Adriatic stretch would give no relief until we were well down below Pescara.

The toll at Poggio Imperiale always made me nervous. No one else seemed to leave the motorway there. We would pull up to a closed booth and wait for the attendant to open it and take our ticket. I always expected a bandit to jump out in front of the car and rob us. After all we had been told so many times to watch the car at the service areas, never both go to the toilet at the same time and always hide valuables. Here, we were sitting ducks waiting for the shotgun.

In truth, though we never encountered any problems in the service areas, only the fear of death by combustion as the pump attendant filled the tank whilst smoking a cigarette.

The last stretch of the journey along the *superstrada* brought back familiar memories as we passed the fertile fields of the plain, and made our way across the spaghetti western scenery. The scene of desolation and abandonment never changed, each year we would see the same houses lying unattended. Some unchanged, some deteriorating badly, others with a new roof - that is, no roof as the terracotta tiles had been removed with or without the owner's consent.

Year after year, we would see the same familiar landmarks of Carpino and Ischitella from afar. And then one year the *superstrada*, instead of ending abruptly below Ischitella, carried on to the outskirts of Vico passing through tunnels and over viaducts as it went. We missed the snaking drive up to Ischitella but the shorter route after a long journey was welcome.

We always felt tired, hungry, grimy and dry by the time we arrived in Vico, but a shower, a little moist *pan' e pomodor, na tzek d'uh voyn*, followed by *n'ah pinnakeredd - un pisolino* - a nap and we were ready to holiday.

~~~

I have to admit that after the gridlock of the UK combined with the effort of the journey to Vico, once we had arrived we were never too enthusiastic about driving or sightseeing in the heat. Most of our time was spent unashamedly lying on the same stretch of beach, soaking up the sunshine, dozing, reading or catching up with other members of the family and friends.

Occasionally we would take exercise; play *bocce* or don our masks and fins and go fishing for clams (or *vongole* as they are known in Italian). Some years we would find them in abundance. Their habitat is in the sand beds, but every so often they surface or more accurately their telltale siphons break through the sand like two eyes and we would dive the few feet down and pluck them out.

We would take them home; steep them in lightly salted water for a day to allow them to filter out sand and then have *spaghetti alle vongole* (olive oil, garlic, parsley, a tingle of peperoncino and optionally a splash of white wine - with the ingredients infused throw in the *vongole* and cook until they are all open).

Once we'd discovered that they liked *vongole* then we would pass the odd half-kilo on to Tittino and Antonietta who considered them a great treat. Like most of the older generation in Vico they hadn't been to the sea for years - it was much too draughty, too great a risk of catching a cold. And they wouldn't dream of buying them at the market at the preposterous price of 16,000 lira (8 Euros) a kilo.

Lunchtimes were, well, lunchtimes. Afternoons were spent snatching *n'ah pinnakeredd*. In the evenings we would join the community doing the *striscio*, explore the Centro Storico or visit friends and family.

When the weather waned as it inevitably did, we might set off to discover Rodi or Peschici. On other occasions, we would head inland to the Foresta Umbra - a vast deciduous forest, mainly beech and oak, - the heart of the Gargano National Park.

A regional railway line, built by Mussolini, serves the northern coast of the Gargano and the first thing that struck me about Rodi was the railway tunnel that cuts under the cliff below the village. From a distance along the beach, the image of Rodi resembles a perfect life-size original for a Hornby-Dublo model railway layout. Opposite the entrance to the tunnel, a white rock rises from the sea and in the early morning light, it resembles a sphinx facing the cliff-top village.

The picturesque seaside villages of Rodi and Peschici are both perched on headlands enclosing a series of white, sandy beaches. Peschici is some 16km along the shoreline to the east of Rodi. The coastal road descends from Rodi crosses the railway and separates it from the beach for about 6km before entering the holiday village of San Menaio. Over the railway, there is a scattering of hotels, villas

19

and gorse covered limestone cliffs, beyond which lie plentiful citrus orchards.

After San Menaio, the road diverges from the railway and beach and cuts through pine forests briefly emerging into the plain of the beautiful bay of Calenella. Here the railway rejoins the road but comes to an abrupt halt at the premature and isolated Peschici station. After the station, the road begins a steep climb up to the headland of Monte Pucci, from which the views back to Rodi and forward towards Peschici are spectacular; but it also provides an aerial view of two prominent features common to the Gargano coastline.

Immediately below the viewpoint is a Saracen lookout tower, one of many solid stone fortresses that dot the coastline. Far below, hovering over the sea is the platform of a *trabucco* - a wooden stilted structure with huge arms splayed seawards supported by a suspension structure of wooden poles, ropes and wires. Using this Heath-Robinson style contraption, local fishermen lower nets into the sea where the currents run strong and wait for a catch.

From Monte Pucci the road hugs the cliff tops until it descends into a dense holiday resort in the bay below Peschici. Then there is a steep winding climb up to the village. The first time we drove this road we were amazed to see a boat-builder building a 30-foot wooden craft on the side of the road - roads here are not just for cars; alas the boat-builder is no longer there.

Peschici, like Rodi is a honeycomb of pretty, tiny houses constructed in narrow alleyways with porticoed stone doorways exiting directly onto the street. It is also the most successful of the tourist villages here and, like so many pretty Cornwall fishing villages, is in danger of being blighted by the gift shop culture.

When we toured we would often pass between Rodi and Peschici, sometimes going on further round the coastline to visit the port of Vieste, the beautiful bay of Pugno Chiuso (Closed Fist) with its crystal clear water or the Baia delle Zagare where enormous limestone stacks populate the bay.

In our few trips inland we would drive through the Foresta Umbra to visit Monte Sant' Angelo, the home of the shrine to San Michele, or San Giovanni Rotondo where now an ultra-modern cathedral stands in honour of the newly beatified Padre Pio.

These drives would be long and arduous in the heat, but following a rainstorm, they were comfortable and the fresh air invigorating.

The inner Gargano is a sparsely populated rugged mountainous region, with a mixture of forest and stretches of open farmland. Every so often, we would spot bell-tagged cattle, pigs and horses grazing unattended and unfenced. On one trip to Monte Sant' Angelo we came upon a bull (of Aberdeen Angus origin) sauntering up the serpentine climb to the village. A couple of hours later, as we left, the bull was just coming into town.

As with all things Gargano, no one seemed to think anything about a bull wandering about on its own - it was the most natural thing in the world.

~~~

The family as a whole didn't do much either so one year it was a surprise when Vincenzo suggested that we should go to San Nicola to eat Pizza. All were agreed that we should go, but long discussions followed - shall we go tomorrow, the day after, the day after that or the day after the day after that.

The Vichesi have as much use for weekday names as they have for surnames (but that's another story). Instead of simply saying shall we do something tomorrow, Thursday, Friday or Saturday. They have dispensed with the precise definitions in favour of flexibility: *krah* - tomorrow, *pes'krah* - the day after tomorrow, *pes'kroid* - the day after the day after tomorrow, *pes'krahtt* - four days hence, *pes'kroon* five days and so on.

Eventually, we made a decision. *Kwan e pes'krah* - the day after tomorrow we'll go and eat a piece of pizza. Such is the climate in summer that we can make plans well in advance.

The women would spend *krah* preparing the ingredients, not only for pizza, but also for bread and biscuits and organise the facilities to cater for the masses that had said they wanted to go.

~~~

The valley of San Nicola is a hundred or so metres below Vico towards the sea at San Menaio. *M*'s great-great grandfather owned a large piece of land there and the pizza participants were mainly his descendants.

The land was handed down through generations; the various parcels being inherited whole or split. Deaths, marriages, emigration and sales have meant that little of the land now belongs in the hands

21

of direct descendants. The only significant parcel left belonged to Pasquale, Vincenzo's cousin and although his little house had fallen down, he still had a working bread oven.

When *pes'krah* arrived, Pasquale set off at dawn with his mule, goat and dog. He would prepare the wood and re-start the oven, which he had lit the day before to warm up the terracotta lining, as is the tradition especially if the oven has lain cold for a time. We followed later in cars, which we had to park just off the San Menaio road and make our way by foot with baskets of ingredients, drinks, an assortment of baking trays, cooking and eating utensils. The stony, steep path went into a fold in the valley and then re-emerged with a long steady climb up towards Pasquale's ground. It was a difficult walk, but even the now frail widow Zia Masuccia, Pasquale's mother made the journey.

~~~

It was that morning that we first caught a glimpse of the Hunting Lodge. An impressive country house fronted with a stone-columned vine terrace. After depositing our load at the oven, Vincenzo took us off to see the house.

The owners had abandoned the lodge many years before and now the wine terrace was devoid of the wooden beams. Old untended vines were creeping along the ground. Vincenzo recollected how these vines were once so beautiful and he seemed genuinely sad to see them in this condition.

When he was a child, Vincenzo and his family used to pass summers in *campagna* - the countryside. Vincenzo recalled that they spent a lot of their time at the Hunting Lodge eating out under the vines with the caretaker's family. The house belonged to the Della Bella family (sort of former squires of the Gargano) and as far as we could make out from Vincenzo's story, it the Della Bella's and their guests (frequently Mussolini and members of the Italian Royal Family) only used it during the winter hunting season.

The door to the house was open and we wandered into a hallway. A staircase with frescoed walls led to the upper floor, but it looked unsafe so we didn't attempt to scale it.

Downstairs on either side of the hall there was stabling for horses and animals - mangers stretched along the back walls.

Attached to the rear of the building there was a chapel and outside in the garden a stone gazebo.

It was the first house of this type that we had seen in the area and we were dumbfounded that it could be abandoned like that. Our immediate thoughts were, 'could we buy the house and restore it?' Of course, we didn't say so to anyone, especially Vincenzo; we would try to find out about it from other sources.

We moved on past the lodge heading for the *cazedd* - the little house that Vincenzo's great grandfather once owned. Although Vincenzo was not in any way interested in *campagna*, the visit prompted memories of his childhood and he was full of stories about the place.

~~~

As we walked up the stone wall terraces, whose stones now lay scattered by animals, humans and the weather, Vincenzo scrumped whatever he could from other people's trees: figs, lemons, pears, grapes - there was plentiful fruit in season.

He told us how his family used to live in the *cazedd* throughout the summer months. Here they had plenty to eat and there was lots of work for them to do. He cursed the stone walls, which his elders used to make him repair and recalled the monotony of continuously clearing the ground of stones as they were tilled up.

Close to the *cazedd* I noticed a tall man sat on the base of large olive tree. He was watching our every move from his shaded position and I thought, "the games up, it's his land and now Vincenzo's going to get a roasting." But no, it turned out to be Michele (pronounced "Mickeh'lay"), who is married to Vincenzo's cousin Francesca, and he was only interested to see what Vincenzo had managed to pick. He was there doing a little work to the trees on Francesca's parcel of inherited land.

The tree he sat under captivated me. It wasn't one tree, but two. We would need three people to join hands around one of its trunks. It was obvious that the trunks came from the same root base but now they were more than a metre apart. How could this be?

"*Y'eh nah chesp d'ooliv*," said Michele. Vincenzo explained, "it was once one tree, but as the centuries passed the wood in the middle had dried and year in year out they used to cut away the dead wood until the trunks become independent."

We left Michele, who didn't appear to be about to do any more work, and moved up on to a stone floored terrace.

"This is the *d'aryah*," said Vincenzo. Now this was a man who

23

didn't want me to learn Vicaiolo. He positively condemned the language when I first talked about learning it on our return to the UK and now, as if going to *campagna* changed everything, here he was delivering it with abandon - *cazedd, chesp d'ooliv* and *d'aryah*.

"*D'aryah?*" I attempted to pronounce it.

"Yes, it's a base for threshing the wheat that we grew under the olives. At harvest time we used to lay the sheaves loose on the floor and then one of us stood in the middle and walked the donkey around and around on them to loosen the ears." For Vincenzo, memories were flooding back.

"And if the donkey did its business?" I asked, not able to resist the question.

"Ah well, we used to pick it up and spread it under the trees."

Vincenzo continued to recall with a bemused countenance as if it seemed impossible that they lived like that. "We used to choose a day when there was wind off the sea, and then we tossed the stems into the air with forks to release the chaff to the currents. When the wheat was relatively clean, we raked off the stems and repeated the tossing process using shovels until the grain was ready to sack."

"And what did you do with the grain?" I wanted the complete picture.

"If we went up to Vico for any reason, we used to load the donkey and take it a little at a time. Sometimes we went to the mill to make flour for use here and that would be a good time - fresh bread or pizza from the oven. The rest we would store in Vico for the long winter ahead."

He pointed me to the bread oven some 10 metres away from the *cazedd*, "we used to make so much bread and pizza in that oven, and now look at it. Ruined!" He seemed genuinely saddened that a fig had taken root in the tiles of the roof and had now split the oven asunder. He cursed the present owners, whoever they were, for letting it go like that.

We moved on to the *cazedd*.

It was a single-storey building with a sloping roof. Outside the front door, embedded in the wall there was a stone loop for tethering animals. To the right of the door an ancient vine, that still produced mouth-watering white table grapes. We picked the ripest to eat after the pizza. Nobody tended the vine anymore and it grew wildly up a mulberry tree, which along with an almond tree provided the only shade at the front of the house.

24

The door was wide open. We went inside and there we found a room with a simple arched ceiling. To the right of the door there was an open fireplace. Next to it was an arch in the wall containing a deep sink with a drain tap.

"That's *ah toyn,*" explained Vincenzo, not able to resist the word.

"*Ah toyn?*"

After correcting my pronunciation again, he elaborated. "It's for washing clothes. You know we used to bring all the linen and other whites down from Vico and give them a special clean here once a year."

"We loaded up the donkey with everything that we needed to rejuvenate and came here to do this job every autumn. We used to layer the linen and clothes in *ah Toyn,* then cover the lot with a cloth. On top of the cloth we heaped a few centimetres of wood ash and then poured bucket after bucket of hot water on to ashes."

"Once the load had been thoroughly steeped it was left overnight and the water seeped steadily through the drain hole. The next day we took the washing to the spring below the *cazedd* and rinsed it.

"What a process. And you did it once a year?"

"Just once," he confirmed. "The Vichesi have a habit of doing things once a year at the appropriate season - for instance they always paint, or rather whitewash, their houses from top to bottom each spring," he added.

Further along the wall there was another arch, a recess for storage of essentials such as olive oil, vinegar and salt.

Hanging on the wall opposite was a *fazzatoor* - a large deep wooden tray with a handle on each corner. They used the *fazzatoor* for making dough and carrying it to the oven. Although woodworm had infested it, we were amazed that someone had not whisked it away.

Next to the *fazzatoor* was a door into what looked like a storeroom. To the side of the door were two low walls about a metre apart.

"What are those walls for?" I asked, not having a clue what they could be.

"That was the bed," explained Vincenzo. "It used to have bars of iron spanning the walls, then wooden planks on top and the whole was covered with straw bedding. Then there were some other beds over here - he walked to the vacant space opposite the fireplace."

"So this was it? Nothing else?" I asked.

"Well there's the stable," came the reply pointing towards the storeroom.

"What did you keep in the stable?" I asked. Now it may have seemed a rather daft question, but I had noticed a stable-like door adjacent to the front door before we entered.

"The donkey of course, and goats and straw and tools."

Hmmm, it certainly was country living. "And the place next door? Isn't that a stable?" I enquired.

"Yes and no," he said, "anyway it didn't belong to us. Another family had the attached building and they used to make and store wine in there in an enormous wooden cask. In fact the land encircling the houses was theirs as well - we simply had a right of way in and out - our ground starts at the *d'aryah*."

We had a look in the neighbours stable. The wine cask had gone, but the remains of a large press were strewn across the floor.

"So, who owns the house now?"

"Oh, lots of people. I don't know who they are. Francesca must be one, but I really have lost touch. It could be dozens," was Vincenzo's rather uncertain assessment of the situation.

~~~

We left the *cazedd* door wide open, as we had found it, and rejoined the others at the bread oven. where things were moving on. The party had gathered up a range of old tables, planks of wood, chairs, tree stumps to make a seating arrangement.

Final touches were put to the pizzas and one by one they went off to Pasquale at the oven. There was pizza with mozzarella and tomato (*Margherita*), tomato and garlic (*pizza alla marinara*), pizza with potatoes, pizza with courgettes - the recipes seemed endless and all made with produce grown by the family.

Pasquale removed trays of bubbling lasagne, which were taken to the ladies at the table to dish out on plastic plates. Then he stoked up the oven with some bone-dry olive cuttings until its entrance was glowing white - the oven was ready. He moved the charcoals to one side, swept the oven base clean with a makeshift brush of twigs and spooned in the pizza trays on a long shovel.

The feast was underway: lasagne, pizza of choice, fresh fruit, tiramisu and cheese to follow. Wine flowed as the meal lasted well into the late afternoon. We were left only to imagine how *M*'s family had lived here all those years ago.

The pizza event helped to consolidate the bold claims made by the Vichesi. They would repeat year after year to me that here in the Gargano they had everything they needed: beaches, forest, olives, vines, fruit, vegetables, fish, natural animals and animal products. They had clean air - there was no industry to pollute. They had sunshine and, god willing, abundant water. They didn't need to import anything from beyond their borders.

But they have much more: language, character, traditions and customs that date back centuries - it really is a time capsule and one that I found irresistible.

As we discovered the Gargano we still secretly harboured the dream that somehow we could one day buy a property, maybe the Hunting Lodge at San Nicola, restore it and come to live in this wonderful place, this little piece of paradise. But how could we really live and work here? It was too remote. I was a computer programmer, not an olive or fruit farmer.

Discovering Vico

When I first visited Vico, there was only a partial sewerage system. As *M* had pointed out that first evening, she used to have to go outside, down the stairs into the stepped street and enter a little candle-lit cubbyhole under the stairs to use the first sewer-connected toilet in the street.

Although by the early 80's, the infrastructure had greatly improved it was not quite universal and would not be for a few years. One morning I heard a hand bell ringing across the valley in an area of Vico called the Carmine.

"What was the bell?" I asked.

"Ah, that's the *carro*," replied Vincenzo with a hint of amusement.

"The *carro*?" I invited an explanation.

"Ah, well, it's the shit wagon. They're calling for people to empty their potties."

"What, they still have to …?"

But I had literally disturbed a swarm of flies around a cowpat.

"Do you know what we used to have to do Ian?" asked Vincenzo, shamefaced, in Italian so that everyone in the room could understand. Everybody else in the room seemed to sense what was coming - his two sisters seemed repulsed and started chattering wildly. *M*'s uncle, Zio Mimi, chuckled at the thought.

Vincenzo has a way of asking a question knowing that I couldn't possibly know the answer. Without waiting for my reply he went on to reveal a dark secret.

"We," referring to himself and his elder sister Rinuccia, "used to be sent by my father with buckets to where the *carro* dumped the waste and we had to collect the dung! And guess what we did with it?"

I couldn't, but before I could say so, he flushed out the secret. "We used to take the donkey load of human waste and spread it under our olives."

"But do you know what was even worse?" he asked.

Could it get any worse? Yes, indeed it could.

"Sometimes we would go ahead of the *carro*, shouting out to people *tein dah dyetta*? - have you got anything to throw out?" And so they would relieve the population of their waste and the unpleasant task of drudging outside the house with it and pouring it into the *carro*.

Vincenzo and his sisters spent the remainder of the pre-lunch conversation revealing other revolting titbits of their life in Vico as they collectively told tales about their childhoods.

No wonder these people were so keen to get away to the north! Well, in any direction actually, so long as it was away!

The council regularly sprayed the streets at night with insecticide to kill the flies. When combined with the smell of the overstrained sewerage system, the communal bins (always open and whose contents were endlessly being picked over by mangy cats) and the many stables housing equine species, goats, sheep and poultry the atmosphere could be heady in summer.

I have painted a bleak picture, but it is the undeniable truth. This is not Tuscany, Umbria or the Marche; this is the South – known as the Mezzogiorno (Midday). Here traditions run deep, modernisation is slow and when the locals make so called improvements it is inevitably to the detriment of the architecture and character of the locations.

As Vico's population burst out of the Centro Storico, the walled historic centre, they built apartment blocks anyhow and anywhere. The construction was not pretty, but it was economical and practical.

Huge garages form the ground floors of these new buildings so that the *campagnoli* can store their tractors, *treruote*, tools, nets and olive oil; others house carpenters, ironmongers and all manner of small enterprises. In the apartments above, balconies provide space for boilers, hanging washing and storing wood (for nearly all apartments still have an open fire or wood burning stove). Running water provides a luxury that was rare in their old quarters, where washing was traditionally taken to a local fountain and water for the house was drawn from communal well pumps sited in the many squares.

Many, especially the young, flocked to these new apartments and the Centro Storico was abandoned except by the old, the poorest and the *appassionati*. To those who remained, whether by choice, need or love, Vico ought to be thankful for they put a brake on the running down of a treasure.

The Centro Storico is divided into three areas: Terra, Civita and Casale. They each consist of a network of narrow streets and alleyways. The whole structure built on rock and so entwined that it is difficult to detect the boundaries.

At the summit of the Centro Storico is the Chiesa Madre (Mother Church); adjacent to the church stands a castle with huge circular buttress towers built by Federico II of Svevia as a hunting lodge in medieval times. From here one can fan out in all directions via the myriad of alleyways, staircases and passageways into the areas of Terra and Civita, enclosed in massive walls bounding the Centro Storico, and on into the Casale area tacked onto the outer ramparts of the walls.

I never tire of visiting the Centro Storico - a single visit could never give a full appreciation of its scale and diversity. It's not simply gazing at the facades although I always seem to find something new, it's about timing. Maybe someone has left open a door to a labyrinth of caves. If I'm lucky enough the owner will likely let me explore and I will find all manner of antiquity, tools, bottles of preserves, wine, hanging cheeses or salami, maybe even an olive press.

Moving on I may find a nook or cranny where people are going about some ritual seasonal activity: bottling wine, making preserves, whittling wood, stripping the cuttings of the broom plant to make ties for their vines. Like the diversity of the Centro Storico there seems to be no end to their undertakings and I cannot resist asking them how, why and what they are doing and they in turn are always happy to enlighten me (provided I can understand them of course).

At every turn along the cobbled streets there is some new shape, form or feature to absorb: arches, staircases, flying buttresses or Venetian arches, wooden-roofed cloisters, piazzas, towers, gargoyles, vast chimneys with diverse anti-draught designs and ornate coats of arms decorating the doorways.

There are places where only donkeys, Fiat *cinquecento* and *treruote* can go. Narrow alleyways, steep staircases and dead-ends. In some cases the street corners have been hewn off or built to allow a particular form of transport to pass.

I often used to stroll around just before lunchtime. Despite the heat, it was interesting to see the men coming in from *campagna*, tending to their animals (for goats, chickens and rabbits would also be kept in the stables along with mules, donkeys, dogs and cats); and then there was the smell of the cooking oozing from every occupied house - an appetizer in itself.

In the late afternoon and early evening the women and children would be out in the street. They would sit in the doorways on the stone steps, on a range of cast-out furniture that was kept in the street for the purpose or, where there were outcrops of rock, they would sit like Barbary apes above the street on seats hollowed out over centuries and made shiny by generations of bottoms. The women busy themselves crocheting, repairing olive nets or darning socks, attending to sun-dried tomatoes or stringing chillies. The children chase cats and dogs or play games of tag or hide and seek tearing around this natural play centre. The old, and I mean very old, look on.

I have never seen such longevity. Whatever their diet is, it's a good one as the aromas floating through the air perhaps confirm.

In these areas, where whole families have kept a foothold, the Centro Storico thrives and is in good order. Where dereliction has set in it seems to become endemic; the doors and windows are the first to go - perhaps rodents begin the destruction and then humans take over. Once open the weather penetrates and erodes until the roofs collapse.

A great deal of the damage is also caused by inheritance. When an owner dies the custom is to divide the assets among the children or immediate relatives. In some cases, common sense prevails and the inheritors sort out land, property and belongings before the death. They agree values, parcel it up, maybe draw straws and then compensate each other financially as prearranged.

But, in many cases, perhaps due to sudden death, indifference, pure stubbornness or family feuds the spoils are simply divided equally. The result of this archaic practice is, for example, a stable being left to, say, seven people.

Now, getting two people to agree what to do with a stable that's probably only got one key would be difficult enough in a rational society, but to hope that seven Italian siblings will find accommodation is stretching it. Grief, greed, envy, mental illness, old scores, hard headedness and astuteness would all hinder the process; the likelihood is that they would fail to agree any settlement; they would fall out; they would not speak to each other for years and they would simply desert the stable. The key would go missing.

Other properties are simply abandoned by emigrants. Whole families who would have occupied a little street or alleyway eventually followed a relative who established a new life in America or Australia. Their descendants probably don't even know that they own, or more likely part own, a small piece of the Centro Storico.

But all is not lost. What remains intact and cared for is a fascinating representation of the evolution of Vico. The architecture began here centuries ago with the excavation of caves. Stone houses were added, built adjacent to or on top of the caves, the haphazard development following the contours of the rock. As the village took shape and thrived, it was strategically fortified to protect against marauding Saracens.

With the wealth that came first from oranges and lemons and then from olive oil, the houses became more impressive and arched stone *portali* became the standard. Elaborate designs decorated the stone columns and the keystones bore coats of arms.

A key feature of Vico architecture is the chimney of the *Cucina Monacesca* (literally a monk's kitchen as it resembles a cell). From the outside the chimneys are excessive in proportion to the houses and tiny windows flank them. Internally these kitchens are miniscule, most of the space being taken up by the thick walls; the focal point is the open fireplace, which would have been used for all cooking. On each side of the fireplace there is a wooden bench or chest, a *cassapanca*, which serves as storage, a seat and a bed. There would have been no sink, perhaps a simple table where the whole family would eat from a single bowl. As the smallest room in the house, in winter it was the warmest.

In the streets of terraced houses it is common to see the *portali*, or stone mullioned entrances, adjacent to one another, absolutely nothing between them. The mystery of this rather curious arrangement is solved when a door is left open to reveal a staircase, usually a very steep staircase; the houses have been built on top of each other but, wherever possible, with independent entrances.

Outside the Centro Storico much larger houses were built with very grand *portali*, ornate mullioned windows and elaborate balconies. Many of these have a single entrance leading to apartments, which lack the traditional *Cucina Monacesca* external chimneys, but inside the traditional open-fired kitchen is still common.

~~~

It was easy for me to imagine what a close society this must have been and how the Centro Storico influenced the development of the character of these generous people. The Vichesi quite literally lived in each other's pockets. The large families (for a family of less than seven surviving children was rare until recently) endured the most cramped conditions; they literally ate each other's food; there was little or no privacy.

And little has changed! In our holiday family, food is often passed across the balconies, especially if there's something special on the menu. It becomes a merry-go-round: one aunt making a traditional dish with local ingredients that can't be had up north, another homemade *orechiette* (ears of pasta), Emilia making chocolate éclairs. They all have to pass their dishes round. If Vincenzo's heard that *pan' n'fuss* is on the go, you can be sure that an extra big plate will arrive for him alone. *Pan' n'fuss* is literally wet bread. It's made of stale Pugliese bread, thinly sliced and layered in a large dish, topped with ladles of a stock of vegetables, such as broad beans, zucchini and tomatoes. It sounds disgusting, and with my aversion to soggy bread, I wasn't looking forward to it all - but guess what!

Then there are the children. The parents have things to do, so the offspring congregate at the most convenient relative's house. Antonietta's house is never without them. The older girls look after the babies; as soon as they can manage they are pushing them round in prams and smothering them with kisses. The boys play football against the house wall - anything to make a noise - or run around playing tag at break-neck pace.

Inevitably accidents happen; the subsequent screams bring everyone out onto the street.

"He's grazed his leg. There's blood," the attendants cry out. Antonietta takes them in, she suffers their screams, she tends their wounds and within five minutes the injured urchins are back on the street tearing about.

Of course, some traditions have gone. Bread used to be made regularly, kneaded in quantity by the women at home and then carried in cotton-lined baskets balanced on long planks to the nearest bakery. Today the ancient ovens that catered for mass production are no longer in use, but one day a friend showed me his. It's easy to imagine how the older hobbit-sized Vichesi, could once have walked

33

in the huge but low circular ovens.

However, there is one tradition that will never go. Noise!

The Vichesi know how to throw a voice. If they want to find someone, men and women alike, they simply hang out of the window or stand out in the street and holler. It doesn't matter whether it's four in the morning or the middle of the siesta driven afternoon, they let rip from formidable lungs "*O'oh Woonchay* - Hey, Vincenzo".

Fortunately for them the Vichesi seem to have a tolerance for noise - perhaps a genetic property, which must have evolved in the cramped conditions of the Centro Storico. There, the bustle of life started at dawn: cockerels crowed, donkeys brayed, men prepared to go to *campagna*, people chopped wood, started building, shouted out for workmates; there was and still is no perception of quiet conversation.

In modern day Vico these habits continue, but the bustle is more mechanised; *treruote* and *motorini* hurtle through the narrow streets; car drivers simply blow their horns to call someone, wood is delivered at dawn, chainsaws whine. From about eight in the morning, traders arrive with small trucks loaded with fruit and veg; to get the full attention of the population they call out with megaphones. I used to think this was charming until they discovered that they could record a message and relay it endlessly through the wretched ear-splitter.

Despite all this, the Vichesi go about their lives without showing the slightest hint of irritation. They are oblivious to noise.

~~~

Outside the Centro Storico, Vico is more of a conventional town. Some areas, such as the Carmine and Coppamen'ele were built in the traditional style a century or so ago. Other developments created main thoroughfares that all converge on San Francesco - the roundabout I encountered and survived on my first visit.

Life in Vico revolves around this roundabout where seven roads meet. From five in the evening until after eight it is a busy hub where people gather to chat, do business, find workers for the following day or simply to idle. Depending on the season, it is the traditional place for selling a day's crop of local delicacies such as fungi, wild asparagus, bunches of oregano, chestnuts or cherries.

There used to be a hair-brained rule in most of Europe, including Italy, where cars on a roundabout had to give way to vehicles entering from the right. Europe abandoned these rules many years ago but no one seems to have told Vico.

The Vico roundabout is probably unique in the Gargano (and maybe in Italy) because it still maintains this ancient rite of priority in the new millennium. There are no signposts for unsuspecting visitors - it just operates by tradition and, for the most part by accident. Though it amazes me how few accidents actually happen here.

The traffic in the early evening alone is enough to ensure gridlock. The petrol station, once the only one in Vico, for now there are two, forms part of the roundabout and from late afternoon hosts a constant queue.

The two *vigili* (municipal police) who appear on duty seemingly at random don't help. In fact the roundabout seems to function better, if that's the correct word, without them. When they're not having a cigarette lit by a passer-by or catching up on the past year's news from a car full of relatives from the north, they turn to observe the chaos that's developed and attempt to referee order with their whistles. It's like closing the gate after the horse has bolted.

Pedestrians and dogs also seem to hold ancient rites of priority. They walk the roundabout 'as the crow flies' holding up whatever traffic is attempting to negotiate the gridlock. Without exception even the most menacing of motorists will stop (if they can't steer round!). Groups gather in the middle and pass the time of day - the *vigili* do not even attempt to move them on and the cars simply drive around them as if it was the most natural thing in the world. As for dogs, they seem to have an innate sense of immortality - they will trot through the traffic, sit or sleep in the middle and occasionally have liaisons!

The roundabout is also the focus of attention at dawn when workers meet here, leave their vehicles wherever they please as the *vigili* are never there, have coffee and then move off. But, by far the best time to sit at one of the cafes and enjoy the *confusione* is market day. Every other Thursday a general market (or *Festa delle Donne* as the locals refer to their women's morning out shopping) comes to Vico.

The market occupies the streets bordering a park called La Villa, which is adjacent to the San Francesco roundabout. It's a hotchpotch of stalls selling food, clothes, shoes, household goods, pets, music and agricultural items for the season. Basket makers and wood carvers mingle on the periphery avoiding the market fees. The crowds swelter in the intermittent sunshine as the stalls have reserved the shade of the numerous Ilex, Pine, Horse Chestnuts and fragrant

Linden trees.

Old and young men, with no work to go to, hang about at the bars, sit on the shaded wall edging La Villa or just stand around the petrol station inhaling its vapours while smoking a cigarette; all are there to bear witness to the calamity that unfolds each market.

In the busy summer months, it seems more like a spectator sport as the *vigili* battle with traders, locals and visitors with the knowledge that the ring of onlookers are scrutinising their every move.

The traffic is running normally; then one of the *vigili* decides to do some work. A shrill whistle and a casual hand bring the main stream of traffic to a halt, perhaps while the *vigili*'s allows a relative or friend passage. He has to let a few more cars go. Someone stops to talk to him. The *vigili* on the other side of the roundabout performs similar favours and bang. Gridlock.

As the heat of summer wears on, the *vigili* smoke more, their whistles become shriller and they show visible signs of stress - a rare thing for a Vichese - under constant observation from their fellow citizens. But summer always ends and they know that they will be able to return to a calmer, if not altogether stress-free, work style in the winter months.

~~~

And summer always ends with a bang in Vico, usually around the Festa of San Rocco in the middle of August. The storm clouds gather over the forest and then without the slightest notice the first bolt of lightning cracks the sky, a thunderclap shakes the rocky foundations and the clouds burst.

Within minutes the streets are awash. Water gushes from the rooftops of the Centro Storico, bursts from the gullies, cascades down the stepped alleys and literally washes the streets clean.

For the Vichesi, it is a welcome sign. They emerge from their shelters refreshed and chattering animatedly - for water is a precious commodity here.

~~~

Despite the seemingly unsanitary conditions, we go to the fruit and vegetable market each day to buy fresh produce. The Vico market is situated just outside the Centro Storico, off the Piazza San Domenico. It was at one of the entries to the market that I took the plunge with the car on that first night and nearly collided with the fountain. Now mains water is everywhere, but *M* remembers queuing for the household water at this fountain during the summer holidays in her youth, for even though they had the cubbyhole loo there was still no running water.

The permanent market building is on two floors. At ground level there is a cavernous room, its timber roof crowned with a ventilation cap to cope with the heat in summer. Here fixed stalls sell locally grown fruit and vegetables. Downstairs is the fish market where attendant sellers are constantly batting away the flies.

Outside in the market piazza other stalls are set up daily to sell fruit and vegetables, market vans are disembowelled and a myriad of goods from pasta to pure alcohol (for making liqueurs such as *limoncino*) are displayed on trestle tables in front of them. Other vans arrive with their innards packed with cheeses, salamis and other preserves.

As the heat of the day builds, so does the population of flies. Though fewer than in my early days there is always a buzz. But having survived so many summers here nowadays they seem less menacing.

Of course, buying at the market in those early days was almost impossible for me. I could point at something and ask for one or 2 kilos, whatever I required, and then hope for the best. If the market stallholder responded with any kind of unexpected outburst (like buy 5 kilos for a special price) I was lost. Fortunately I wasn't given the market chore too often as everyone realised that the stallholders would take advantage - for every four peaches I would get a bad one; for every kilo I would get 900 grams or something like that. Also I wouldn't get the best price - the secret at the market was to question the price and barter, but you had to be a Vichese to do that.

Tittino and Sopranomi

By western European standards Tittino was a peasant. He, like so many men in Vico, scratched a living from the land. He had *campagna*: olives, some sweet chestnut woods and a garden. Not a garden, in the sense that he could just pop out the back door to tend his roses and dig his vegetable patch. No, it was a piece of land on the outskirts of Vico, dedicated to the serious business of growing vegetables and fruit for his family, heavily fortified against predators with four legs and two. His olives and woods were scattered in the outlying hills and valleys - all a collection of inheritances.

He also had Rosina, his only means of transport and the work engine of the family. Each dawn Tittino would load up Rosina with the implements he needed for the day. He would never go without his axe and secateurs; then maybe he would take his *zappa* (a type of pick with a double head, one pointed the other flat for working around the olive roots) or maybe a scythe.

Tittino had to be organised, as it might be an hour's walk to his ground on any one day. To go without the necessary tools would be careless just as to take a beast of burden without burdening it, would be inefficient. One day he might take water in plastic containers; the next he might take *letame* (compost from mucking out the stable); if he were harvesting olives he would load the donkey with nets, sacks and *mazze* (supple sticks of various lengths to beat the olives from the trees).

In the Summer he would leave home a little after 4am and return towards midday having worked in temperatures rarely below the upper 20's. In the Winter he would leave before dawn and endure wet weather, cold winds and damp, treacherous roads and rock tracks.

When he returned, Rosina would be loaded with whatever tools he had taken in the morning plus the results of the day's work. During the olive harvest, she would be laden with sacks of olives, plus the work nets; at other times she would carry wood - a priority for the cold Vico winter; if not wood then hay, bamboo, or *louperi* (the wild suckers that grow at the base of olives, which are used in basket making). Then depending on the season, nuts, fungi, figs, oranges, lemons, mulberry, grapes, rocket and all manner of herbs and wild greens that grow on the roadside.

Peasant, yes, but resourceful.

At midday, after he had unloaded and tended to Rosina, he would eat, take a siesta and reappear between four and five suitably rested but a little groggy from the intake of lunchtime wine. For Tittino took pleasure in drinking. After a quick trip across the street to the bathroom he would reappear and sit on the steps outside his front door waiting for the card game to start.

In the evenings, after Tittino had eaten I would often be invited in and he would entertain me with wine, olives, *cash'e-cavadd* and whatever else was left on the table. The scene was generally as on that first night we met. Grandchildren, nieces and nephews came and went at will, raiding the table, the fridge and the sweet bowl.

The children never spoke, they all shouted! It was surely in their genes - a legacy of the time, not so long ago, when whole families, including Vincenzo's, ate from the same bowl and only the fittest, strongest and loudest ate their fill.

Communication was difficult, Tittino was one of those people who had no truck with speaking Italian, but there were other adults, maybe his sons Matteo or Franchino or his daughters Maria and Lucia, who all spoke Italian as well as the dialect; they would try to find a way to help out.

~~~

It struck me that he had a small family by local standards and one evening I discovered the possible reason; Tittino was in rip-roaring form and he told me the story of his war years. The details, that I understood, were sketchy but I got the gist of his story while we demolished a bottle or two of *Vino Naturale*.

He had only just got married when the Second World War broke out and he joined the army. He was shipped off to the Balkans where he started off fighting the Greeks, which he described with lung bursting booms and imaginary rifle shots; then when the Italians surrendered he was unfortunate enough to be in the area where the Italians then started fighting the Germans.

Another round of booms and bangs, but the nub of the tale was that on his platoons' first encounter with the Germans, they simply laid down their weapons and surrendered without a shot being fired. Tittino gestured with his hands held above his proud head. "We weren't stupid. We weren't going to get killed".

The Germans took them north to labour camps. He seemed unsure where, as Geography was not on the curriculum when he left school at 9 years old, but maybe he was taken to Poland. Wherever it was, it was bitterly cold in winter. They were starved, frozen and forced into labour. When the war ended he narrowly escaped being taken by the Russians and eventually he and his comrades made it to safe territory. From there, wherever it was, they walked back to Italy (or creatively found whatever means of transport they could).

The scenes and celebrations when they got back to Vico in 1948, three years after the war ended, must have been extraordinary and Antonietta (who had tended his *campagna* throughout) had waited all that time for her beloved Tittino, never knowing whether he was dead or alive. They set about making a family.

So, it was that I learnt that these old people really weren't that old at all, at least by local standards. Tittino would have been in his late twenties when he returned from the war - that put him and Antonietta in their middle to late fifties when we first met in 1981. It must have been the hard peasant existence (and the war) that had wreaked havoc on the countenances of this once handsome couple.

But if life had been hard this kind-hearted pair didn't complain - indeed they considered their lives to be good. Tittino may have been a peasant, but he didn't know it. He was a survivor, a winner, a success, the head of a huge family (now with several generations it was much bigger than I had first imagined); he was resourceful, the breadwinner, a landowner, but most of all he was a generous friend.

~~~

Tittino and I were *'grande amici'* - his words, not mine, but I liked to believe that it was true. So it was no surprise one August day when he suggested that I go to *campagna* with him. I agreed - we would meet at dawn.

Vincenzo, who is a nocturnal insomniac but won't take my advice and give up his afternoon *pinnakeredd*, woke me at 4am and I dragged myself out of bed after a restless, airless night. I dressed for the heat and went out into the street to meet Tittino and Rosina - already saddled and loaded with tools and manure from the mucking out of the stable.

Tittino, on seeing me, immediately dismissed my dress. "You can't wear shorts," he said, "you must cover your legs. There will be brambles, thorns that will scratch your legs to ribbons. There are vipers you know, you can't take chances. And put a hat on, the sun will fry your brain!"

Vincenzo interpreted his counsel from the balcony above the street with that air of I told you so. Vincenzo had escaped *campagna*, and apart from going there to pick somebody else's figs, he wouldn't care if he never went there again. I had to be crazy to go there at anytime, let alone at this time of day.

Suitably dressed in my stoutest pair of jeans and walking shoes, I headed off for an adventure with a man with whom I would have a few communication problems, his donkey and a new-found fear of snakes.

It was too late now though. "*Ya muh chu'nuh*," said Tittino to Rosina, who needed no further instruction, and we were off.

We headed off out of Vico, exchanging salutations with all manner of early-risers as we went. Though light, the sun was yet to rise but the buildings still radiated heat from the day before. Through narrow streets and alleys we ran the gauntlet with dogs fiercely guarding their territories. Each one would receive a curt "*Za'ah. Ah kooch*! - to bed!" from Tittino and they would scurry back within their boundaries.

It was a relief to get out into open countryside. With thoughts of rabies out of the way, I could concentrate on snakes. As we left the protection of Vico cool morning air swirled around us.

We walked for about two kilometres. Chitchat was a little hard going. Tittino would point out various landmarks and say their names, but I found it difficult to imagine the words that he spoke and I instantly forgot them.

"*Yam a bash* - let's go down," Tittino suddenly said as we plunged off the road on to a steep stony path. We headed on down and down into a valley. At first the track was barren and wide, but as we descended the atmosphere changed as vegetation closed in on us.

"*Attent' ee' serp'* - watch out for snakes!" warned Tittino. The trek seemed to go on forever and the humidity oppressed.

41

Eventually we came into a clearing with steep rocky sides covered in moss, lichen and ivy vines. Water trickled from a spring at the base of the ravine. It was cool, even fresh. I was glad of my jeans.

We moved out of the ravine into the open countryside and soon came upon a little house - we had arrived at one of Tittino's many properties. It was approaching 6 am and we had a day's work ahead of us.

The fiery sun was coming up over the valley sides. Tittino led Rosina to a shady spot at the back of the *cazedd* and tethered her to a stone loop in the wall, unloaded the tools, the manure and gave her a bag of hay to eat.

He then lit a fire that he had made on a previous visit. It was a bone-dry mixture of weed and olive prunings. "*Y'eh benzoyn'* - it's petrol!" said Tittino as he put a light to it. Within seconds it was ablaze. He made signs to me to state the blindingly obvious - that there was no wind, a good time to light the fire but if there was any wind "woosh" we would set fire to the valley.

When the fire had calmed, we went off to water some plants. Tittino had planted new lemon trees and an olive. We collected water from an old tin bath, fed by the spring, and flooded the parched hollow base around each plant. The water sank without trace.

After watering, we picked figs and lemons. There's a knack to picking figs, without ripping the skins but sticky milk covering my hands was evidence that I still had much to learn.

This was a piece of ground with everything: fruit, olives, nuts and the invasive Fichi d'India. As Tittino picked he also cleaned any excessive growth, moving lithely through the trees with his secateurs and axe strapped to his waist.

He had a routine and seemed to take the work in his stride, while I stumbled around on the unforgiving ground and perspired as I clambered about in the lower part of some trees.

At about 8 am, we stopped for breakfast in the shade of a vine growing up the side of the house. From an old leather saddlebag he took some tomatoes, salami, a jar of olives and fresh bread (now where did he get that before 4 am?) and sliced it with his penknife. We ate *pan' e pomodor,* washed down with a swig of peasant wine from the bottle.

Like one of those survival experts in the jungle, Tittino trotted off to an olive tree, cut off a sucker and trimmed it to a stick about 50cm long. With his penknife, he slit one end and inserted a lath of the trimmings to open the split ends. He sharpened the ends to points and then showed me the finished tool as if to say, "guess what this is?" It was plainly a fork. But what was he going to do with it?

He sliced the salami, impaled a thick piece on the fork and offered it up to the embers of the fire. A few minutes later, I experienced the new taste of toasted salami with another glass of Vino Nero and some salt-dried olives.

To finish off the banquet he plucked some grapes from the vine.

With the hard work of eating done, we pottered around tidying the trimmings from under the trees, weeding and preparing a bonfire for the next visit.

At 10 o'clock, hot sun on our backs, Tittino loaded Rosina with the day's produce plus a few billets of olive wood and we set off back to Vico.

Not much of a day I thought. But we hadn't finished. The walk back up the valley to Vico was blistering. The jeans were sticking to my legs. I hadn't seen any snakes and wished I had my shorts on. Tittino seemed unphased by the steamy conditions as he kept a countryman's eye on the surroundings - he would stop occasionally, get out his knife and cut some greens or pick some fruit from someone else's tree. He would say what the greens were, but I didn't recognise them and without anything to reference I instantly forgot the names.

We followed a different route to Vico and just outside the town we stopped at a grand iron gate set in a dry-stone wall. Tittino produced a set of keys and undid the heavy padlock. "*D'ort' meh* - my vegetable garden", he announced with pride.

"*Ah roo-ook* - rocket", he declared as he picked off some peppery leaves and bid me to eat them "*man-yuh, man-yuh*". One by one he reeled off the dialect names: "*d'atch* - celery", "*ee' k'cotch - zucchini*", "*ee' melaunguanuh* - cucumbers," as he picked fresh vegetables for the table.

At least I could recognise what he was talking about, but it would be years before I could master such an array of the vernacular.

Just after midday, we locked up and moved off to the stable to unload Rosina before having a thoroughly deserved lunch.

~~~

Tittino always loved to grandstand and no other occasion suited him better than Via Fania's very own "Festa dell'Umanita". This was a

43

rare event, for it could only take place when there was no official mourning happening in the street and I only ever attended one.

The Festa dell'Umanita falls on the same day as the national annual Communist Festa dell'Unita. The non-political summer visitors had little truck with the national festival or the communists and so they held their own.

The festival began with the formation of a committee, which struck me as very collective; this took place in the street at the card table when the men had finished playing. They appointed someone to co-ordinate food, someone responsible for drink, another for organizing tables and chairs, someone for entertainment and last, but not least, they appointed a treasurer and his minders - the latter to make sure the treasurer wasn't mugged and didn't fiddle the books.

This particular year Vincenzo was treasurer and collector of taxes. For the occasion he dressed up as a priest and as usual made a song and dance of the invitation as he toured the neighbouring streets with his minders. A gregarious character with a red-light-district sense of humour, he shocked the women and made fun of the men. He made everyone laugh and they coughed up happily.

On the day of the festival a banner was hung across both entrances to Via Fania citing "*Chi trasce, ava pagha!* - who enters, has to pay!" It was the first time I had seen written Vicaiolo and now at last I discovered the meaning of the words '*trash, trash*' that I heard a few years earlier on my first night in Vico - '*trasce, trasce*' as properly written in Vicaiolo meant 'enter, enter'.

Catering began early; the women commandeered Zio Mimi's cantina, set up a huge gas ring on to which they put an even bigger pot and then prepared the ingredients for a *risotto alla marinara* - fisherman's risotto.

We erected a series table in the street to seat about fifty. Everyone contributed something - chairs, tablecloths, and cutlery - the table was laid with paper napkins, plastic plates and cups.

Just before the meal, Tittino's son-in-law Franco arrived with bread from the bakery: several large wheels of *pane Pugliese*, each weighing 5 kilos. The women sliced them and placed heaps at intervals along the table. We filled jugs of wine from large *damigiane* and distributed bottles of water and soft drinks for the children and those with a gentler constitution.

Tittino swept a corner of the street spotlessly clean and lit a wood fire. When the cooking began it was clear that he would be the master of the barbecue.

The *festa* was noisy, everyone shouting as usual and the children barely resting for a moment before setting off on another round of tag. Slowly but surely, we had our fill. A small army of helpers served the risotto, then Tittino's barbecued spicy sausages with *cowdedd* (barbecued bread dribbled with olive oil) and salad, followed by helpings of strawberries and ice cream from the Pizzicato Bar. Naturally, we finished off with cheese - balls of *cash'e-cavadd* and wedges of *pecorino* sheep's cheese - and buckets full of grapes.

Tittino broke off at some point and brought Rosina to the feast, tethering her next to him at the head of the table and feeding her with whatever was to hand. With the meal over, he led Rosina around giving donkey rides to the children.

The wine flowed; music started and the tables were removed for dancing. It was truly *confusione, confusione* in the only style that the Vichesi know.

As the festivities drew near to an end, Tittino silenced the music, took the DJ's microphone to the nearest balcony and made a speech. His head held high, his nose prominent and by now a little red; he thanked the committee, the helpers and so on to rapturous applause and heckling from the crowd.

He raised his glass to Humanity.

~~~

Tittino's surname is Fania, but if you were to ask someone in Vico and if they knew Tittino Fania, the person would likely shrug their shoulders and give you a blank look. If you asked for Giambattista (a variation of Giovannibattista or John the Baptist) Fania as he was christened, you would likely get an even blanker look.

But, if you were to ask for Tittino *Tavola Moiss'* then you would get instant recognition. "*Shoin, shoin. Lu conosk - Si, si. Lo conosco* - Yes, yes. I know him".

Tavola Moiss' is one example of a '*sopranome*' - an umbrella name or nickname for a family. Tittino bears the name, so does his brother *Chickeen'* (little Francesco) and his sons *Matte'* and *Frankeen'* (yet another diminutive for Francesco).

Tittino's *sopranome* literally means, 'table laid'. And that's how *M* had always interpreted it; she believed that it reflected his table being ready for anyone who turned up, just as we found on my first night in Vico.

But there is lots of scope for misunderstanding Vicaiolo dialect and traditions. One evening when the topic of *sopranomi* came up, as it often did, we discovered the true meaning. Apparently one of Tittino's ancestors was given the name *Tavola Moiss'* because he was in the habit of turning up at other people's houses at meal times.

Sopranomi reflect some notoriety, deed, habit, tradition or misfortune that befell a member of a family. Once applied, they stick and become the currency of recognition. Some *sopranome* are so old that nobody can remember their meaning or why they were applied.

Once I asked Vincenzo where the wine we were drinking came from - his response was *Vincenz' Zi'Gadd*. Vincenzo could translate the sopranome as 'Uncle Cockerel', but he couldn't tell me why the family picked up the name. Nor for that matter could he tell me their surname.

He went on to say that he preferred to buy wine from *Leonardo Ahrahstyn;* although Leonardo was not really an *Ahrahstyn*, he was married into the family and so it was a convenient way to describe who he was. As for the meaning of *Ahrahstyn*, I have never found out to this day. Perhaps it meant dwarf as the unmarried brother and two sisters who lived in a hobbit-sized house in our street were the size of undernourished children.

But for the most part the Vichese can explain the meaning and origin of *sopranome*. *M*'s great, great grandfather had the *sopranome* '*duh Cazedd*' - of the little houses and he earned it when he made his first visit to Vico from *campagna* (for in those days they lived in *ah cazedd'* - *la casetta* - the little house that we visited at San Nicola the day we made pizza). According to legend, on arrival he was overcome by the number of houses and as the story goes he couldn't stop saying "*Mah quant' cazedd* - Well what a lot of little houses."

From then on his descendants would carry the *sopranome* unless they themselves did something significant to get their own. When *M* needs to explain her origins she will always use '*duh Cazedd*'.

The Vichesi can and will deliberate on the origins of *sopranomi* for hours. They treat the subject with sincerity, humour and mischievousness. Often the explanations are simple and straightforward, but where there is legend, there will always be great debate.

I was watching a festival concert in Piazza San Domenico one evening with Zio Mimi (*sopranome Cagnazoll'* - money changer) when he nudged me furtively and nodded in the direction of a group of people sat on a raised pavement outside the Ideal Bar. They resembled a family of gypsies, but they had the best view of the bandstand as if they were a private party in the royal box at the theatre.

"See that old woman all dressed in black," he smirked, "the one sat in the middle," I nodded towards her. He continued mischievously, "*Qued y'eh midyerr dah Cazz' Noyrr*" - *Quella é la moglia di Cazzo Nero* - That's the wife of black penis!" Whoever she was, and whoever he was and why he was bestowed with such notoriety remains a mystery, but she, sitting like a queen on a throne surrounded by adoring courtiers, was a living legend.

Could such a naming system really work? I wondered. Could every generation simply be known by their *sopranome*, their surnames being as redundant as an appendix?

I had my doubts. But Vico is full of surprises.

A French Affair

One year in the early nineties we were returning from a month in Vico when the trusty Volvo quite literally blew its top. We were just about to pass the French town of Bourg en Bresse when there was a loud bang under the bonnet.

I looked in the mirror and a trail of blue smoke was swirling around behind us in the slipstream of the 90mph hulk of metal. We managed to pull into a service area and inspect the car. Oil was dripping menacingly from the rear of the engine.

We called the breakdown service and they arranged for a mechanic to come and have a look. While we were waiting, I managed to locate the leak - the oil was spewing from an unplugged hole in the rear of the cylinder head. Presumably pressure had built up in the engine and blown out the plug. Well it didn't seem too serious.

Eventually the breakdown truck came. The mechanic was very apologetic for the delay but it was Saturday - a busy time. He took a look and immediately confirmed my diagnosis.

"*Ah, bon.* So can you fix it today?" *M* enquired optimistically.

His reply was swift, "*Lundi, je suis desolé*". He was very sorry but we would have to wait until Monday; he would need to order parts and so on.

He loaded the car on to the back of his breakdown lorry and unceremoniously took us away, still sitting at the controls of the not so trusty Volvo. He transported us to a village east of Bourg called Jasseron. From there we called the breakdown service again and arranged for a hotel in Bourg; a further call and we managed to get a taxi.

It was hot, so before the taxi arrived we rescued whatever we could from the bowels of the packed estate car - *caciocavallo*, salami and so on. We had to leave the olive oil, though. We had 50 litres in plastic containers - normally olive oil should not be stored in plastic, but for one or two days it's usually okay. Surely it would be fine until Monday?

We took a room in a hotel recommended by the garage people. We had requested somewhere quiet and if possible not far from a few restaurants. Well it was a modern hotel on a noisy main road, a fair distance from the town centre. Not what we'd asked for at all - perhaps we needed to brush up on our French.

We got the opportunity. Monday came and went with no news on the car. When we rang for news in the late afternoon the mechanic said he had just ordered the part, but he had no idea when it would arrive.

In the meantime we did a lot of walking and discovered Bourg en Bresse, its cuisine and historical buildings. There was a great bistro "Le Petit Creux" half indoors, half out on the street, run by the spitting image of the Glasgow comedian Robbie Coltrane - beefy with a mop of curly dark hair.

Then there was Chez Guy, an independent haute-cuisine restaurant attached to the Hotel de France in the centre of town. The restaurant was excellent but hard on the wallet. The hotel was convenient and despite its condition, we thought it would have been much the better to stay at.

Then there were bakeries, cafes and the market; life while bustling was nowhere near the *confusione* that is Vico.

~~~

We had holidayed in France some years earlier, but only accidentally. On that occasion we had decided to have a couple of weeks in the south-west of the UK touring Devon and Cornwall. Lot's of our friends went there and always came back saying how agreeable the weather was. So we chose blazing June and set off.

Even as we left the Cotswolds, the rain started and it rained and rained. On the way south we managed to pick up more of the weather forecast. It was raining, it was going to go on raining and it was going to get colder.

But we had a plan B. We could go to Brittany. We had our passports so we headed for Plymouth and caught the ferry to Roscoff. We left the rain behind. Landing at Roscoff, a small port with all the character of a fishing village, we parked the car and did a little shopping. We bought a baguette, some paté, cheese and wine and had a picnic while looking out to sea and perusing the map. The weather was gorgeous. What should we do next?

We decided to head for Carnac to see its stone circles in the warm evening sunshine. There we spent an unmemorable night. The next morning we headed out along a narrow peninsula protruding into the Bay of Biscay. At the tip was the town of Quiberon - we would eat there and see if we could find somewhere pleasant to stay for a few days. We were lucky; we found a seafood restaurant right on the beach and a table in the sunshine. Plan B was working. There we sat and gorged on a multi-tiered platter of crustaceans accompanied by a bottle of Muscadet.

The afternoon waned and with it the sun. Storm clouds gathered and it began to rain. We didn't find anywhere to stay, so we got back in the car and headed south. That night we stayed in some non-descript *table d'hôtes* - Plan B in shreds.

"Well lets go further South; we still have lots of time," I suggested. Out came the map. We'll head for the Dordogne - we'd heard that it was charming.

The next day we set off determined that we would enjoy the weather somewhere. We arrived in Beynac in the early evening. Just in time to find a hotel and wash away the long drive with an ice-cold Kronenbourg in the warm evening sun before having a meal.

The following day we struck out towards Libourne and St Emilion following the Dordogne. Plan C was to do a little wine tasting. But things didn't turn out as expected; we wound along the river taking in the sights and in the evening stayed at a hotel with a restaurant. I ate a medium rare steak smeared with one of those French sauces that failed to disguise the fact that it was raw. How did they cook it? By walking it slowly through a warm room? That night I went down with the 'Dordognes'.

It was after midday the next day when I felt it was safe for me to leave the room and checkout of the hotel. I was a pale shadow of my former self having emptied most of my body one way or another in the bathroom. The headache was splitting my infinitives. The madam tried to charge us another day as it was after twelve. With a few chosen phrases vis-à-vis the state of the kitchen and condition of the meat they served we left without paying extra.

The sunshine was fading as I dragged my stricken body round St Emilion. Eventually we left for our evening accommodation. In a guidebook we found a *table d'hotes* in the Medoc: Chateau Cap Leon Veyran at Listrac. Despite my ordeal I managed to enjoy the home cooking, the company and, of course, the wine.

There we met a Canadian couple with whom we spent the next few days tasting a variety of great Chateaux in the region and having picnics whenever the weather allowed. The 'Dordognes' were never too far away, but I survived.

We travelled back up through the Loire and went up to the Normandy beaches before returning to the UK. Plan A, a little warm weather had never stood a chance. Plan B was short-lived, but Plan C introduced us to a France we rather liked.

~~~

We escaped Bourg en Bresse after 4 days, the Volvo's reputation and the holiday budget in tatters. The one consolation being that we had had the sense to remove the perishable valuables from the car. The 4-day delay in the heat would have seen them off. Surprisingly the olive oil survived and we soon had it transferred into glass back in the UK.

It was a frustrating delay, but it did remind us of the brighter side of our unplanned French sojourn years earlier and that France had its good points.

In the years following we made sure that we stopped en-route instead of just hurtling straight through to Italy. Bourg en Bresse was an ideal stopover. The Hotel de France was cheap, clean and we enjoyed many gastronomic delights at Chez Guy - after a few visits I became confident enough to order the meat. On return journeys we would stop somewhere between Macon and Dijon or further north in Reims.

Each stop reminded us how much we liked France and that it could be a good place to live. It was less chaotic than Italy - no *confusione*, quieter by far (almost to the point of being dead at times). If we believed what we read, property was a snip and a house in the country would be easy to find, maybe even a vineyard?

And so it was that *M* and I agreed that we would, one day, sell up and move to France. We could still visit Vico with ease and journeys back to the UK would be less arduous than from deepest Italy. It made good sense. We were convinced.

~~~

Whenever we could spare the time (and money) we made forays into

France taking in Provence, Cotes du Rhones, The Gard, The Vaucluse and The Languedoc. We researched the climate in these zones, attempting to find microclimates that were least affected by the wind - an almost impossible task but we tried.

We brushed up on French, cultivated the art of drinking *pastis*, eating three-course lunches, visiting the markets. The food market at Narbonne was particularly mouth-watering. There we could buy oysters for 7 francs a dozen; the fish merchant would open them on the spot and lay them on crushed ice on a polystyrene tray. We'd take them back to the gîte and wash them down with a bottle of champagne. *Mais oui*! The French life suited us well.

Estate agent's windows were full of pictures of desirable properties, so much so that we didn't bother too much about interrupting our holidays to investigate what we might be able to buy – we would deal with those matters when the time came.

It seemed idyllic; we loved France and we had already given up any thought of living in Italy. We would escape the UK and find a new life in France - the only issue being when and where.

House Hunting in France

The opportunity came in 2001. Our plan had always been to find work in France, sell up in the UK, rent a place and spend the weekends and holidays searching for a new home. It would be easy and we would have cash when the time came.

But I didn't actually find a job in France, I found one in Switzerland. Well, it was close enough and it was too good a chance to miss. We sold up and put our worldly goods into storage.

For the next 18 months we worked the plan. My job was flexible enough to arrange long weekends and I could take holidays at will provided that my project was not affected. We began to hone in on the areas that we liked, selecting the microclimates that might give us an ideal life.

We scoured southern France from the Haute Savoie to the Languedoc and in the end we chose Nyons - famous for its olives and apparently possessing a microclimate that escaped the penetrating Mistral winds.

But by this stage we were having problems. Where were all these properties that we had read about? We simply couldn't find anything; admittedly we were being a tad specific. We wanted a detached house (preferably an old farmhouse) set in land of not less than 1 acre with some interest that would put us in touch with the locals. Olive trees or vines would be ideal, as we would have to harvest and sell them somehow. The only real proviso was that the neighbours and watercourses had to be kept at a distance from the house.

Surely we were not asking for too much? But by now we had used up a valuable 18 months with nothing to show for it. We had shifted our position from no, or little restoration, to "we'll look at anything". We were tired and it seemed like another of our plans had backfired.

We had trawled the estate agents (along with many other foreigners) but all those pictures of desirable residences were simply window-dressing. The properties had already been sold, perhaps years ago judging by the unbelievable prices! But the agents were predictable. "Je suis desolé – the property has just been sold." We didn't believe them, but we would never know.

The other problem was the agent's inaction. Despite cultivating them, cajoling them and efforts to convince them that we weren't time wasters, they simply did nothing on our behalf.

~~~

Then out of the blue we seemed to have a breakthrough. One of the estate agents we had been nurturing called us in Switzerland to say that he had found a charming farmhouse with terraces of olive trees about 1 km from the village of Mirabel-aux-Baronnies just down the road from Nyons.

"It's a little over the budget you mentioned, but completely renovated," he added.

It certainly had to be - you'd have thought we were looking at a house in the leafy suburbs of Surrey, judging by the price.

"Could you come immediately, as it is a house that will sell?"

They faxed a picture. "Yes! Of course we'll come," was our instant reply.

We made arrangements and, as always, contacted our other agents in the region. Did they have anything new we could look at?

There was Errol in Nyons. "Yes" he had one or two interesting properties and he would be available after the weekend. Then there was another long shot - an agent in the Ardeche, a Dutchman called Hendrik, had something very interesting. It all looked like our hard work was paying off at last, so we arranged a long weekend and departed Friday morning. But the question was always on our minds, 'So why on earth hadn't either of these agents contacted us about these new properties as promised?'

~~~

On Friday evening we stayed in the hotel Colombets in Nyons, dined at a reasonable restaurant then watched a serious *boules* competition in the town square that must have involved the whole population. The next morning we checked out of the hotel in Nyons and drove the short distance to Mirabel where we met Marcus, the estate agent who had phoned us about the farmhouse, a young clammy-handed man in a very smart suit. We followed him the "1 km" to the house - about 5 km later we arrived!

Well, it looked very attractive as in the picture they had faxed us, but where was the view? It did indeed face south, with a splendid view of the back of a hill. The outlook was disappointing, but from a distance, this was the best house we'd seen, so we thought we'd give it a positive look-over before making up our minds.

There was a man standing in the driveway; he was saying farewell to a couple in a Belgian car. Was it already sold? We waited patiently, while our young estate agent attempted to put a gloss on the southerly view and made a note about correcting the distance from Mirabel in the details.

Eventually the Belgians left and we were able to meet the owner. He seemed an odd sort of person for the house. Dressed in a leather suit with longish greased curly black hair and sunshades. He was as polite as he needed to be, but his mobile phone took precedence over us. He seemed a sleaze ball to me, but who cared? Let's get on with it.

Marcus walked us across the lawn where, he told us, we could put the swimming pool - only problem being that the septic tank was in the middle of it. "Hmmm, we'll let that pass for now."

We passed the garage, which had a roof that was about to collapse (rather negating the claim that the property needed no work) as he took us to view the detached studio. It was a character stone building and we weren't disappointed - it had been well renovated.

Having inspected the studio, we turned towards the house. From nowhere a woman appeared, waving her arms in the air and severely testing my powers of comprehension. In the fracas we noticed another woman. She was verbally assaulting the owner who was still clinging to his mobile phone.

Translations flowed. Apparently, the first woman had told us that we couldn't go into the house; that it wasn't for sale and we should clear off. Marcus decided that retreat was the sensible option at this point and he shepherded us off to see the olive terraces. The rumpus continued behind us.

The olive terraces turned out to have only just been planted, the new saplings looked sick, either from lack of water or unsuitable terrain. The terraces were non-existent - it was simply a sloping field. Whether that was important we didn't know, but we were losing interest fast as Marcus tried to save the situation.

As we returned to the house my thoughts were simply of despair and I just wanted to leave, but not *M*. She was determined to find out what was going on. Her French is much better than mine and she was listening attentively to Marcus. The sleaze ball was Marcus's estate agent boss; the problem was one of divorce. The husband of the woman who was abusing the sleaze ball was a friend of the sleaze ball. It appeared that she wasn't too happy with the thought of parting with the house and her husband had, apparently, made arrangements to sell without her knowledge.

One the situation was clearer we decided to leave. We weren't going to see the house and even if we did, it might be years before the marital feud allowed its sale. The only problem was that we couldn't get out. The women assaulting the estate agent had blocked us in - the car doors were wide open and her baby was crying in the back seat.

As we couldn't escape, I attempted to charm the first woman with my schoolboy French. "Look," I said, "we have come all the way from Switzerland to see this house - at least you could be reasonable with us? Let us at least have a look?"

"The house is not for sale!" she retorted. "Bugger off," or words to that effect.

"Well move the bloody car then!" I bellowed in English for all the good it would do.

Eventually Marcus got them to move the car; he attempted to apologise to us for the misunderstanding, but it was lost on us. "No, you needn't bother keeping in touch," were our parting words.

We left, by this time completely numbed by events. As we drove down the narrow lane we consoled ourselves with the thought that at least we had other arrangements for the weekend.

"It won't be a completely wasted trip," we were agreeing, when a car appeared from nowhere at breakneck speed. It left the road and tore through the bushes to avoid being squashed by the Volvo; I looked at the dust in the mirror as he sped off. "That must be the husband," we laughed simultaneously, trying desperately to look on the bright side of things.

~~~

That afternoon we made our way across the Rhone to Joyeuse in the Ardeche. On one of our earlier exploratory visits to France, we spent a week just outside Joyeuse at a *gîte* owned by some Belgians. It was a lovely area and we particularly liked the colour of the stone used in building houses and dry-stone walls. This trip we had booked B & B with the same Belgians.

It was there that we had made our only offer on a house in France some months earlier through the Dutch agent Hendrik. We never had a reply. But we were still in contact with Hendrik and so we could brush up on that house to see if it was still for sale and he had two or three properties he wanted to show us - we would not be disappointed, surely.

On the Sunday we rested up at the B & B. The weather was perfect, so we could swim in the pool and our hosts invited us for lunch. We were relaxed for the following day.

We met up with Hendrik on Monday morning at his office in Les Vans. We had inquired about our previous offer and Hendrik said that his boss wanted to speak to us about it. Were we getting somewhere at last? The boss hadn't arrived so we went for coffee. One hour later his boss still hadn't arrived so Hendrik decided to take us to see a 'gem' - a farmhouse close to Joyeuse.

It turned out to be a massive complex of house and farm buildings, in need of complete restoration. Someone had already attempted some repairs; parts of the house had been partitioned and ugly steel girders were suspended in some rooms giving the impression that something was seriously wrong with the structure. It had lots of land, all of it completely derelict. Here and there were signs of a failed campsite enterprise: toilet blocks, tap stands and concrete bases.

Hendrik seemed to be getting close to what we were looking for, but this project was too big to even contemplate; the price was ridiculous and we told him so as we returned to the car. He didn't bother to try and call his boss about the house we were really interested in and continued with his schedule. He assured us that the next house was a little out of the way, but it really was well worth seeing and the owners would come down in price.

Well, we had talked to Hendrik a lot about what we wanted and we were sure that he had understood. So we set off in a westerly direction from Les Vans and drove up into a remote hilly region. Even as we left civilisation we were saying to Hendrik that it was already too far out for us. But he was determined to go there.

"Yes there is a village nearby with a bakery," he affirmed. "No, it really isn't that remote," he argued.

After a gruelling 45-minute drive into the forested hills we were on a remote road when he asked us to stop at a chalet style building.

"This is it?" we inquired astonished.

"Yes,"

"But it's in the middle of nowhere, has no views, no *raison d'être*. It's not remotely like a farmhouse. What the hell are we doing here?"

It turned out that we couldn't even look at the property even if we wanted to. The owners weren't there. He didn't even have the keys to the garden.

We returned along the same arduous route. Hendrik was quiet. This seemed like the end of the road. We stopped at a bar for a beer and to let him smoke for a while. It was there that he had a brainwave.

"There's another property, we have the keys; it's on the outskirts of a little village about half an hour from Les Vans. It has only just come on the market, I haven't seen it yet but I'm told that it has spectacular views, lovely roof terraces and a garden," he enthused. He would collect the keys at lunchtime and we could see it in the afternoon. He was trying hard.

"Do you have any details?" *M* asked.

"Well no, you see it has just come to us; they won't be ready for a while."

We had another beer and he another smoke as we juggled with this latest possibility.

"Well we're here, we have nothing to lose. Yes, ok then, we'll meet you this afternoon."

~~~

After lunch in Les Vans we felt refreshed and ready to return to the grind. We had had another chance to digest the slack methods of the estate agents here; we knew we had little choice but to go along at every opportunity. Something would turn up. We set off again with Hendrik, his clothes giving off a most unpleasant aroma of stale tobacco.

Again, it wasn't a half hour drive. It was an hour. Are they using a different clock? I was just about to turn the car around when Hendrik pointed to a hamlet clinging to the side of hill in the distance. "There it is," he blurted out, "not far to go now."

We'd nearly passed through the hamlet when Hendrik ordered

us into a lay-by where there were two parking spaces. It certainly did look a pretty place, the whole hamlet constructed from honey-coloured stone.

Hendrik leapt out of the car.

"Hang on I'll just get directions," his voice trailing off as he went. He lit up. We waited a few minutes, trying to be patient about him bringing us to yet another very remote location. But still there was the hamlet. Eventually he re-emerged from the cluster of houses.

"I've found it, come on," he beckoned.

"What, we have to go by foot, why can't we go in the car?" I asked in vain as he disappeared ahead. Not that I had to drive everywhere, I welcomed the stretch, but surely we could get the car to the house?

We caught up with him and he looked pale. "Well, it's not exactly an independent farmhouse," he admitted as we paced along. "You see I haven't been here before and, well, they appear to have got the description mixed up."

We were just about to turn and flee, when he stopped; "there it is," he pointed to a bijou, terraced cottage.

Before we could protest Hendrik whipped out the keys and was trying to find the right one when suddenly the door burst open and a woman appeared.

"What are you doing?" she screamed.

Hendrik reeled back in shock. Then a man appeared by the woman's side with a menacing look, asking a similar question I supposed.

After a few tense moments, they managed to work out who was who. Hendrik had never met them; they were supposed to be away. We just wanted to run away.

"No, no, no it's no trouble," they insisted. "Do come in and have a look."

Well we didn't want to; we're not voyeurs and we knew that the place was completely wrong for us. Hendrik was desperately sorry and asked us just to take a look so that he could get a feel for the place. So we did.

It was very picturesque. The roof terrace was a strange arrangement though - we had to climb up a ladder to get to it!

"Where is the garden?" I asked with feigned interest as I gazed out over the rooftops. I had to admit it was a spectacular view. Hendrik asked the owner, who pointed far down into the valley -

59

apparently there was a piece of ground below somewhere.

After a short viewing, we departed saying farewell to this young couple (and wanting to advise them to change their agent).

"Yes, we'll think it over," we felt obliged to say.

Back in the car we were all silent. There was nothing Hendrik could say, and nothing we wanted to say. It was a long drive back and another fruitless visit to the Ardeche was about to end.

Suddenly Hendrik broke the silence.

"You know I'm giving up this job next week."

"Really, why's that?" I inquired politely.

He muttered something about his boss, presumably and maybe quite rightly blaming him for the whole charade.

"What are you going to do?" I asked, trying to console him.

"Start my own agency." It was not very convincing reply.

We said goodbye to Hendrik in Les Vans, lying to him that we would be his first customers, and returned to the B & B for a late swim followed by a meal in a restaurant in nearby Laurac. We were exhausted, not just with the viewing; we were tired of the whole process. But tomorrow was another day.

~~~

The following morning we set off early for Nyons, where we would meet up with Errol. In our hearts we knew that Errol was our last chance. He claimed to know exactly what we wanted and he had said on the phone that he had a couple of ideal properties.

Well, surprise, surprise, he hadn't! Once again he wasted our time and his. As we said farewell to Errol and Nyons, we sensed that our affair with France was over.

On the journey back to Switzerland we struggled to understand why, after so much effort, so many trips, so much research and such expense, we had drawn a complete blank.

We had to change tack, but which way to go?

We determined to go to Italy whenever we could manage our next holiday. We needed a break from France and while we were there we would spend some time investigating the property market. We wouldn't bother with Tuscany, Umbria, The Marche or Abruzzo; they would be just like France - full of foreigners looking for their dream homes and estate agents willing to feed their appetites.

No, we would go straight to the Gargano.

The Bolthole

That August we headed down to Vico for a holiday and a little research. We would ask around among our relatives, friends and acquaintances. Someone was bound to know of properties for sale. After all, for years everyone had been saying that they couldn't give the stuff away and the countryside is littered with abandoned buildings. If all fails there is one estate agent in Vico - we would, reluctantly, give him a chance.

Falling back into the Vico routine, so familiar now with years of practice under our belts, was easy. First thing in the morning we would go to market to buy fruit and greens and maybe some fish, pick up a piece of *Pugliese* bread and, if there was a shortage at home a little *caciocavallo piccante*. We would bump into old friends and relatives and nod to familiar faces; it all seemed so natural. Yes, it was a good place to be.

On the face of it Vico had changed little over the years. There had been modernisation of sorts: mains sewers had been installed throughout; the council no longer needed to spray for flies at night; the communal bins were emptied regularly and people were asked to put out their rubbish in the cool morning only.

Streetlights had been installed (practical yes, but some of the character of the shadowy alleyways had been extinguished), attempts were being made to control unruly parking and rein in stray dogs.

The Vichesi had become visibly richer: the young were now driving smart cars; old bangers were generally a thing of the past. However, the elderly and wise still stuck to their old ways - no new cars for them, but maybe a new set of teeth!

Treruote and donkeys were still plentiful, as the surrounding countryside had not changed at all. The three-wheeler workhorses can go almost anywhere and seem capable of hauling loads many times their weight - the motorised equivalent of the ant; but once the gradient of the land becomes too steep they become unstable. Then only the donkey will carry the load, so their presence may be assured for years to come.

Goat and sheep herds still roamed around as if they owned the road and everyone else's countryside. The goats being particularly destructive as they erode dry stone walls, climbing all over them in order to reach succulent leaves or ravage unguarded vineyards and olive groves.

No, the only thing that really changes in Vico is the population. Hardly a week passes without a funeral. These are announced with sombre black and white posters at various billboards throughout the town.

At one time I believed that deaths were contagious here as the billboards were constantly being changed, but then I discovered that many posters were simply reminders of the anniversaries of death.

The posters starkly announce the name and age of the departed. Their age always grabs my attention. So many people live well into their eighties and nineties, even after enduring such a harsh, peasant-like existence. Or was it because of it?

~~~

A few years earlier my dear friend Tittino had died. A combination of a hard life and an even harder lifestyle had taken its toll.

When we visited that year, his wife Antonietta was still there at the door to welcome us, looking no older than the first day that I had met her all those years ago, but now wearing the solemn face of the bereaved.

Now she was dressed from head to toe in black. She wore some black the first day I saw her and I'd never seen her without, but this was different. When immediate family die, the women dress in black for a respectful period, often for a year, sometimes for years, depending on the closeness of the deceased relative. Now, in her case, now it would be for life.

We went to visit Tittino at the cemetery. Antonietta had given us directions, but it's a big place with many alleys of block upon block of high-rise, marble-fronted tombs. We shuffled from grave to grave for ages in the heat looking for his photo. Eventually we found him in a wall in a new part of the cemetery.

There was his picture, taken many years before his death, perhaps at a wedding or first Holy Communion of one of his children, grandchildren or indeed great grandchildren. In it he looked about the age when we first met him 16 years or so previously. Then my eyes fell upon his death year inscribed on the marble tombstone … for Vico he wasn't old at all, he died aged only 75!

We also paid our respects that summer. The street was solemn apart from the children, who raced around playing tag or football screaming at the top of their voices, innocents not required to mourn. The remaining men still met every evening for their mandatory card games, but instead of playing in the street they had to play in Zio Mimi's cantina.

When arguments erupted at the table, as they inevitably did, they were short-lived and always brought to an abrupt end with a nod in the direction of Antonietta's house.

~~~

Having settled into the routine, our minds returned to the big question in hand - could we find a house here?

Of course, if we did find a property, we knew that we would be in for a ground-up rebuild and be at the mercy of all the local tradesmen, whose collective reputation was as good as any you'd find in the UK or was rumoured to be in France. But at least we knew people - they would help us, guide us to the right tradesmen. We convinced ourselves that it could work.

After market we would head for 'our' beach between San Menaio and Rodi, but this year instead of taking the shortest and most convenient route past Zio Mimi's olives at Partechiano, we drove a different route each day scanning the countryside for properties.

It was actually on the Partechiano road that we found the first interesting house. In fact we had passed it for years without noticing it; maybe we hadn't really been looking, but more likely someone had cut trees or a hedge to reveal it. There was a ready-made track going to the house. A wire stretched across the entrance - a sure signal here that no one was about. We stopped the car to explore.

We furtively circled the house on foot, as always astonished by the state of abandonment. But the house was in good condition from what we could see through the brambles that almost surrounded it. The roof was still intact and the thick walls showed few cracks. We couldn't see inside, as the front door was locked and the windows were shuttered. But that is normally a good sign, as humans and animals would have ravaged a house left open to the elements.

The house was located on flat ground, surrounded by what seemed to be fertile land stocked with well-tended orange, lemon and fig trees, the lot encircled by small manageable olive trees. It had a panoramic view from West through North to East. The sea shimmered about 200 metres below a kilometre or so away. It would be much warmer than Vico in winter but close enough to get daily supplies. We liked it. We would find the owner. As we left, we spotted electricity posts close by. This was a good find.

Back in Vico that evening we wasted no time. We found M's uncle Mimi playing cards in the street, as the men do every evening in grief-free summers. He had land at Partechiano. We would ask him first. He was sure to know the owner. We waited till they had finished and then broached the subject.

It took some time for him to hone in on the property as we described the location - it would have been quicker to take him there. The assembled sages debated *sopranome* after *sopranome* until they eventually agreed that it belonged to the Cataldo family - they didn't have a *sopranome*, as they came from the nearby village of Cagnano. So we knew who they were, but no one could tell us how to find them.

To us that didn't seem too much of a problem. Someone was tending the ground, so it ought to be easy to find that person even if the owners had emigrated.

~~~

Widening our search, we decided to try the local estate agent Ciccomascolo. He had an office close to the hub of Vico - the roundabout at San Francesco, but there were only postcards in the window with a limited description of the various properties and land for sale. Not a photograph in sight.

We decided to go in and ask. He sat alone in a cavernous office at a solitary desk. We described the sort of house we were seeking and he nodded - he "knew" exactly what we were looking for. He rifled through his files, but he had nothing to show us on paper. He simply read out descriptions "house on one floor, one room and a stable, 1 hectare of olives, some fruit trees". Had he been listening?

Eventually he found a house that at least had two floors and so we set off to see it.

He took us to San Nicola, the valley where *M*'s grandfather used to have land and the location of the Hunting Lodge that we visited on the pizza picnic day. In the intervening years the Hunting Lodge had been sold without us even knowing it was for sale. We were a little sad to have maybe missed an opportunity, but we had been fortunate! The new section of the *superstrada* passes literally right over it and the new owner has to live with the constant noise of traffic thumping across the expansion gaps in the viaduct above.

Ciccomascolo took us down the track past the Hunting Lodge; we went on and on deep into the valley till we reached an abandoned house set in 3 hectares of olives. It was idyllic, but we knew the area too well. In Summer it would be unbearably hot with not a breath of wind, humidity would engulf us, mosquitoes and midges would eat us alive. No, Ciccomascolo didn't quite know what we wanted.

We conceded that the style of property was good, if a little small, but he had to understand that we must have a view, air and so on. They would guarantee us a reasonably insect-free environment.

"Is there anything else we can see?"

To our surprise, he announced that despite all the derelict buildings in the Gargano, this one was all he had on his books.

How could this be? "Do you already have a market and are they snapped up the day they come up for sale?" *M* asked unbelievingly.

"No, no," he insisted, "nothing like that. The sort of house you want very rarely comes on the market."

With that unwelcome scrap of news we gave him our contact numbers and bid him farewell saying we would be back again soon, probably in November. He assured us he would keep his eyes and ears open and let us know if anything turned up, but we had little faith!

~~~

As the holiday drew to a close we were having little luck finding the owners at Partechiano, then one evening we mentioned the Cataldo family to *M*'s cousin Mimmo who recognised the name as the people who owned a furniture shop in Vico. While we were talking to Mimmo we described what we were looking for generally and he said there were lots of places and we would talk again later in the year.

Just before we left Vico that Summer, we managed to locate the Cataldo shop and we stopped to ask the owner whether they would like to sell the property. The reply was immediate and firm "We don't sell. We only buy!"

So much for the long held belief put about by all here that 'they couldn't give property away'.

The holiday ended with nothing tangible - only disappointment. We could only console ourselves with the fact that at least we had put the word about. Hopefully when we returned there would be things to see.

Vico Out of Season

In November of that year we managed to return for 10 days. On the first evening we passed the estate agent, Ciccomascolo, who is always loitering on the street outside his office, but he had nothing new. The postcards in the window had only yellowed with age.

We visited cousin Mimmo; he had many possibilities but he still had to talk to people. Well, he has a full-time job and is always busy so we can't expect much.

Nothing seemed to be happening. Then one day at market we bumped into *M*'s cousin, Michele *Kappa da For'* (literally meaning "out of his head", but it was really given to an ancestor who never wore a cap). He knew of a house with an olive mill set in about 7 hectares of olives; the price, he thought, was 300 million lire. He like many others still ignored the Euro.

This was the first price that we'd heard for property in Italy. Three hundred million sounded a tidy sum and we had to do some quick mental arithmetic to convert to 150,000 Euros. Once in perspective, though, it seemed reasonable especially remembering the prices in France.

"Okay Michele, let's arrange to see it as soon as possible." Fine, he would check with owners in Rome and make the arrangements.

Meanwhile we continued our tour of the area. Occasionally we would leave the car to walk up tracks taking advantage of different viewpoints; it was an opportunity to collect wood and *strummeli* (pine cones) as winter was approaching and even though the weather was sunny and warm, the evenings in Vico were cold.

It was a very different experience from August - there were no tourists, but still it was very lively and not the dead place that Vincenzo assured us it would be.

The countryside was a-buzz with the locals cleaning the ground and laying their olive nets, transforming the landscape under the trees into a patchwork of reds, oranges, greens and whites. Some had already begun to collect their olives and take them to the mill; *treruote* and donkey alike laden to the hilt with sacks of the precious fruit.

The market, although not displaying the same range and abundance of fruit and vegetables was non-the-less good for wintertime and there was always fresh fish if the seas were not too stormy. We had expected the fish prices to be cheaper as the visiting migrants all said, rather cynically, that they put them up in the summer because the visitors had more money. So we had taken careful note of the prices in August and now in the autumn on the face of it there seemed very little difference. Of course prices went up and down according to seasonal availability and weather conditions, but overall little changed.

Up at San Francesco men gathered at one corner each evening with their day's harvest of mushrooms from the forest. This year though was not particularly good, so quality *porcini* were expensive.

Despite everything that we had been told, Vico seemed a pleasant place to be out of season.

~~~

Zio Mimi, *M*'s uncle, arrived from Bologna and we immediately struck up a deal that I would go and help him harvest his olives at Partechiano in exchange for some oil - it would give us a rest from traipsing around the countryside and me some experience of the harvest.

With no time to lose we set off the next day at dawn in his hatchback Lancia, loaded with nets, ladders, an assortment of *mazze* (supple sticks for beating the crop from the trees), sacks and of course a chainsaw and axe.

The weather down at Partechiano was every bit as I had expected. At 500 metres the wind was now biting at Vico and our holiday apartment was proving ill-equipped to deal with the cold. But at Partechiano, some 300 metres lower down, I soon stripped down to a T-shirt as I laboured away carrying out the torrent of orders coming from Zio Mimi.

Of course, he doesn't speak Italian (or if he does it must be the Bolognese sort) so there was a great deal to learn. But everything was a rush, we had to get on and he would mime the actions to me.

"*Toirr, Toirr!*" as he tugged at the corner of the nets. "*Alz', alz'!*" as he lifted the corners.

Zio Mimi had always looked young, unlike Tittino. At 70-something he was moving around on the difficult stony terrain like a 20-year old but he kept all his winter layers on.

It wasn't long before we had the requisite four nets spread under the first tree, pinned down by rocks in case of sudden gusts and the remainder of the nets organised to catch any stray olives and in position for the adjacent trees.

All the while Zio Mimi had an eye up the trees. He had worked here in the Spring, pruning the trees and cleaning the ground. Throughout the hot summer months he had spent from dawn until midday sweating away on this unforgiving land. And now he was swearing away under his breath and gesticulating with his hands raised towards the tops of the trees. "*Porka miseria, poco roba!*" he lamented. There was no doubt he wasn't pleased with the crop.

Then with ladders in place, secateurs in his belt-holster, razor-sharp axe tucked into a loose string belt and a suitable *mazza*, he was off up the tree. Olive trees generally have three or four main branches, he chose one and in seconds he had left the ladder, was perched in the top of the tree, one knee looped over a branch for balance. Olives began to rain down to the nets as he brushed the *mazza* through the pendent branches.

It looked precarious, it was certainly not something I fancied doing at least not until I had had some practice lower down. I grabbed another *mazza* and started to sweep through the ground-level branches as he did. Within moments he was on to me.

I interpreted him correctly "No, no, not like that, you'll damage the plant."

I was outside the circumference of the tree beating inwards. He gestured to me to stand inside and brush outwards.

I was learning, but it wasn't long before he was calling to me again.

"What now?" I was standing on the olives, crushing them underfoot. This was no good, it would ruin the oil; it would make it acidic. It seemed impossible to move around on the nets without doing some damage. I reasoned, incorrectly, that in a few hours time we would be crushing them anyway so what was the problem? As a compromise, I decided to climb the tree and have a go at the lower branches.

Zio Mimi seemed to approve. By now he had his axe out and was cutting away some of the top growth, suckers that would not produce fruit. This would save work later next year and made harvesting easier. I would be in mortal danger if he dropped the axe, so he told me to work from one of the other main branches.

After about an hour we had knocked all the olives off the first tree - the crumpled nets below awash with green and black rivers of fruit. I got out of the tree, gingerly picked my way to the edge so that I did as little damage as possible. Zio Mimi came down and walked across the nets without even monitoring his feet seemingly squashing olives as he went. I looked for a trail of devastation and found nothing - it was as if he had walked on air. We began to collect up the nets. As we did so, we had to remove the *frasca*, the prunings that he had cut and all the other debris that comes down from the beating of the branches.

When the net was clean we lifted it, piled the olives on a net under the next tree and moved on, taking the empty nets with us and laying them in the general direction that we would head that day.

I was already tired, hot and thirsty but there were several hours to go.

"*Sant' pisciatur, poco roba*! - Holy bedpan, so little stuff!" was just about all that Zio Mimi could utter as he looked at the pile of olives that we had gathered - it wouldn't even fill a sack.

If Zio Mimi was unhappy with the crop he didn't let it spoil his day. He went about the task with zeal. He'd grown up with olives in his blood and even though events forced him to desert his land for a factory job in Bologna, he would never abandon it. Once at the top of a branch in the brilliant sunshine, he would burst into an aria and trill away like a thrush in Spring. He was never happier than when he was here in *campagna*, breathing the clean air, tending his flock of precious olives.

As we moved through the trees he instructed me to collect all the frasca and make a bonfire - we would clean as we went. Six hours later, my eyes smarting from the wood smoke, my back sore, my feet blistered and bruised by the rough rocky ground, we had collected three bags of olives (maybe 150 kg).

Zio Mimi carried the bags one-by-one on his shoulder to the car some 50 metres away and loaded them into the back. I tried lifting a sack and, somewhat shamefacedly, decided to leave it to him. We collected up the nets and tools and tied them to the roof rack; the

70

only thing we left in *campagna* was the ladder - this he chained and padlocked to one of the trees.

When we got to Vico, we unloaded the olives at his garage; we would not be taking such a puny amount to the mill. Better to wait until we had at least five *quintale* (500 kg) - so just as well that I hadn't crushed too many under foot.

We worked for three days and on the last evening, Zio Mimi, *M* and myself took the olives to the mill at the market place where we were initiated into the process of producing olive oil.

The olives were weighed, loaded into a hopper, from where an escalator took them to a blower that filtered out any remaining leaf debris. From the blower the olives cascaded into a shallow bath-like washing machine, where the interlocking mesh floor agitated the olives in water, any dirt draining through the mesh and the olives bubble along to the end of the floor where they fall into another hopper.

After washing, the olives are transported from the hopper to a grinding machine and then on through a series of milling machines with revolving circular blades, emerging from each one as a more refined paste. In the last stage, the paste was pumped into a centrifugal press from which the precious golden liquid emerged, separated from the waste water.

We photographed the whole process, providing much amusement for the assembled company - what was all the fuss about; didn't they make olive oil in *Inghilterra*? As the oil poured from the press, the workers tore apart some Pugliese bread, dipped it into the oil and handed it to us to taste - it had a delicious peppery flavour. This was cold-pressed, admittedly using modern methods, Extra Virgin - the best in Italy we were assured by all.

For our efforts we had turned a little under 450kg of olives into 85 litres of olive oil - an acceptable yield of about 19%. Despite Zio Mimi's misgivings about the crop, it had been a good year.

That evening over supper, Zio Mimi presented me with five litres for my three days work.

~~~

I was happy to return to the important business of finding a home and having a well-earned rest. One thing for sure was that making olive oil involved a lot of work and the financial reward seemed disproportionate.

Two days later on the way to market, we visited Michele *Kappa da For'* at his carpentry workshop as we were eager to get on with things.

"We can go and see the Roman's house," he said.

At last a breakthrough - we were actually going to see something. "When?" I asked.

Michele, who only speaks Vicaiolo, uttered "*Moh, moh, yah muh chu'nuh moh* - Now, now, let's go now."

He dropped whatever he was doing, whether it was important or not and we crammed into his Fiat Panda and headed out of Vico on one of the roads going down to the Bay of Calenella. About 150 metres above sea level he pulled off the road onto a track and stopped the car. This was the start of the land. We walked down through the gently sloping olive groves eventually arriving at the back of a quite derelict house.

Half of the upper floor of the house appeared to have been demolished. It didn't look good. But when we went round to the front of the house we were taken aback by the uninterrupted view of Calenella and the coastline cliff of Monte Pucci - never mind the state of the house, this really was stunning.

As we absorbed the view, we noticed some old millstones lying around in the long grass. Time to move on and in. First we went into the left-hand two-storey part of the house. The door had long gone, but the stone mullions at least were still in place. Inside the rooms were tiny as the staircase took most of the space - it lead to equally cramped rooms upstairs. We were not impressed.

We exited and approached the adjacent front door. From repairs to the outside masonry, we could see that it had once been a huge entrance, now toned down. Maybe to allow the passage of carts. The door was adrift on its hinges, but again the mullions were in place. Inside we found a huge arched room about the size and shape of a Nissen hut. This was more like it we enthused.

As our eyes became accustomed to the light, we could see that the building had been rifled; most of the flagstone floor had been ripped up and only the footprint of the milling machinery could be seen. But there was much more ...

From this arch, there were steps down into another arch of the same proportions; above that arch and visible through the top of the arch we were standing under was another large room with arched columns supporting a now defunct wooden roof. The building was simply massive.

The second lower arch was full of bins and derelict animal pens and beyond it, we found an enormous cave; then to the right there was a two-storey stable building just to add to the immensity.

This really was a staggering place and our imaginations were running wild. How could we convert it? What might it cost? It would be a massive project!

We stood outside on the flat ground where we imagined we would dine on long hot days and cooler evenings and once again admired the breathtaking view - it was perfect.

"Well, Michele, we would like to buy it. Did you say 300 million?"

It sounded a lot now that we had seen the structure, but there were 600 olive trees and 2 acres of woods. Really, the price reflected the value of the olive trees at about half a million apiece.

Michele didn't really answer the question. He muttered that the price was there or thereabouts the last time he asked.

We walked back up through the olives; Michele picked some of the black olives that were on many of the trees.

"These are Leccina olives - they make fine oil," he said. We thought his sales-pitch was good. Was he in for a backhander?

Just before we reached the car, I spotted a house across the valley. Unlike the one we had just seen, which was rather spoilt by the loss of half the top floor, the one I spotted really did look like an intact house.

"That's more like it. Take a photo of that house," I suggested to M, "it looks worth investigating".

"Michele, do you know who it belongs to?" No, he had no idea.

~~~

Our holiday was coming to an end. We hadn't heard anything more from Michele *Kappa da For'*. We were doing the rounds saying goodbye to friends and family (so many that it's a process that we seem to need to start the day we arrive).

It was the penultimate evening and we went to visit Michele *oo' Noyrr* (the Black) and his wife Francesca, a cousin of Vincenzo.

Michele was a giant among the dwarf-like people of Vico. He matched my height even with his bandy legs. He had broad shoulders, huge hands and a lolloping gait. From the day I had first encountered him at San Nicola on the day of the pizza picnic, sat on the stump of an olive tree with his huge hands cupping the knob of his walking stick, he had given off the aura of an oracle and so it was to Michele that we always went for advice.

We had mentioned to him earlier in the year that we were looking for something in *campagna*. His reaction was like many other people. We were mad! So, he wasn't going to help. But that evening he seemed to waiver as we told him about our exploits. It was almost as if he thought, 'well they are mad, so if they're going to do it we might as well help, maybe that way they won't get into too much trouble.'

"I know a place," he suddenly said. It was a house in the country with 4 hectares of olives and woods.

"Would you like to see it?" he asked as if earlier conversations about our madness had never taken place.

"Yes, of course," *M* replied eagerly "it's always worth seeing what's about."

He told us little else that evening, but we arranged to go to see the house the following day.

A Breakthrough

The next day, we set off in the company of Michele *oo' Noyrr and* Zio Mimi to see the house. We took a road out of Vico that we had never used before and headed down towards the sea. The narrow and twisty road, flanked by steep ground and stomach-wrenching drops, was surrounded all the way by olive groves.

Michele pointed out his ground where he had about 500 olive trees. Then we passed an area called La Chiusa - strangely we had been here back in August to view a *cazedd* with a couple of hectares of olives, so we must have used this road but from a different direction.

Eventually Michele asked us to stop. "Leave the car here, it will be easier on foot," he said.

Well that didn't augur well - we had to be able to get a car to the house!

We walked off the road along a track for a short distance until we reached a dry river-bed.

One of our few rules was, 'avoid water!'

Instead of continuing up the road, we turned left along the river-bed until Michele came across a huge olive tree with yellow paint daubed on it.

"The ground begins here," he declared.

Fine, fine but where's the house? Surely, this is not the access road?

We climbed out of the river-bed and walked into a grove of ancient trees. They were big and even impressed Zio Mimi. Obviously, Michele's opinion was that the olives were more important than the house.

As we walked across the flat river-valley, I glanced up and there was the house perched high above us. It was the same house that we had taken the photo of 3 days earlier. There was no mistaking it. We could not believe the coincidence!

As we climbed the steep valley sides, we lost sight of the house, but the first images were firmly implanted. This was something different, something that we had not seen in Italy or, for that matter, France.

Eventually we reached a driveway; at least there appeared to be access from the road that we had left at the river-bed. The target was now visible again but still high above. We went up the track, negotiating an extremely steep S-bend to arrive at a terrace in front of the house. The ascent had taken its toll on all of us except the sprightly Zio Mimi. We stopped for a breather - our thoughts dwelling on the inhospitable access and the river-bed, as we slowly absorbed the scene.

This house appeared to be intact; it seemed in good condition despite a crack on the southern wall. As we walked onto the grassed terrace that fronted the house, we passed between a freestanding bread oven and two great olives trees. The unkempt grass went as far as the central door to the house, beyond was a virtually impenetrable barrier of brambles. I subconsciously logged the contrast and moved on.

We reached the arched doorway and were disappointed to see that the stone mullions were missing - only the feet remained. The left part of the door was hanging off its hinges - par for the course. Inside, the scene was of further disrepair. The hall floor was dirt – not a flagstone is sight. The staircase leading to the right from the entrance hall was strewn with rubble. Someone had taken the stone steps.

But all was not lost. The entrance hall and the ceiling of the staircase was vaulted and halfway to the first floor was a landing with an impressive 'cross' vault.

It was a sad but inspiring sight. Ahead was a closed double-door that we managed to prise open. Inside we found a large room with a truly magnificent vault. Any worries we'd had about poor access and floods were fading.

The room was full of broken furniture and building materials. The flagstone floor was half intact. In one corner, we found two small rooms under the staircase; one was a *Cucina Monacesca*, the other a low-arched store. On the other side of the room a doorway led to

76

what seemed like a more conventional kitchen with a large fireplace; rubble from a hole in the wall was scattered across the dirt floor.

"That's how 'they' broke in," Michele announced.

Peering through the hole, we could see the next room was a stable.

We made our way tentatively up the rubble stairs. On the second flight, after the cross-vaulted landing, we found the stone treads almost all intact, but one had been dislodged ready for transport.

"Are 'they' still plundering this building?" I muttered to *M*. She asked Michele – he shrugged his shoulders.

At the top of the stairs, we found another double-door leading into a further large room; this room too boasted a vault, at least 4 metres high, still bearing traces of an ancient fresco. Door-less entries led to three further vaulted rooms, one of which had a small balcony with views to the sea; a small staircase led to another *Cucina Monacesca*.

From the *Cucina Monacesca*, a steep staircase led towards the roof space. Everywhere we looked there was rubble. We felt that it would be unwise to go any further.

We gingerly and thoughtfully made our way back downstairs to the front door. As we re-emerged into the bright sunlight we gazed at the view - olive trees as far as the eye could see, uninterrupted views to the valley sides opposite that swept down to the sea.

The house was magical - every ceiling vaulted, the staircase imposing and the living space cool and inviting. Despite its state of abandonment and the apparent ongoing rifling - this was a house that made our imaginations gallop.

Then we noticed the overgrown staircase leading from the front of the house to a further terrace below. What a wonderful spot for the swimming pool! Sold!

On the way back down to the car using the road, we badgered Michele for more information. Whose is it? How much do they want? How many olive trees are there? He was reluctant to answer any of our questions; perhaps he thought we couldn't possibly be serious. All he would say was that the owner had already turned down an offer, but the clue about the price was good.

It was a start. *M* and I hadn't discussed it - it was a subliminal decision - the olive mill we had seen a few days earlier already forgotten. We told Michele that we would buy the house. Please could he arrange the matter?

That evening, the last evening of our stay, *M* went to the

hairdresser and while being quizzed about our presence in Vico at this time of the year, the hairdresser said he had a friend with a fantastic house for sale. Without asking if she was interested, he was on the phone and, within minutes, he had made an appointment to view the house the following morning at 8am before we left for Switzerland. Things were really beginning to happen.

To close the evening we called in on Michele and Francesca to bid our final farewells for this visit, with the hope that Michele would have some news. We were to be disappointed, but they promised to ring as soon as they did.

~~~

The next morning we were up, packed and ready to leave early. At eight we met Signor Narducci as arranged the night before. He brought along his wife and daughter.

We followed them down the usual road to Calenella and then turned away from the sea towards 'the house' we had seen the day before. We thought we were going to the same place we'd visited with Michele *oo Noyrr'*. Maybe it was Narducci's?

Not so. We drove on by and eventually stopped a further kilometre or so up the valley, parked the cars and made our way by foot up a track - it was steep, rocky and broken. After about 50 metres we turned off into an olive grove. This was the start of the land. It needed no yellow paint on the trees; the land was distinguished for being so clean amongst its neighbours.

The olive trees were a little smaller, but large just the same. To the untrained eye, they were very good trees and Signor Narducci spared little time in telling us. He was doing a marketing job on olive trees and we wanted to see the house.

After a steep climb, we eventually came across the house. It was, as his wife had been telling us all the way, an historic house. She had also said that it was in great condition. It came into view - a magnificent stone coat of arms marked the main entrance; the windows were 4-leaf stone mullions - it was, from a distance, impressive.

In the main entrance was a square reception hall, easily as big as the main room in 'the house' down the valley. Off the reception hall were three large doors. As we looked in through the first on the left, Signora Narducci said that we could easily brick up the door.

"What? Why would we want to do that?" I demanded.

It turned out that two rooms, one on the left and one on the right of the entrance hall, did not actually belong to them!

"Sorry, we're off," I said immediately without feeling the slightest bit rude - M had taken the precaution of stating in the hairdresser's that we were not interested in joint ownership. We had a long journey to make.

The daughter moved in with her sales pitch. "It's historic, you know. The coat of arms above the front door belongs to Italian royalty. If you had this house you could get 10,000 Euros a day renting it to film companies from Rome," the sales talk continued relentlessly until we reached the cars.

We managed a "sorry, but we really are not interested even with the cinematic potential." If the house is that good, why don't you do the place up and hire it out yourselves?

As we shook hands, Signor Narducci handed us a bottle of his olive oil. Once we had tasted it, we would have to buy the estate. We bid them farewell.

~~~

Back in Switzerland Christmas passed with no news.

"Should we ring?" I urged.

"No, if Michele had some news he would let us know," M assured me. Eventually though, we rang to wish them a Happy New Year.

"Yes, the owner did want to sell," Michele confirmed. But that was it - no other information. We didn't even know the owners name, let alone where he lived.

While we awaited news, we spent lots of time gazing at the pictures we had taken of the house. It was then that we noticed something odd while scrutinising the gaping hole in the roof. "Could it be a tree?" we agonised.

In the original digital photo taken from across the valley, the trees blended into the background, but when we zoomed in on the roof there was indeed a tree in the middle of it! No - two trees! How could we have missed them?

This came as a bit of a dampener. Perhaps we would have to continue our search ... but with a certain determination, I inserted the picture as my computer desktop wallpaper.

As the months passed and we heard no more, we made the first big decision since we had sold up in the UK. We must go to Vico full-time - if we don't, nothing will ever happen.

So in May 2003, with my project completed and only requiring ongoing support that I could do remotely, we packed up and left Switzerland.

The Move

We moved into Vincenzo's little holiday apartment with all our possessions from Switzerland. However, in less than a month Vincenzo and Emilia were due to arrive for their annual three-month holiday, so we had to find alternative accommodation, and fast. With the best will in the world we, and all our clutter, would be in the way, to say the least.

We started searching on two fronts: a restoration project and a temporary solution, which we would need anyway during the restoration.

I began to scour the Centro Storico, revisiting the honeycomb of streets and alleys as I had often done on holiday. There was far more building activity going on than I had experienced in the height of summer and most of it was more sympathetic than earlier examples of renovation.

Things were changing in the Centro Storico and if we could buy a small house there, as our temporary solution, then it would be a good investment that we could rent out later.

Unlike the rest of Vico, the streets of the Centro Storico were very quiet at this time of year apart from those where building work was going on. Only the die-hard residents remained and many of the properties stood empty and closed up awaiting their summer visitors.

I found many broken down properties with faded *Vendesi* cards pinned to them. In many cases, the telephone number or contact address was completely illegible. I wasn't really getting anywhere and then I bumped into Peppe.

Peppe was a young builder and he emerged from a restoration project just as I was peering in.

"Would you like to see inside?" he asked.

"Yes, I certainly would."

We entered through one of the many doors that led from the street into the ground floor of this 3-storey building. Peppe explained that originally the ground floor was the stabling for the house. He and his workmates had transformed the structure into a set of apartments by gutting the internals, revealing stone, renovating timberwork, building character fireplaces and staircases. He was very proud of his work and I had to agree it was good.

I was amazed that we were able to communicate. He was a true Vichese, who still lived in the Centro Storico, but he spoke a little Italian.

"Was any of the building for sale?" I asked.

"Already sold." "If you want to buy in the Centro Storico, you have to be quick!"

"Well I've only just started looking," I said dismissing his sales pitch, "do you know of any other properties?"

"Yes, meet me at *Mezz' Cavoot* at six that evening and I will show you".

Peppe had to explain that *Mezz' Cavoot* was the local's name for La Vecchia Cantina, the only bar at that time in the Centro Storico and a place that, uncharacteristically, I had never dared to visit, but I knew where it was.

I learnt later that *Mezz' Cavoot* - Half a Hole is an affectionate name for the arched entry into the Terra quarter of the Centro Storico and it was a few steps away from the bar.

When I arrived that evening, the little piazza outside the bar was congested with *treruote* selling vegetables, fruit and fish - a little market of its own. Men sat at the tables outside. All turned their gaze on me. I plucked up courage and went in.

There were three customers in the bar; none of them was Peppe. I turned to leave, but something spurred me inwards. I boldly ordered a beer.

"*Noo boo'kweer?*" muttered the barman unhelpfully.

"*Cosa* - What?" I uttered, simultaneously realising that he was offering a glass. "*No, no, grazie*" I held up a hand to refuse and took the bottle. I stood at the bar with the others. All were drinking from their bottles.

I drank the beer before I knew it - part thirst, part nerves! I was in true Vicaiolo-company and felt exposed. Peppe was late.

I ordered another and took the opportunity to ask the barman if he knew Peppe. "Which Peppe?" he asked.

"Peppe, the builder?" My description didn't help, but overhearing my question the members at the bar began a debate about "Peppe the builder". I didn't understand a word. One of the men, a tall muscular man wearing a flat hat turned to me and started speaking pidgin German. One thing I had learnt was that nearly every man in Vico had, at some time or other, worked in Germany and all of them have just the slightest grasp of the language. The moment they encounter a stranger, they automatically assume German and want to practice their slender vocabulary.

"No, no, no," I pleaded, "I'm not a German. Can we speak in Italian?"

He agreed and introduced himself as Nicola *Zi'Gadd*. Now here was a stroke of luck - I recognised the *sopranome* Uncle Cockerel.

"Have you got a brother called Vincenzo *Zi'Gadd*?" I asked.

"Yes," he said.

"And another brother called Giuseppe?"

"Yes, indeed," he replied seemingly baffled by my knowledge of his family and use of *sopranomi*.

"They both make wine," I clarified, "and my father-in-law buys it from them each summer. I met both of them on different occasions when we went to taste and buy."

I had fallen amongst friends. Who was I? Who was my father-in-law? Where did I come from? Why was I here? They peppered me with questions: some in Italian, some in Vicaiolo and inevitably some in German. I had forgotten about the appointment by the time Peppe arrived. He was sorry; he had been kept at work until late.

"No problem" I assured him. I was enjoying myself with Nicola and friends. "Have a drink!"

"So this is the Peppe you wanted," said Nicola "Peppe *Ci'Catt'*". I had shown an interest in *sopranomi*, now there was no holding them back.

By the time we left the bar it was getting dark and we were the worse for wear. Peppe still insisted that we go to see something. It was very cheap and he would be able to make a good job of restoring it. We headed off deep into the Centro Storico. Once at the house, he called out to someone from the street, a woman answered from inside a neighbouring house and appeared with a bunch of keys.

We went into the house. It was a single room, full of dusty old bottles and bric-a-brac. There was no light, no electricity, no water and no toilet! There was just a hole in the floor in one corner. It wasn't what I thought! Using a flashlight the lady had brought, we climbed down a ladder to the ground floor - it was a cave.

Peppe was still enthusing as I managed to extract myself from this unwanted restoration project. I made it clear that this was the first property I'd seen and I would get back to him on it later. Meanwhile I asked if I could see any other properties.

Peppe reminded me that if we wanted to buy something in the Centro Storico, we had to hurry.

~~~

If we did find a telephone number on a *Vendesi* sign to ring we still had to do it using a UK mobile phone. It was expensive so we decided to get Italian chips for our phones, but when we went to a shop to buy one, the shopkeeper wouldn't sell us one.

"Can we see your *Codice Fiscale* please?" the shopkeeper asked.

"*Codice Fiscale*? But we're not Italian residents, we're just visiting," we offered the excuses that came to mind.

"You still need a *Codice Fiscale*," he insisted.

We offered passports, driving licences, anything he wanted, but it was no good. No *Codice Fiscale*, no chip. We'd had no problems buying a chip in France, but then France isn't Italy!

We asked around and discovered that we had to go to San Severo, some 75 km away, to get a *Codice Fiscale*. We also found out that we would need a *Codice Fiscale* to buy a house, a car and goodness knows what else. It's a wonder that they don't ask for one to buy tomatoes at the market!

We decided to make the trip to San Severo and face the inevitable bureaucratic nightmare. We set off early in an attempt to start the queue at the *Ufficio delle Imposte Dirette* (Inland Revenue Service). After touring San Severo for some time we finally found the flag-bedecked offices (the EU flag, the Italian flag and presumably the IRS flag) with about 20 minutes to go before opening.

There was no queue! The doors were open. We went in and found one of the most modern government buildings we'd ever experienced - it was light, airy and air-conditioned. We browsed the ticket system that enabled us to choose the bureaucratic queue of our choice. Overhead, new displays matched numbers to desks. We gazed at them and waited in comfortable chairs.

The receptionist arrived and as we began to make an enquiry

about *Codice Fiscale*, he brought us back to earth with, "we're closed. Come back at 8.30."

At our request he directed us to the nearest bar for coffee. Then, as we headed towards the door, for some inexplicable reason he called us back and said that we could start filling out the forms. We took the opportunity gladly and as we struggled with the first question, he took over, asked us for passports and filled out the forms himself. We signed and he took them away for processing.

We settled into the comfortable chairs for a long wait, but within minutes he came back with our *Codice Fiscale*. We thanked him and left. I looked at my watch - the *Ufficio delle Imposte Dirette* was still closed!

~~~

We contacted Michele *oo' Noyrr* a few days after our arrival to see if he had any news about 'the house'.

"Yes," the property was definitely for sale and he would see about arranging a meeting with the owner.

"*K'yahn, k'yahn, - Piano, piano* - Slowly, slowly, there's no rush" he would say. Well we begged to differ after more than six months surely things had moved on, but ...

So with no further progress we decided to pay 'the house' a visit on our own. Something we were reluctant to do without permission, but we needed to have a second viewing, especially of the trees in the roof. Perhaps we were wasting our time anyway.

Armed with the digital camera and sturdy clothes to protect us from potential hazards we set off. We stopped at the location where we took the original photograph and surveyed the house through binoculars - indeed the camera had not lied - there were at least two trees in the roof. We drove on and parked the car in the same place as before, then made our way on foot.

It was warm May weather and the climb to the house was again tiring, especially the final S-bend in the driveway. A host of doubts were gnawing away. Would we be able to get vehicles there? Would the builders be able to transport materials? Was the roof recoverable? Were we out of our depth? Were we out of our minds?

The house was as we had left it. Half the main door hanging off its hinges, the other half propped up against an internal *cisterna* (a pear-shaped store under the entrance hall floor that had once collected water from the roof). The downstairs seemed exactly as we had last seen it - the impressive vaulted ceilings shouting "buy me, buy me!"

As we moved carefully up the broken staircase, we noticed the cracks in the vaulted ceiling. Were they getting bigger? I'd noticed them on the first visit but I couldn't decide whether they had changed. On the second flight we were pleased to see that 'they' hadn't returned to remove the dislodged stone step.

Upstairs, though, we did find a change. The unusually wet winter had taken its toll - plaster was beginning to fall off the ceiling and walls in the main bedroom, the study and the bathroom (as we had it sketched in our minds). Roots from the trees on the roof had exposed themselves. The house certainly didn't look as attractive a buy as previously.

We made our way up through the *Cucina Monacesca* to the roof space, climbing over broken tiles, glass and all manner of debris. It was a sorry sight. Terracotta tiles sagging on a flimsy bamboo structure that looked like it would collapse come the next storm. And there were the two trees slightly obscured by part of the collapsed roof - but how had we missed them the first time? We didn't dare enter for fear of further collapse.

With some relief we went out into the sunshine unscathed but we were still undeterred. This house was crying out to us. We decided to explore round the back. It was a jungle. Were there snakes? I picked up a stick and thrashed my way through the brambles, nettles and weeds until I found a rear entrance. It was the door to the stable - directly ahead was the *mangiatoia* (manger), to the right was the hole in the wall to the kitchen (where 'they' had apparently broken in!); two plaster of Paris casts were embedded in the wall above the manger, but their central iron rings for tethering the animals had been removed. The ceiling was another magnificent vault but debris lay everywhere. Could we save the *mangiatoia*? We spoke as if we had already bought.

At the rear of the house we found a *grotta*. It had a low roof that sloped down to the north; as our eyes accustomed to the light we spotted another little cave leading off the main excavation. "It would make a fantastic cellar," I enthused.

Re-sold!

The scene behind the house was *confusione*. The house appeared to be hewn out of a 3-metre high wall of rock; a dry-stone wall held back soil above it. Towards the middle of the house, the wall seemed to have collapsed, but it was impossible to investigate because of the impenetrable undergrowth.

Apart from the wet getting into the house through the roof, we couldn't see any other major problems. All the walls except one were sound; that one had a crack down the chimney, but it was coming from the roof and we had learnt in France that it was typical for buildings to splay once the roof had lost its strength.

It wouldn't put us off, but there was a lot to do. This was a house without electric, water and sewerage let alone the work involved in reconstruction. We would have to seek advice and quickly.

~~~

Back in Vico preparations were underway for the Festa di Santa Rita. We had never been in Vico for any *festa* other than San Rocco, which takes place in August.

The Festa di San Rocco had seemed to us to be **the** *festa* in Vico, but we were about to learn that *festa* was endemic here. In August, of course, visitors swell Vico and the preparations for the *festa* only add to the already chaotic street life.

Several days before the *festa*, the work begins with the erection of lighting gantries from the roundabout at San Francesco through a network of streets eventually arriving at the Piazza San Domenico, where Zio Mimi had introduced me to the darker side of *sopranome* all those years ago. In the *piazza* a bandstand is erected and posters advertise the guest band and the forthcoming concerts.

Across the piazza opposite the bandstand, under a banner depicting San Rocco, a group of men sit at a table and collect donations, the funds allegedly paying for the highlights: bands, the *batteria*, a pop singer and the final night's fireworks.

The *festa* opens at 6 am in spectacular style. If you happen to be in bed, which is a very reasonable place to be at that time of the morning, it is more of a shocking style. An explosion rocks Vico, the shockwave penetrates every household and the aftershocks reverberate around the outlying valleys. To the uninitiated, or those caught napping it seems like a bomb has gone off; maybe a gas bottle has exploded in a neighbouring street.

It is only the second explosion that jogs the memory; by the third, you are tuned in to the mortar firing and prepared for the bang. Each bomb is louder than its predecessor is. If the collection for the *festa* has gone well, fireworks intersperse the explosions. Every day, twice a day, the hostilities are repeated until the *festa* ends.

The *batteria* for San Rocco is a spectacular firecracker display that encircles the town's War Memorial in Piazza San Domenico; rather like barbed wire and minefields surrounding a machine-gun nest. The display takes place at the end of the last procession, with the statues of San Rocco and The Madonna taking pride of place facing the *batteria* before the bearers return them to their sanctuary in the Chiesa di San Pietro e Paolo.

The *batteria* always begins with a mortar round that's fired off somewhere distant from the crowds - it serves to remind the festival-goers that the fireworks are about to begin. Then there's a long wait while the crowd jostles for position close to the statues and even closer to the *batteria*. Despite our British reserve and cautiousness, we usually take up position as near to the front as we dare.

The fireworks begin with a sort of damp-squib Catherine wheel and fountain pyrotechnics. Then the first crackers go off. Slowly at first, the flashes pursue the wire framework and the reports ricochet from the surrounding buildings. Gradually the pace increases, the flashes get brighter, the reports get louder - the *batteria* reaches a multiple mortar launcher and three or four bombs explode above the *piazza*. The spectacle accelerates as it encircles the War Memorial seemingly blowing the whole square to pieces. Cardboard debris flies through the air, smoke and the smell of cordite fill the nostrils, the ground shakes, windows rattle - another multiple mortar launches bombs into the air - the furious crescendo continues relentlessly until the final mortar, which launches three, consecutive, ear-splitting blasts.

The crowd applauds ... they think it's all over ... but if the collection has gone well a firework display bursts out above the Chiesa di San Pietro e Paolo. More applause and then the crowds disperse in relative silence to continue their festive *striscio*.

~~~

The *festa* of Santa Rita surprised us in that it seemed as busy as the bigger San Rocco festival; the parades, the bands, the *striscio* and the *batteria* were all impressive.

During the *festa* we bumped in to cousin Mimmo and he was keen to help us with 'the house'. Michele had by this time told us that the house belonged to his brother (why he hadn't told us this earlier we will never know), but that was all, no name, no price and no other news.

We told Mimmo all that we knew from Michele. Mimmo suggested that we meet at his house and there he could at least 'map' the house for us. We were in the dark, but agreed to go after the *festa*.

So one evening we went to visit Mimmo. He had a copy of the *catasto* on his computer - a local land registry that details the owners of every parcel of land in the Gargano. Well, this was a find - just what we needed! Could we get a copy we wondered? But for now let's concentrate on 'the house'.

Mimmo had not been to the house, but we managed to describe where it was and we honed in on the appropriate '*foglio* - leaf' of the *catasto*. Eventually we found the parcel of land containing the house. This revealed that it did indeed belong to Michele's brother Emidio (now we had a name!) and his wife Filomena. But, on closer examination, we discovered that they only owned the upper floor and a share in the ground floor. Who owned the rest?

Mimmo searched another part of the *catasto* and here we found the same parcel of land containing the house, but there was just one owner - Angela Pino! Who on earth was she and what did this mean?

The *catasto* revealed all the parcels of land surrounding the house and who, supposedly, owned them. We noticed that at least four parcels that bounded the house did not belong to Emidio (or Filomena). Two belonged to five members of the Pirro family; another belonged to a Francesco Palmieri and the last he still could not identify.

What an almighty disaster! My memory flashed up the scene outside the house - semi-cared for grass leading to the front door, dense thicket after it.

One rule we had set ourselves was that we must own all the land surrounding the house having experienced unreasonable neighbours in the UK who bounded the back wall of our house. They grew trees against it, claimed the wall partitioning our gardens was theirs when it was patently ours, and constructed abominable corrugated iron woodstores against its beautiful Cotswold stone. We were not going to allow that to happen to us again.

To add to the gloom, Mimmo sucked in hard as he completed his search of the *catasto* and revealed the owner of the fourth parcel. It was one Guido *oo Capone*.

"What's the problem?" I asked not sure that I wanted to know.

"He is a *cosa tremenda* - a piece of work!" Mimmo reluctantly replied.

"What on earth ... is he a mobster?" I suggested having heard the ominous *sopranome*.

Mimmo explained. "*Oo Capone* - the Big Head" was a *confinante* (he owned land neighbouring ours) and he was a *coltivatore diretto* (a sort of registered farmer), which gave him certain rights. If the land adjacent to him was to be sold, he had to be informed of the price and then he had the right to buy at that price. This knowledge was demoralising enough, but then Mimmo added that although it was rare for *confinanti* to exercise their rights, Guido could be the one exception. He had gained a reputation.

Well, we were sunk, or if not sunk we were floundering. We left Mimmo's carrying a wodge of documents detailing our discoveries, our spirits somewhat dampened.

~~~

It was the end of May and we were no further forwards in our quest. M and I were discussing how to tackle this with Michele *oo' Noyrr* when we bumped into him at San Francesco.

"My brother's across the roundabout," he said. "I'll take you to meet him."

We walked 'as the crow flies' through the traffic in true Vichese style to encounter Emidio. The brothers met. There could not have been a bigger contrast. Michele was tall and imperious, Emidio short, stocky and gnomish. He didn't squander time on polite conversation. Michele introduced us and he grunted his name as we shook hands with little enthusiasm and then they fell into a deep dialect conversation. Whatever they were saying, and M didn't understand it, we correctly assessed that these two brothers had little time for each other.

Eventually their conversation ended and apparently, they had agreed that the next day we would go with Emidio to the house and talk business. Well, it was a breakthrough, but perhaps too late.

~~~

That evening we studied the map and documents that Mimmo had printed for us. We pencilled in the names of all of the neighbours - we would need to be ready to question Emidio about all of them. By the time we had finished we had 11 names attached to various parcels. Even though we were not interested in all the parcels, surely the task would be beyond us.

The next day we set off with Emidio to 'the house'. He was a different person: cheerful, even jolly, and full of life. His dialect was thick though, and he had a cleft lip that affected his pronunciation. I didn't understand a word and *M* was struggling, but managing. He was very chatty and it was all she could do to give me the odd explanation.

Perhaps his manner the evening before was due to his brother's presence.

The first thing he clarified was that everyone called him Midew. He didn't care to be called Emidio.

"Fine, Midew it is," we concurred.

He drove his little car right up to the *piazzale* in front of the house - it struggled through the S-bend, tyres smoking and stones flying, but it got there. If he wasn't impressed by this feat, we certainly were!

On the journey, we had broached the subject of the joint ownership, but he brushed the subject aside as being a minor detail - he insisted the others would sell their shares.

We toured the house again. He cursed the people who had stolen the door mullions, the flagstones and the stone treads of the staircase. He cursed the other owners who had left the house to go to rack and ruin. If he had had his chance he would have restored it himself, after all he used to be a builder.

After inspecting the house we had a look at the land; he tentatively showed us the boundaries, we talked about who owned what, especially those parcels bordering the house. We told him that we would have to buy them - without them, there would be no sale.

As we walked towards the house along the boundaries of the Pirro's olives, my eyes fell on a tree trunk - it had something growing on it. I called to Midew. When he saw it his eyes lit up, he let out a childish squeak.

"*Foon'yah' d'pistazz,*" he cried out as he ran towards it with a mixture of cackling and giggling. He was just so excited. I had found him a 'Chicken of the Woods' or 'Laetiporous sulphureus' - a prized bracket mushroom.

It was a huge specimen, perhaps weighing a kilo. Midew deftly cut its anchor from the tree with his penknife and held it up like a trophy.

91

As we made our way back to the house Midew explained that *pistazz'* was the dialect name for the carob tree and he pointed out that there were several of them on his land, presumably making it more valuable.

"At this time of year, especially after rain you must keep an eye on the carob tree and you will find them," he instructed. And just for good measure, he added, "but you'll have to be early in the morning, before all the others get them."

It was another little hint. I made a mental note. "Why would other people be on our land taking our mushrooms?"

As we were leaving in the car, *M* reminded Midew again. "Don't forget, we will have to buy these other parcels of ground otherwise there's no deal."

"Don't worry about a thing," he assured us. "I will talk to everyone and arrange it all."

"And what about this *oo Capone*?" I asked.

"Ah," he replied, "I'll talk to his son Mimmo, he'll sign the necessary papers saying that he doesn't want to buy the land," he assured us.

Our spirits had been lifted. Maybe we could do business with this man Midew. He seemed to have everything under control.

"And the price?" we asked in unison.

He said we would talk about it later. He would be in touch. As we parted he ordered us to go to his house that evening to eat the *Foon'yah' d'pistazz*.

~~~

We visited for dinner as instructed. Midew's wife Filomena showed *M* how to clean and prepare the fungus.

"The important thing is that it's a young specimen," she said. "Look at the colour" - to my eyes it was a deep yellow almost the colour of egg yolk. "And when you squeeze - see the yellow juice - that's a sure sign that it's fresh," she enthused.

M had to translate all this for me, as Filomena's dialect was particularly strong.

"The main thing to do is to make sure it's cooked," Filomena added, "I normally blanch them before cooking." She put some of the meaty slices into a tomato sauce that was simmering on the hob. Then she dipped others in an egg batter and began frying them in olive oil.

Midew was pouring out his home-made red. "*Benzoyn'* - Fuel for the body", he chuckled. We could almost sense his taste buds salivating as he waited for this most special of treats.

We had never tried it before, but I had heard of Chicken of the Woods. So, when the time came to taste we were apprehensive but assured by their confidence.

Filomena served the fried slices first. They were delicious; the firm meaty texture with a hint of sourness did indeed taste like chicken.

Midew loved it, chattering all the way through and reminding us that we had to keep a good eye out for these treasures and harvest them before anyone else got to them.

"Would we have people roaming about picking our mushrooms?" I asked. He gave me a sheepish smile then more wine, but kept his counsel.

Filomena served up spaghetti with the mushroom and tomato sauce. A double helping for Midew with the pasta slightly overcooked - a common requirement of older men in Vico. They all have a special big plate and most need the pasta well cooked for their teeth, or in many cases for their gums, to cope.

We had normal helpings. The flavour was delicate, the texture distinctly of chicken. It was a feast.

The fungus had been a chance find and yet another experience in our new life here.

~~~

Our minds now returned to finding a temporary home. I visited Peppe the Builder at *Mezz' Cavoot* as often as possible, not solely with the search in mind, but also because I was enjoying the atmosphere there and meeting lots of other people.

M took no time to settle in. She had always said that she felt instantly at home here, as if there was some sort of hidden force, pulling her back.

When Vincenzo first escaped Vico (for that really was how he felt about it), he went to work on a Scottish estate. Then *M* was born and although the laird and lady of the house were none too pleased at having another mouth to feed, Vincenzo and Emelia managed to continue in their work while raising M. But, when *M*'s sister was expected 14 months later - for the lady this was a mouth too far. Vincenzo faced the sack for excessive productivity.

He turned to the only thing that could help him - family. He spent all their savings on train tickets, took M to Vico on his own and left her in the hands of his mother and sisters. For Vincenzo and Emilia it was heartbreaking and he could never find it in his heart to forgive his employers, or for that matter, himself.

Vincenzo began the search for a new job and found one within months, but the deed was done and he could not afford the trip to go and get M back.

Her exile lasted for two years, cared for by her grandmother, her aunts and of course by the other women in the street, great aunt Zia Masuccia, great cousin Addolorata and family friends Antonietta, 'Cheline and Angelina. Every word she heard was dialect, the food she ate was *Cucina* Vichese - all her senses were tuned to Vico.

M has no memory of it, nor of the distress that it caused both herself and her parents when they came to collect her and she didn't recognise them anymore. But, she and Vico had formed an indelible bond.

Now she was sitting outside on the doorstep plaiting garlic with Antonietta, as if she had done it all her life, when Peppe arrived. He was amused and shouted out "*Margheri' k'eh fah? D'ahdyuh?*"

"*Shoin, shoin!*" she replied in Vicaiolo - "Yes, yes of course I am doing the garlic!"

In Vico, there is a season for everything and in June, it is time for the women to plait garlic. Lorries arrive from afar and cruise the streets with loud hailers advertising their price. "*Aglio, aglio, dieci kili 3 Euro*".

M was enjoying herself with the neighbours, the same women she had known since infancy, doing the seasonal things that her grandmother would have done years ago. She bought 30 kilos for 9 Euros, more than we would need, so that she could make strings for all the family.

~~~

Peppe had come to tell us that he had found an apartment and, M being tied up, he took me alone to the Casale quarter of the Centro Storico to approve the property from the outside. I did and we agreed to meet him that evening to have a look inside.

When we met that evening he hadn't been able to get the key, however he was renovating the apartment below it - he didn't have the key for that either, but he crawled in through the bathroom window and let us in. He wanted to show us his work, and it was good - he had revealed the beams in the roof and had built a traditional fireplace in one corner. The standard of finishing was excellent and it was just so much better than the last hole he had shown me. We arranged to meet him the next day after work when he would have the keys for the house above.

On second viewing, the apartment from the outside did not look that good - the outer walls were covered with electric wires (when electricity was installed in Vico, any house left unattended was adopted as an electric pole). Peppe assured us they are now putting the electricity underground and clearing up the mess of the past.

We went inside. The apartment was good. It had a living/bed room, a kitchen and a bathroom. But, there were the usual quirks - there was a metal ladder in the middle the middle of the bathroom! The ladder led to a roof terrace where there was another independent room.

The views to the west from the living room and the terrace were uninterrupted to the sea; it was in the Centro Storico, but not deep inside - there was light and air and it was even possible to get a car to it.

"Well, we would like to buy it, as long as we could remove the ladder from the bathroom," *M* confirmed to Peppe.

Throughout the visit, he had simply agreed that we could do all the things we wanted.

We arranged to meet the owner, Rocco, and after very hard bargaining, we agreed to buy it for the asking price. We weren't quite prepared for this result, but as Peppe kept reminding us, "we had to be decisive and move quickly if we wanted to buy in the Centro Storico."

Within a day, Rocco passed the necessary papers to the clerk of our *Notaio*, Nicolino, who happens to be a cousin of *M*'s father. All seemed to be in order, but within a day or so he came back to us bearing bad news. The room on the roof terrace was *abusivo*! Built without permission. There was an order to demolish it - he produced the papers that damned it.

When we confronted Rocco, he was most indignant.

"No, it wasn't *abusivo*, certainly not!" he announced angrily. He had been to prison for it! He had also paid a fine. That made everything OK he insisted. We were in the bar at *Mezz' Cavoot* - Rocco's builder joined in the fray insisting that everything was in order - the other clientele took in every detail. Meat to their drink!

"Well, get us a document that will prove it," *M* conceded, "and then we'll look at it again. But if we have to demolish the room, we'll have to talk about the price again."

The next day we heard that Rocco and his builder had been to the *Ufficio Tecnico*, the office that deals with all building matters, including *abusivo* ones and had demanded a piece of paper - any piece of paper - that would satisfy us. They came away empty handed.

We sought further advice from Nicolino and we were staggered when he said "well there's no risk really; the Centro Storico is full of *abusivo* building work with demolition orders already served, but no one ever does anything about them." This seemed to ring true, as the copy of Rocco's demolition order was already 18 years old.

Not wishing to give up easily, we decided to take the risk if we could drop the price by 10 million or so (even with the Euro, we were still negotiating in millions of Lira). Rocco stood firm. He had done his time, paid his fine.

We regretfully withdrew, hoping that we had not caused offence. He was a tough old boy, but he seemed to bear no malice. A few weeks later he declared triumphantly that he had sold - for 10 million more! Peppe was right; if we wanted to buy in the Centro Storico, we had to be quick.

~~~

A few days later, we had a slice of luck. While visiting *Michele oo' Noyrr* one evening he had visitors who, when hearing about our search, asked whether we had seen a For Sale sign on a house not far from where we were sitting in the Carmine part of Vico. No, we hadn't, and so they gave us directions.

On the way home that evening we found the For Sale sign on a staircase in a little alley, Vicolo Sancarlo, off the main street of the Carmine. We rang the number and within a minute, a little old woman met us on the steps outside the house. She told us that the house belonged to her son, Giuseppe; he was a builder who lived in the north of Italy. He would, as it turned out be there the next day, Saturday. We made an appointment for 11 am.

The next day we viewed the house - it was perfect. It had an independent entrance and two storeys, both rare features in Vico, and a large roof terrace with unrestricted views to the Centro Storico and to the Adriatic - we could even see the islands of Tremiti. Giuseppe had personally restored the house for him and his family but they were growing up and not interested in coming South anymore. If we liked, we could move in immediately.

We made an offer and it was accepted (surprisingly the negotiation wasn't tough like that with Rocco; but then this wasn't the Centro Storico; the Carmine was only built a hundred or so years ago). Giuseppe agreed our terms and even threw in all the furniture – "after all, what are we going to do with it?"

The next day, Sunday, Nicolino prepared the papers for an exchange of contract (the *compromesso*) and we signed. We arranged to transfer a deposit to his bank on the Monday. Giuseppe gave us the keys there and then; we could move in. He was due to return home to Reggio Emilia and would be back in July to complete the transaction.

So, in a whirlwind weekend we had finally committed to Italy. It had taken a little over a year; we still had a long way to go, but at least we had resolved where we would live that summer and during the rebuilding of 'the house'.

Walking Among Giants

We settled into Vicolo Sancarlo very quickly. The little alley of terraced houses was deserted except for Raffaele and his wife Angela. In typical Vico fashion, they had lots of kids and grandchildren who came and went and it took us some time to work out who they all were.

Raffaele and I became quite intimate sleepers, as the late spring and summer that year was a scorcher. As temperatures soared to 40 degrees Celsius, I spotted Raffaele pulling an old bedstead up to their roof terrace with a rope. He was heading for the roof at night and it wasn't long before I joined him.

I followed his example, slung a hammock in one corner of our roof terrace, and took a light sheet to bed at night. As Vico settled down for the night there was only the ruffle of Raffaele's snoring and distant barking dogs. I swayed myself to sleep gazing at millions of stars. By the time I awoke Raffaele had gone, the sheet was on the floor and I could feel the cool morning air - maybe about 25 degrees C.

As dawn approached, Vico would stir; town dogs began their daily rounds, the cockerel in a neighbour's stable crowed, donkeys brayed and the Vichesi rose noisily to go about their daily business.

~~~

Immediate neighbours were curious and wasted no opportunity in saying hello.

"Are you just here for the summer?" they would ask.

"No, no we're here for good." We would usually add that we were looking for a house in *campagna* to restore; if they knew of one, would they please let us know.

"Here for good? What never going back? In *campagna*? But you've got a house here! Why ever would you want to live there?" There were many variations to their questions, but all were leading to the same point. But, you could sense that they welcomed our presence even if they were a little mystified. In their experience, people only left Vico.

Having satisfied themselves that we were staying, they would then move on to the personal details of our lives. The Vichesi need to know everything – surely a throwback to the cramped conditions of the Centro Storico where everybody's business was everyone else's. They would have no hesitation asking us how much we paid for the house in Vicolo Sancarlo - we found ourselves put on the spot and were remarkably honest and open with them.

Satisfied that they were keeping track on the property market, they would then move on to the next question.

"You must be *in pensione* then?"

Now this was not so strange a question, even though I was in my early 50's. In Italy, the pension used to be available after 35 years of contributions, so people who left school at 15 and managed to hold down a job for the qualifying years could relax at 50. No wonder the country is in such a financial mess.

"No, no," I would reply falling deeper and deeper into the honesty trap, I have to wait till I'm 65 and then I'll be lucky if there's anything left in the pot the way the government's going."

"But how will you eat?" their appetite for the details seemingly insatiable. Here I had to be a little more ingenious as it wouldn't do to leave them with the impression that we'd won the lottery.

"Ah, well I have some private pensions about to mature," concealing the fact that respectable UK financial institutions were sending me annual statements telling me that they had failed to make any money whatsoever on my lifetime investments and inviting me to throw more good money after bad by increasing my contributions.

However, you could see the calculations going on in their minds, "you've bought Vicolo Sancarlo and you want to buy in *campagna*?"

So, I would add, "we were just taking advantage of the price differential between the UK and Vico. You know that you can't buy a house in the UK for less than 200,000 Euros and we sold our house reasonably well." This information would usually seal their curiosity - we had invested astutely as only a Vichese would do.

~~~

News of our purchase spread through the town. People began to accost us in the street to congratulate us. Some we knew and some we didn't. "*Auguri, auguri!* - Congratulations!" they would repeat.

It was typical of the hospitality and generosity. Most people we met would say, "if you want something come and ask? If I haven't got what you need I'll know someone who has."

So, with this in mind, when we needed shade for the roof terrace I popped into the Zanzibar - they had large umbrellas advertising ice cream shading the tables on the pavement outside. We had often used the bar in the past to telephone the UK, back in the days before mobile phones. It had a row of three kiosks; the bartender would tell us which kiosk to use and, at the end of the call, we would pay for the number of units used. It would be impossible to close the kiosk door in the summer heat, so we would attempt to make phone calls with the deafening background noise of table football and a dozen card tables.

The bar belonged to *Michele ah Nerr* (as opposed to *Michele oo' Noyrr* - now there's a conundrum. *Ah* is the feminine direct object while *oo'* is masculine - so how did these genders of 'the Black' come about?). I asked him where I could get some umbrellas like his.

"I'll get them for you, he offered immediately. How many do you want?"

"How much will they cost?" I asked, expecting to pay the moon.

He told me not to worry about the price and anyway he would get them for us at cost! I ordered two.

A few days later as I passed the Zanzibar, he called me in to say they'd arrived. "When and where should he deliver them?"

Delivery too! "No time like the present, if you can spare the time?" I suggested. We loaded up his truck with the umbrellas advertising Nastro Azzuro beer, and their concrete bases and headed to Vicolo Sancarlo.

"Where have they got to go?" he asked. I pointed to the roof and grimaced apologies.

"No problem" he said. Between us, we carried the first base to the top, but it was a very awkward passage and I was inhibiting his movement. He was sweating and I was having nightmares about the condition of my back as we struggled to the roof.

Michele had the build of a Rugby prop forward, but the belly of a landlord and I became really quite concerned. He was breathing heavily, his tea-shirt soaked in sweat. I should have suggested a cooler time of day to do this job - say, four in the morning, after all Michele would be setting out for his bar at that time.

I suggested a rest, but he dismissed this idea with a hint of derision, for him it really was no problem. He lifted the next base to his shoulders and carried it alone. He emerged sweating, his breathing even heavier, but he assured me he was fine. I took the umbrellas to the first floor and had to convince him that I was capable of taking them the rest of the way.

What could I offer him? Would he like a drink? No, he wanted nothing - I paid him for the umbrellas and he was off. How could I thank him? I guess I would visit his bar more often.

~~~

The neighbours in Via Fania congratulated us with one breath and then bemoaned the fact that we were leaving them in the next. Antonietta, 'Chelina and Angelina, now all widows, would be the only residents at the end of the street until the summer visitors arrived.

"We're only a stone's throw away", we insisted. "We'll pass by often", we promised. But, Vico is a strange place, it seems to absorb time and they were accurately aware of the fact that we would not see them that often.

~~~

Perhaps we were too busy taking in the experience, one of which was, *ee' ren'n'nuh*. Before we arrived in May, the swifts had settled into Vico, had built their nests under the loose terracotta tiles of the old houses and had bred. The first young were appearing in the skies.

It was the first time we had seen the swifts in Vico and nobody had ever mentioned them to us, so we worked out that they must leave sometime in July, perhaps by the middle of the month and we had never been in Vico at that time of year.

There was nothing remarkable in the swifts themselves, other than their spectacular acrobatics when feeding and their numbers, for truly I can never remember seeing so many in one place.

No, they were just interesting to note and to watch. One pair had built their nest under the tiles of Antonietta's house and from Vincenzo's balcony, we had a bird's-eye view of them coming into land, beaks loaded with insects. At the landing point they are at their least graceful as they shuffle up under the tiles, but fluid flight returns as they shoot out from under the tiles to continue their harvest.

The change was almost imperceptible. They are birds of habit, swooping around in the morning until the sun is hot, retiring for a siesta and then returning to the skies in the evening. But their habits were changing. We began to notice that they were gathering in huge numbers, especially in the evening. The skies over Vico filled with black bodies, hurtling through the air at break-neck speed, performing hair-raising acrobatics.

They flew in gyrating, screeching patterns, formation after formation flying headlong at each other only breaking off at the last second to reform and repeat the manoeuvre over and over again.

The formations skimmed the rooftops, sky-dived the streets; bombarded the alleyways filling them with a cacophony of shrieks.

As June went into July the air-show became more intense, the formations bigger as they blanketed parts of the sky.

Then one day, there was nothing! They had simply gone. It was about the middle of the month; the full moon had passed and the skies were silent.

~~~

In mid-July, we experienced the *Festa della Madonna del Carmine* for the first time. This was now our part of Vico, therefore our *festa*. The mortar launchers were much closer to us and quite literally shook the rock foundations of Vicolo Sancarlo. The processions passed close to our alley and the main thoroughfare was packed with stalls and locals performing the customary *striscio* well into the night.

We watched the fireworks on the last evening from our roof terrace. It was much easier than attending personally. The last night fireworks of each *festa* are timed for about 1 am, but they never happen on time as the sequence of concerts that take place throughout the evening usually fall well behind schedule. So, we waited in comfort on the roof terrace, until the opening mortar salvo signalled the start.

Ten minutes later (at about 2.30 am) the sky above the Centro Storico was a scene of cascading fireworks, silhouetting the castle of the Della Bella's, the fortification of Federico II and the Mother Church.

~~~

We had seen Midew at the *Festa della Madonna del Carmine* - he was one of the bearers of the Madonna. He had no further news for us.

102

"They would be here in August," was all he would say. We weren't quite sure who he meant by 'they', but we believed that two members of the Pirro family and Francesco Palmieri lived in Rome - surely he must be referring to them.

In truth, we hadn't spent much time trying to find the other owners, as we did not want to attract interest in 'the house'. What we had learnt about Vico is that news travels and very fast.

Despite the fact that the house was derelict and there wasn't a big market in such country houses, there were people who would be interested. At least two had been bought and restored in recent years and we had just missed buying another on the Partechiano road - so we convinced ourselves that we must let Midew set the pace.

~~~

One day in August, I headed for the Zanzibar, only to find that it had shut down. I was disappointed, as this had become a favourite haunt, a local where I felt reasonably comfortable. It felt as if a bulldozer had come along and demolished my favourite village pub to make way for a housing estate.

I carried on up to the roundabout at San Francesco. Once there I inquired about the fate of Michele *ah Nerr*. "He's over there," came the reply - he had moved to a newly appointed Gran Caffe, close to the roundabout.

That evening, I made a point of going to visit him and wishing him "*Auguri!*" Whilst at the bar, I spotted Midew going to play cards in a back room with some of his cronies.

I decided to join them and watch. He introduced me as Gianni to the circle - I am sure he didn't reveal anything more despite their inquisitive welcome - then carried on playing. They were playing *Tressette*; I am no card expert, but I would say it's a game similar to Whist. The lead plays a card from one of four suits and the remainder at the table must follow suit or throw away.

But, that's where the similarity with Whist ends. Their play baffled me, and any explanation that they offered made little sense. I decided to research the game on the Internet and before long, I had the official rules, but little knowledge of the strategy. That I would only learn by playing.

Unlike Whist, there are no trumps, it is a points scoring game and instead of using the 52 card traditional pack, they play with a *Briscola* pack consisting of 40 cards of the suits *Denari, Bastoni, Coppe and Spade* (Coins, Clubs, Cups and Swords). There are many styles of Briscola cards and, fortunately for me, the locals here only play with one style - *Napoletane*.

Using traditional 52-card sets players form a fan with the hand and can see the values clearly in the corner of the cards, but with Briscola cards there are no values in the corners. So, in order to have a picture of the full hand, the players arrange the cards in an array; but even then, a player's ability to recognise a card by the slightest clue is essential.

For instance, in the *Napoletane* sets the Kings have a rectangular coloured bar at the base of the card: yellow for *Denari*, red for *Coppe*, green for *Bastone* and blue for *Spade*. So, experienced players can tell both card value and suit from a view of a fraction of the bar; but there are lots of other subtle differences. For example, each King has its feet set in different positions on or near the bar.

In turn, players can tell the difference between the King and the *Cavallo* (Horse) using distinct markings. Naturally, they use the same colours for the suits but the Horse has a parallelogram at the base, so the King has a rectangular edge and the Horse a sloped edge. Easy! And if that's not enough the player can tell the suit from the position of the Horse's feet.

Using this wealth of characteristics, expert players can form their hands into a tight array and onlookers who are less adept at distinguishing the cards must await the identity of a card until it is delivered to the table.

And that's where the game is different to Whist. It's in the play that one becomes aware that this is not an English parlour game. Players bang cards on the table with the knuckles, toss cards with derision and slide cards across the surface with cunning. All movements giving a signal. The lead player can make some comment as he plays his card and, although, the true rules of Tressette limit these comments, here in Vico they play the Roman variant where almost anything goes.

The evening I found Midew in the Gran Caffe was the first time I had really watched a game of *Tressette*. Naturally, I had seen these schools in action outside bars and in squares, both in Italy and France, but always from a distance. I had never joined them. Luckily, I was familiar with the *Napoletane* cards, as I had learnt to play Cinquanta Cinque (Fifty-Five) in via Fania with Zio Mimi, Tittino and many others over the years. Fifty-Five is more of a Poker game, a little gamble and a great deal of bluffing.

I learnt it because it seemed to be one way to interact with the locals, but Vincenzo disapproved. He recycled the same comments every year "They are cheats, they will rob you! Don't let anyone standing around see your cards - they'll tell the others what you've got."

To a degree, he was right; they would cheat if you were stupid enough to let them get away with it. But I did enjoy playing and the exposure helped ever so slightly with the dialect. In the beginning, I regularly lost unthinkable amounts, such as 10,000 lira (5 Euros), over a few hours play, but as I became more familiar with their game and harmless cheating, I very rarely lost. Unlike *Tressette* it is a simple game, but what these games do have in common is that you have to listen, listen hard and try to stay calm.

And now in the back room of the bar looking at *Tressette* close up the play reminded me of another card game - Bridge. In my early working days in a computer company, a group of programmers used to meet at lunchtime for a game of Bridge in a room specially set aside. Unfortunately, they never closed the door! At least once each day things would go awry; they would play a hand and, when it had finished, the players would erupt with anger, frustration, accusation and culpability. Observers would join in, as one poor soul would try to justify the mistake he might have made.

Imagine a back room of a bar in southern Italy, packed with a dozen card tables. These men are of peasant stock, they do not pull their punches when they think they have been wronged. The failure of a partner to spot the 'subtle sliding of a card across the table' can be tantamount to staring at another man's wife, or even worse, his daughter! Or if the players have agreed to play in silence and someone makes a comment out of order the table erupts. The recriminations reverberate, until some ground is given, one or more players get up and leave or the table subsides into silence.

The next day, the same tables form with the same partners. Yesterday's arguments usually forgotten - this is a small town and it doesn't pay to hold a grudge too long as you will soon run out of places to play.

~~~

Having found Midew's haunt, I visited most evenings at about 6 pm hoping to get some news and to learn the *Tressette*. No news ever came. He and his cronies would greet me with pleasure and ask me to sit and watch. Midew seemed to enjoy the notoriety of having a foreigner as a friend. Whether he had told them who I was or why I was attending him like a dog-at-heel I will never know.

Over time and with the help of a computer game I learnt the rules and strategy of *Tressette*. Then one day when they were a man short, I got to have a game. I started badly. My first hand was good; I was holding a *Napoletana* - the Ace, Two and Three of a particular suit worth 3 points but I forgot to declare, "*Bon Jyock'* - *Buon Giocco* - literally Good Game" before the end of the first round. Points lost! There were no allowances made.

The rest of the hand continued in disastrous fashion as I tried to maintain the fragile array of cards in my hand, listen to the instructions that they were giving and remember the cards played. When the time came for me to lead a card, I was so confused that someone sitting behind me helped me out.

At the end of each hand, I was expecting a tirade of abuse as even I realised my own mistakes, but they were more than generous and let me off scot-free. I was out of my depth and everyone knew it.

Nevertheless, I continued to go and watch them play most evenings and enjoyed the camaraderie.

~~~

Some days Midew would ask what we were doing the next day. If we were free, he would always have some little thing he would like to do with us as he seemed to warm to us.

He took us to San Michele, where he had other land and a particular type of fig that was ripening. *M* loves figs. On many occasions, he took us to Canneto (a spring a few kilometres below Vico where women still go to do their washing). There he has a walled garden, with vines, figs, nuts, oranges, lemons and vegetables.

He always appeared grumpy when he arrived at Canneto. He would study his patch with a trained eye and then declare that someone had stolen his vegetables. I didn't really believe him at first, but then one day as we were picking figs, I found some marrows that had been moved to the boundary. Maybe the scrumpers had abandoned their haul on being disturbed.

Midew spent many days in the summer months at Canneto, often going with Filomena. Occasionally he would ask us to join them in the late afternoon and we would find them there, with the bread oven going and preparing Pizza. On days when they lit the oven, they would also make bread and biscuits. Filomena and *M* busied themselves preparing these essential supplies as we men harvested whatever was ready in the garden. All the while Midew uttered a continuous unintelligible commentary on how to grow vegetables, prune vines and trees, keep the ground clean and the importance of having water. I went along with it all, as he could not imagine that I had once tended a garden in the UK.

But if Midew was unintelligible, Filomena was from another planet. She was from nearby Rodi, about 15 kilometres from Vico, and even though she had lived in Vico for decades, she still spoke *Rodiano*. As *M* had explained all those years ago - the dialects here vary considerably and even she had real problems understanding Filomena. Now I believed her.

□ ~~~

One evening late in August, Midew did not show up for cards. On my way home from the bar to the Carmine, I spotted him strolling round the corner with one arm in a sling.

"What on earth have you done?" I asked.

"I fell out of a tree," he announced with a wry smile on his face.

"How?"

"I was cleaning one of the olives when the branch I was standing on broke," he declared.

"How high up were you?"

"Oh, not very high, about 3 metres," he grinned.

A selfish thought passed through my mind. "What if he was to fall and break his neck? Then where would we be?"

His half of the property would pass to goodness knows whom in his family and then we would have to deal with them as well as the others.

The next day I drove him down to 'the house' as he couldn't drive. Midew used the opportunity to tell me that in August they clean the trees in preparation for the harvest. First, they cut away any suckers at the base of the trees; then they clean them of any masculine shoots - those that don't bear fruit. The tree must channel all the sap to the olives.

His team of pruners was already at work in the *pianura*, the dry river-valley below the house, where the best trees are to be found. I had seen these trees once before when we first came to the property with Michele *oo' Noyrr.* They were certainly big I had noted then, but seeing the pruners perched high up in the branches, like shipmates atop the rigging of a schooner. From this perspective these trees were truly awesome - we were walking among giants.

Midew introduced the *squadra* - there was Andrea the team leader, Damiano and Matteo *da Pecora.* At the mention of Matteo's *sopranome,* a chorus of 'Bahh, Bahh' broke out from the others - he was Matteo 'of the sheep'.

Doubts were creeping into my head about how I was going to control these pruners, if we ever did get around to owning the olives. They spoke Vicaiolo, seemed to have a wicked sense of humour and would probably run me round in circles. Would I actually be able to manage them?

As misgivings swirled about our intentions to buy these olives, my stomach plunged as I contemplated climbing the trees - would I ever be up there with them? Would they expect it of me, after all Midew at 70 still climbed. My head was awash with the wooziness of vertigo.

To make things worse, Midew showed me his broken branch, actually a little higher up than he said. It's a wonder he hadn't broken his neck. Goodness knows what would happen if one of the pruners fell out at the height they were at.

"And if they were to fall?" I asked. He grunted that there would be trouble. I was sure he was right, but what did he really mean by trouble? I pressed for an explanation but I never understood his long-winded reply.

□ ~~~

A couple of weeks later, we drove Midew to his garden at Canneto. The *kaki* (fruit of the Persimon) were ready for picking and I was to help him. I naturally assumed that I would be climbing the tree, but no. Off he went, using his rigid plastered arm to hook around branches and pull himself upwards. Before I knew it, he was too far away to be able to load the basket I was holding.

I started to climb the tree and Filomena said something to *M.* I didn't understand. *M* translated that I had to go very carefully as the wood of the Persimon tree is notoriously brittle. Midew barked for me to get on with it. Selfish thoughts for my own safety flooded my mind as he pursued a fruit that I did not like in the slightest.

□ ~~~

Summer passed. Though we had done our utmost to keep Midew on track with the house, nothing had happened.

Vincenzo and Emilia had gone back to England; their apartment was once again empty for another nine months. We had Vicolo Sancarlo and comforting as it was, we had no plans to stay there for the rest of our lives. We yearned to be out of the town, away from the noise and bustle and looking after our own patch of land.

Whenever we broached the subject with Midew, he always managed to brush it aside. He had other plans; we needed to know more about the Gargano, how things were done. One of his favourite diversions was to arrange an outing. The best we could hope for was that he might just feed us a crumb of news while we were out.

One day we all went to the Foresta Umbra to collect sweet chestnuts. It was a beautiful autumn day and the deciduous trees of the forest were beginning to shed their leaves.

We headed out of Vico, climbing to some 800 metres and turned off the main road at a military base. We followed a tarmac road for a while passing one of the many picnic areas in the forest and then Midew indicated that we should leave the tarmac road and take a track.

We eventually stopped deep in the woods. It seemed deserted - bird-song the only sound.

Armed with walking sticks (to tap the undergrowth as a warning to deadly vipers) and baskets we set off through the fern covered ground. En route, we came across the odd big old chestnut tree; they all had chestnut skins lying around under them but it was obvious that someone else had already visited. Midew urged us on, "there's nothing much to be had here. Follow me."

As we descended into a valley, he let out a shout. He had found *porcini* - he hadn't expected to, as it had been dry recently. He collected them and we hunted around for more, but didn't find any.

We moved on across the valley and into a plantation of chestnuts. Here the fruits were sprawled all over the ground.

As we foraged for the harvest, we heard bells - cows started to come into view grazing the forest at will. Then there were other signs of life - some Vichesi were coming towards us, their tone of voice was unmistakable.

Then there was a call "Midew". It was Peppe *Ci'Catt*, my young

109

builder friend. He came from out of the trees carrying a large plastic basket full of chestnuts. "*Margheri', K'eh fah? - what are you doing?*" he shouted out to *M* who was coming up the hill behind us with Filomena. Like the plaiting of the garlic, Peppe appeared to think it strange that *M* was out in the forest picking chestnuts.

He and his friend stopped to chat for a while. They had been there since dawn and had filled many baskets. Now it was time to go to Vico to meet the traders who bought chestnuts. For Peppe this was a cash crop - he would earn far more picking chestnuts in a day than he would building. I couldn't help wondering whose these chestnuts were. How come we could just come and pick them?

Silence, apart from the cowbells, returned after they had gone. We carried on towards the end of the plantation where the well-tended chestnuts merged with dense undergrowth. The noise of the bells seemed to be coming from everywhere and then we noticed that bell-laden pigs joined the cows - all snuffling away in the leaf mould.

We were just about to call off the hunt when a young man with a very dark complexion emerged from the undergrowth in front of me, an axe casually resting on one shoulder. Were they his chestnuts?

His sudden and rugged appearance took me by surprise. What was he going to do or say? But I needn't have been concerned as he looked past me, smiled and called out. "Midew, *Bona serr'*."

Midew introduced Angelo, the shepherd of the herd. His axe just a tool to free animals should they become entangled in the undergrowth.

Midew and Angelo had a long chat. What about is anybody's guess, but Midew took the opportunity to get as much information as possible.

On the way home Midew explained that Angelo was a Vichese and that if we wanted some good meat we should go and see him at Christmas.

Another outing finished back at Midew and Filomena's where, after dinner, we roasted chestnuts on the open fire and drank Midew's homemade wine well into the night.

We chatted about all aspects of life here, except 'the house'.

□ ~~~

We decided that it was time for action. On our next meeting with Midew, we pressed him about 'the others'. When were they coming? How could we know that they would sell? His answers were unintelligible. He didn't seem interested in giving straight answers. He just smiled and implied that all would turn out right in the end.

We told Midew that soon we would be leaving; we would not spend winter in Vico. If we left with nothing to come back to, we were unlikely to return at all.

Under consistent pressure, he finally conceded that they would come in November. Our hearts sank. There wouldn't be time to sort things out. "How do you know they'll be here?" *M* demanded.

"They always come, to collect their oil," he stated authoritatively.

His manner was beginning to annoy us. Had he been stringing us along all the time? Had he any intention of selling? We pressed hard and said that November was no good. By that time, we would be preparing to leave.

We must have struck a chord. As October came to a close Midew came to find us. He had spoken to Matteo Pirro and 'they' had agreed a price for their four parcels of land and rights to the house!

Well so much for negotiation. Midew seemed ignorant of our need to be involved, as if we couldn't possibly negotiate on our own behalf. But the price seemed reasonable, so we didn't bother arguing about it and for the moment, it was academic.

He had more news. Giuseppe and Lucia Pirro would come from Rome in November in order to do the deed whenever we required.

That just left Francesco Palmieri. He had parcel 111 and we needed to talk to him. Midew had more news - Francesco would be arriving from Rome shortly and would stay for his olive harvest. He would not be at Vico, but had a holiday apartment in San Menaio. Midew gave us his mobile phone number - it seemed this was one negotiation we had to deal with ourselves.

Last Piece of the Jigsaw

Our attempts to ring Palmieri on his mobile phone failed, so eventually we called Midew and asked whether he could do something. A few minutes later, Midew called back and explained roughly where we could find Palmieri at his holiday home in San Menaio. We decided to go and find him after lunch.

Just as we were finishing lunch, the phone rang. It was Palmieri. A message had reached him that we were trying to get hold of him. He was ready to talk.

He began by trying to sell us all his holdings near the house. Apart from parcel 111, he had another three parcels of land that he wanted to sell and he seemed reluctant to sell them separately. We really didn't want any more land and certainly not at the price he was asking. We were also sure that *oo Capone* had an interest in joining up his land and by attempting to buy the unwanted parcels we might overcomplicate issues with him. We stuck to our guns, pleading that we weren't really olive farmers and that if we couldn't buy 111 then the whole deal was off. He reluctantly conceded and agreed that he would sell parcel 111 alone.

So what was his price? He mentioned his figure. *M* couldn't disguise her frustration he had effectively put a price of 1000 Euros on every tree! Parcel 111 was an abandoned piece of ground where it was difficult even to see the olive trees, let alone value them.

"How can this be?" she demanded.

As she negotiated fruitlessly on the phone, I could feel things slipping away. He was not talking about olive trees; he was basing his price on a water storage tank. If we had to build the tank today, it would cost millions he exaggerated.

"Let's talk face to face," I mouthed to *M* and somehow we managed to stop the phone horse-trading and agreed to meet at the bar in front of the station in San Menaio at 3 pm.

The lull gave us time to calm down and agree a strategy. Here was a man who knew his position was strong. He'd spoken to the others, probably knew what they were getting and he wanted a big piece of the cake.

We reasoned the basics. At least we didn't have to buy his other parcels with some 100 olive trees at an inflated price - that was a sum we didn't have to spend. We wanted to pay him half of what he was asking for 111, so we agreed to convey an air of calm and negotiate as toughly as we could with the knowledge that if he stuck to his guns we would have to pay him or throw in the towel after a year of very hard work.

We arrived at the station. There was a man opposite leaning on a Ford Escort talking into his mobile phone. Dressed in a Hawaiian shirt - he looked like a wheeler-dealer. There was no one else in sight. We did a U-turn and pulled in behind him outside the bar. He looked too young to be our man but then we noticed the Roma plates on his car. We got out of the car and he stopped his conversation abruptly and greeted us. As we exchanged handshakes, it became more apparent close up that this was a well-preserved old man.

He was stocky, quite tall, tanned with a large bald head, and a nose that would sit well on any Roman. He looked tough.

"Sorry, the bar's closed," he said. "I don't understand. It's always open at this time." He invited us to sit outside anyway and we recommenced negotiations.

We went over the same ground. He inexplicably talked about the cost of land, property and living in Rome. Our offer simply did not impress him. What would he do with a mere few thousand Euros? I decided to change tack, as talking about trees seemed pointless, and M was getting a little agitated. I didn't think she would blow it, but a little calm wouldn't do any harm. "Let's talk about his rights to the house," I suggested.

We broke down his asking price into land and house. He, apparently, wanted three times what we were giving the others for the latter (that brought the trees down to 700 Euros each!) We argued that the others at least had bricks and mortar - as we understood it he only had the right to walk in (whenever he pleased), light a fire and shelter from the weather! How could that be worth so much more than the other's shares?

He insisted that he, too, owned part of the house! Our

confidence slumped as we contemplated the thought that he might be right. If we gave in to his price and the others got wind of what he was getting - would they want more? Nothing at this stage could have been more daunting. He started talking about an aunt who originally lived in the house and about his childhood memories; yes indeed, he had inherited. Again, to diffuse things, I decided to find out a little more about him.

To our knowledge, he was the uncle of a neighbour in Vico. M had been helping his great niece with her English for several months. Maybe that would help us to soften his negotiations with us. "Yes," he agreed that our neighbours were indeed his relatives. Furthermore, it turned out that he was actually born in our house in Vicolo Sancarlo! He chatted away nostalgically for a while and then, bizarrely, conceded that we were right - he only had minimal rights to the house!

What a relief. Now, would he reduce his price? No, he was adamant. He was sticking with the original price and was not prepared to split the house and plot 111 even if we wanted to do that. We covertly exchanged desperate glances. Could we afford to lose the whole deal for what was, after all, a relatively small amount, or should we just pay up?

We upped our offer a little, sticking to our strategy. No, he replied. At this point, I thought we should leave it for the night and let him think it over when suddenly he declared a lower price - 500 Euros above our latest offer. We exchanged a flickering glance - it was enough.

We agreed and shook hands - the last part of the jigsaw was finally in place. We were exhausted but exhilarated and didn't want to let on just how relieved we were. After a few more minutes of small talk, we shook hands again and parted. We drove to Rodi for a *caffe corretto* - coffee laced with whisky. Not exactly a celebration, more of a fortification, for there was still plenty that could go wrong, but in general, we were pretty pleased with ourselves.

Michele the Builder

With all the pieces in place, we decided that we must get some technical advice before taking the plunge. But going to a builder was tantamount to going public. If we got a gossiper, the whole of Vico would likely know what we were up to. But we desperately needed estimates and to reassure ourselves that the house could be saved.

First, we took Mimmo (*M*'s cousin) - the one who had helped us with the *catasto*. He is a surveyor with a good engineering background and anyway he already knew what we were up to.

At the site he told us what they would have to do to save the vaults, reinforce the house to comply with seismic regulations, as the Gargano is an earthquake zone, and so on. All in all though he said he thought the house to be in good condition - despite the jungle in the roof.

Our next step was one into the dark. We had to expose our plans and take a builder. We began by asking builders we had already met during our searches in Vico whether they could do some work for us at Vicolo Sancarlo in the New Year. If they couldn't be available for that then they would be of no use to us on a much bigger project. This strategy eliminated, among others, Peppe, who said he had indefinite work in the Centro Storico.

We narrowed it down to a builder we had found restoring a similar house while we were out searching. We decided to tell him a little lie, that we were about to sign the *atto* - bill of sale, that the deed was done, the property was effectively sold.

At the site, he confirmed everything that Mimmo had said and gave us a quote. We took it with a pinch of salt, for we knew it would cost more, but nonetheless for the work that he would do it seemed within our budget. But we needed to confirm.

Mimmo had mentioned another builder. Michele *Oo'*
Pes'keh'chyah'n, but in the same breath he said we would be lucky to
get him. He was considered the best in Vico especially for this sort of
restoration work; he was very busy; we wouldn't stand a chance of
getting him and so on. Nevertheless, Mimmo gave us his address.

One evening we went to see him at his home. He was
welcoming. His wife, Rosetta, prepared coffee and offered *corretto* and
he listened to our requirements. We couldn't tell whether he was in
the slightest bit interested.

Instead of addressing our needs he produced a photograph from
the sideboard of a lady - Signora Della Bella. She was from a rich
family that used to own a sizeable chunk of the Gargano and our
once coveted Hunting Lodge at San Nicola. Michele went on to say
he did most of his work for the Della Bella family and talked through
many of his projects. To back up his credentials he asked Rosetta to
find a photo album. She searched the house from top to bottom but
couldn't find it.

We sensed from his stance that he would simply be too busy, he
would cost a fortune and even if he would do the work, we would
have to wait for years. In the meantime, if we waited for him, 'the
house' would fall down. But he didn't say "no" there and then. He
agreed to come and view the project, so we made an appointment for
the following evening.

~~~

The next day, we picked up Michele and drove down to the house.
We left the car on the main road just as we had done on our first visit
and walked up to the house.

Michele stopped on the last curve in the drive and gazed up at
the 12-metre high building as if he were already sizing up the
scaffolding. He declared the outside sound.

"What about the crack in the South wall," I asked.

"*Non c'è problema.*"

We went in and surveyed the ground floor; he couldn't find any
problems there either. We picked our way over the broken stairs,
seemingly few problems there. Michele headed straight for the
balcony of the 'study'. He lent on the railing staring wistfully at the
view.

The evening before we had learnt that Michele was from
Peschici (explaining his *sopranome oo' Pes'keh'chyah'n* - an umbrella

116

name for everyone from the neighbouring fishing village) and he had married into a Vico family. He had been a sailor, he'd mentioned. From the balcony, he looked out at the views to the sea and you could tell he liked it.

"*È una torretta* - It's a little castle," he declared.

Yes, we know it's an imposing house, but what about the rebuild?

"No, problem," he replied, "*si può fare tutto* - you can do everything."

"What, no problem with restoring the vaults, the roof etc? Wouldn't you like to see the roof?" I offered.

"*No, no Signor Giovanni, non c'è problema.*"

"Well can you do it?" *M* urged him for an answer.

He thought for a while and said, "*Sì, certo - Yes, of course.*"

"And can you start in the New Year?" Again, he replied positively.

It was difficult to believe that we could snatch the 'best' builder in Vico away from the Della Bella family, but maybe there was a catch.

"How much will it cost?" We finally broached the subject of money expecting to be bowled over by an astronomical sum. But, with a few caveats and much to our relief he quoted almost the same figure as the first builder - it was good enough.

We could see that Michele liked the building, that for him it would be a prestige job. He wanted to do it. We liked Michele and wanted him to be our builder. We pushed a little more.

"When exactly can you start?"

To our amazement, he told us that he had one or two jobs to finish, but providing all the necessary permissions were in place, he could start almost immediately. We were overjoyed.

I only had one reservation - he spoke Italian as he surveyed the house and confirmed that everything was possible, but once off the site and back in the car he returned to his native *Peschici* dialect - I couldn't understand a word!

Process of Elimination

With everything and everyone now seemingly in place we visited the *Notaio*'s clerk, Alberto, to discuss whether we could complete on the following Monday. He had all the documents, we had all the people and now all he needed were the results of a search that one of his colleagues was carrying out in the provincial capital Foggia.

Our hopes were tested within minutes as he dismissed the documents - they weren't enough to identify the true owners of the house. No surprises there then. And to cap it all, he had gone through Palmieri's deeds and apparently, he had no rights to the house at all!

Midew's documents were all in order, but the other documents apparently were not. They didn't state clearly that the vendors owned the rest of the house. Someone else could be lurking out there with some rights to the house or land and there was, according to Alberto, no way to find out. It seemed impossible - we were missing the '*successione di morte*' for Angela Pino, Palmieri's father and the husband of his sister Caterina Palmieri.

In Italy paperwork is everything and the '*successione di morte* is probably one of the most important. It is a death duty certificate that all beneficiaries to an estate must hold and is in most cases the definitive proof of ownership.

To add to the confusion who exactly was Angela Pino? Was she a typing error? Was she really Angela Pirro and if so what effect could this have on the outcome of all our work? Alberto shrugged his shoulders.

We left frustrated and immediately sought out Midew to talk about the situation. He phoned Antonia Pirro and she agreed to see us straight away. We arrived at her apartment and finally met one of the other vendors for the first time. Shortly after, her brother Matteo arrived. And so we met another.

They were delighted to see us after all this time and wanted to know why on earth we hadn't contacted them before? They had wanted to sell earlier and be done with it.

Midew, who had never revealed to us the identities of the other parties (nor ours to them, incidentally), sat sheepishly sipping a grappa.

We explained why we had come and between them, Antonia and Matteo, contacted all their relatives but the vital document was nowhere to be found.

We left at least with the satisfaction of having met some of the other parties and they assured us Angela Pino was a typing error, but that was all.

~~~

We visited Alberto the next day to see if he had found out more and to mention that the Pirro family were having difficulty finding the missing document.

It was then that Alberto blurted out, "the document wouldn't tell us anything anyway!"

"Then why do we need it?" my pleas fell on deaf ears.

M intervened. "Why can't we go to some bureaucrat and get copies of what we need so as to be sure we have it all."

"Well," Alberto said, "we could go to Lucera and trace the ownership of the house to the present day but that would take weeks, maybe months and then it might not prove beyond doubt who has rights to the house. It's almost impossible."

M's patience snapped. "Whatever it takes, Alberto, do it! There is no way here but forward!" *M* suddenly commanded. "Don't you realise we've been chasing this house for a year, that we've put together most of the pieces and we're not going to give up now?"

Reluctantly he then went back to the deeds, with the aid of a colleague. Meanwhile *M* read the Pirro's documents again and was sure that she had found the vital piece of information needed. For some reason Alberto and colleague both ignored her as they fiddled about researching the *catasto* only to come up with the same result - the house was in the name of Pino Angela.

Tired of the process we eventually agreed that the signing could not go ahead on the Monday as planned. So we made an appointment for the same day to see Alberto's boss, the *Notaio*, to solicit her opinion.

~~~

In a welcome diversion to our dilemma, we escaped to 'the house' with Midew so that we could walk the boundaries again and survey the Pirro's olive crop.

The boundaries were mystifying. A mixture of yellow paint daubed on trees, broken stone walls, large stones or simply subtle changes in contour. So we moved on to the olives.

Midew walked us up through the Pirro's trees and as we passed each tree, he would pull one, two or three leaves off and ask me to hold them. What on earth for?

He was not forthcoming until we reached the end of the grove where he asked me to count the leaves.

"Forty."

"Not bad," said Midew.

He revealed that each leaf represented a half *quintale* so we should collect about 20 *quintali* (2000 kilos) of olives.

"Yes, yes, but how much oil will we make?" we were keen to hear. Midew wouldn't answer, he couldn't be precise, and he became cagey. "We'll see," was his closing remark on the subject.

~~~

The meeting with the *Notaio* was much more upbeat than we were used to having with her assistant Alberto. Although many things were unclear, she was confident she could resolve them given time. We had the time but we couldn't speak for the other parties and urged her to pull out all the stops. She promised she would and rearranged the completion date for the last Friday in November. We left the meeting a little more optimistic and, in a way, more determined.

We telephoned the Pirro family to inform them of our progress. They couldn't hide their dismay at the latest delay. As for Palmieri, he said he couldn't wait. He had an appointment with the doctor in Rome; he had things to attend to. But after much negotiation, he agreed to stay until the last Friday of the month. That was a relief, but if push came to shove and he decided to leave, we might have to just do the *atto* with him and risk a few thousand Euros to buy a piece of abandoned ground with a 30 cubic metre water reservoir!

With so many open ends, we returned to the history of the family as our only true means of finding out the facts. We knew that

120

Palmieri's uncle Luigi had built the house. He had three brothers Giacomo, Nicola and Michele and a sister, Francesco Palmieri's mother, Erminia. Michele apparently sent money from America to have the house built. For some reason Luigi ended up with the lion's share, which eventually was sold by his descendants to Midew.

Michele married Angela Pirro, whose son Francesco had five children - Antonia, Giuseppe, Erminia, Matteo and Lucia, who confirmed to us that they had inherited the rest of the house.

We believed them, but our task now was to find out what happened to the offspring of Giacomo, Nicola and Erminia. The title deeds of Angela Pirro mentioned all three of them - not in respect of the house, but it clearly stated access rights to their parcels of land from the house! Could they have had any rights to the house as well?

~~~

The following Monday, we visited Alberto with documents obtained from Francesco Palmieri. Over the weekend, we had created the family tree and we knew that we still needed information on two branches of the family. We were trying to persuade Alberto to look them up in the *catasto* when Antonia Pirro walked in with the missing '*successione di morte*'.

Alberto scanned it and said, "this tells us nothing." We still needed specific information on two counts and this latest document only covered one of them. Antonia began to get a little frustrated as she urged that the first count was perfectly clear in documents she had already handed over. Alberto shook his head, gave her back the original document and said, "show me."

Antonia and *M* read through the document and bingo another piece of the jigsaw fell into place. They were right and he was wrong.

Our doubts about Alberto increased - did he have an interest in obstructing us? We knew that he had bought a house in the country and that he actively bought land. Did he want to buy 'the house'?

We now had only one case to deal with, the '*successione di morte*' of the husband of Caterina. This document appeared to be unobtainable, so we finished up by making another appointment to see the *Notaio* to try to clear these matters up and present all the information we had gathered.

~~~

Midew had retained the rights to harvest his own olives that year.

121

Could this have been the single factor for holding us up for a year? His trees were creaking under the weight of olives. Yes, that must have been the reason, we concluded.

Surely, he must have realised that had he asked us, we would have granted him the rights. After all, in the negotiations with the Pirro's he had, using his own initiative, insisted that we have the olives from their trees. Why would we want more? Why shouldn't he reserve the crop after all his work? We had neither the means nor the wherewithal to harvest and store the oil, let alone sell it.

It seemed Midew had to be in control. With the negotiations over the Pirro's olives completed, he pronounced that we would go ahead and prepare for the harvest despite the minor detail that we didn't even own the trees yet. We would lay nets under the laden Pirro trees and catch any olives that might fall in the coming week. After all, he said, a wind could come at any time and bring the whole crop down.

So, on the Tuesday I rose early to go down to the Pirro's land. Midew and his *operaio* - worker, Damiano, were already there. They had arrived in the *treruote* at dawn loaded with nets, strimmer and other tools.

With introductions complete, Damiano began by inspecting my new secateurs and condemned them immediately as being blunt and 'hand deadeners'. He showed me his and apart from being a little fancier, they seemed the same to me. He assured me they were professional and he would take me to get a pair. When he got a chance, he would sharpen the 'hand deadeners' for me; meanwhile I was to leave the trees well alone.

We set about preparing for the harvest, cutting away any suckers at the base of each tree and cleaning a 100 sq metre area around each tree of anything that might snag the nets. Midew would carefully survey the size of each tree and then we laid the appropriate sized net.

These "tree nets" (as opposed to working nets) are square with one half split through to the middle in order to wrap around the tree. We placed the split on the uphill side of the bole of the tree and pinned the sides as close to the tree as possible using large stones. Then we stretched the edges of the net and pinned them to the ground with any other large stones to hand. On the steeper slopes, we raised the lower edge of the nets on stakes made from the freshly cut suckers so that the olives could not roll away.

After I had learnt the basics, Midew despatched me to supervise the bonfire, clear up around the trees and to gather up old piles of wood and move them to the *treruote*. I seemed to be all over the place following their orders and learning how they did things.

Still at least Damiano spoke to me in reasonable Italian and helped to translate Midew's Vicaiolo whenever he grasped that I was unable to understand.

It was a hard morning's work, but the sun was shining and it all seemed worthwhile. By one o'clock, we had finished laying the nets and I was thirsty, hungry and ready to go home. But we still had jobs to do - we had to cut the wood that I had collected. The *treruote*, like any ass before it, was to be loaded with wood and was not to go back to Vico empty.

At two o'clock, we reached Vico. I was suffering an energy crisis, but it appeared we still had work to do. Midew had already visited our house and decided that the firewood we had was too green and the fire pathetic. He was going to improve our life so we unloaded the wood and stacked it in our stable.

About an hour later, we had rearranged the firewood according to Midew's exacting standards. Green wood and seasoned wood suitably mixed up and neatly stacked. Only then could we at last have a break. *M* provided us each with a big bottle of ice-cold Peroni, which we all demolished with ease.

They departed for a well-earned lunch. Midew's parting words "At least the trees will sleep well tonight, knowing that they have a new *padrone* looking after them. Your health!"

Well we weren't about to start counting our chickens yet.

~~~

After a late lunch we prepared to go to the *Notaio* again as we were still pressing for clarifications. One thing in particular was *oo Capone*'s signature. He, as a *coltivatore diretto*, had the right to buy the land (not a part of it but the whole) at the purchase price declared. The *Notaio* had to declare the price and if *oo Capone* did not want to buy then he had to sign a declaration.

The *Notaio* assured us he would sign and, with that, she declared that the completion would take place on Saturday, not Friday as arranged.

It would be easier, she assured, with so many people involved it would be better to do it when the office was officially closed.

123

We were nervous, would Francesco stay? He'd promised to stay until Friday. What if anything were to go wrong, would there be any chance of holding the parties from Rome until Monday? She assured us there would be no problem and that she would make all the arrangements. In the meantime, she would tie up any loose ends.

~~~

We had to go to the bank first thing on Friday to draw cheques for various amounts for each of the vendors. We had taken the precaution of talking to the bank well in advance, to ensure that we could draw the banker's drafts and that they would have some in stock. Over cautious, perhaps? But, in the past, banks in Vico had been known to run out of cash and we were taking no chances.

Even though we'd had the conversation only a few days earlier, having even left a detailed list of the names and amounts, the fact that we actually wanted the drafts seemed to come as a big surprise to the cashier (as if they knew what we were up to and had laid bets on the chances of us succeeding!).

They didn't have drafts for the larger amounts, the cashier declared. It would have been futile to ask why, so we concentrated on solving the problem.

While the cashier was thumbing his way through his stock of banker's drafts, each having a specific pre-printed limit, we noticed that there were some with limits of a significant amount.

"Couldn't we draw up multiple drafts for the larger amounts?"

"*Si, non c'è problema,*" he conceded with a smile.

In the evening Nicolino, who had helped us purchase Vicolo Sancarlo with ease, arrived at our house. We had asked him to look for missing documents and he had news: he had secured the missing documents related to Caterina. We breathed a sigh of relief again, but it was short-lived. He wanted to go through all the documents we had, just to be sure, and he had some clauses he wanted added to the contract of sale.

He stopped at Francesco Palmieri's documents and sucked heavily through his teeth before explaining that Francesco's wife needed to sign the *atto*. This unwelcome news was all we needed.

"What on earth do we do now? She's not here, she's in Rome!" said *M*.

Nicolino calmly assured us that there was no other way - she had to come and we handed him the phone to speak to Francesco.

But she's 80 odd - how can she get here by tomorrow? What if she won't come? What if she can't come? As the phone call commenced, the questions and doubts raced through our minds.

The conversation between Nicolino and Francesco didn't appear to go well as Francesco tried to argue that it wasn't necessary for his wife to come. According to him, all his documents were in order. Nicolino switched rapidly into his 'how to treat people from Vico when it comes to talking about buying and selling' mode - he'd done it all his life. We were worried (about the way he told him what to do instead of begging) but Nicolino didn't seem concerned. Eventually Francesco agreed. He would ring his wife and she would come. How? When? We could only guess.

After the call Nicolino revealed that he knew Francesco quite well - they had both lived in the Carmine as boys - and it seemed Francesco hadn't realised who he was speaking to until well into the conversation. Anyway, Nicolino's intervention seemed to have worked. Now we had to wait and see if it worked.

The Eleventh Hour

At about 10 on Saturday morning, we went to the *Notaio*'s office. We had a brief meeting with her; she had worked into the early morning putting the pieces together, had traced the missing documents and could verify that there were no outstanding claimants. She confirmed that Mimmo *oo' Capone* had signed the necessary documents declaring that he had no interest in the property at the declared price. There were no loose ends and we were ready for the signing.

She asked us to go to a conference room on the third floor where we would be able to accommodate everyone in comfort. Francesco Palmieri was already there, he certainly seemed eager. We shook hands and inquired after his wife.

"She will be here tomorrow," he said completely relaxed.

"Well, how will that help?" I reacted agonizingly, "she needs to be here today surely!" Francesco said he had spoken with the *Notaio* and that it would be all right for her to sign separately. We breathed another sigh of relief.

In dribs and drabs, the signatories to the *atto* began to arrive. They were very noisy and excited as they climbed the stairs. True to form, many had brought their children just to add to the mayhem. There is simply no way that Italians can do anything, from as simple as eating (in or out), weddings, funerals and even serious moments 'when one is about to change one's whole life' without surrounding themselves with *confusione*.

Thankfully the children were eventually excluded, quite what they did with them we don't know. Maybe another relative took them off to the Pizzicato for an ice cream.

For some, especially the Pirro family, it was something of a reunion. Lucia and Giuseppe had just arrived from Rome, and then there was Francesco their Uncle and his sister Caterina. She was the oldest present, at 86, very frail and accompanied by her daughter, Antonietta.

Finally we were all gathered; the *Notaio* and her assistant, Midew and his wife Filomena, Francesco and Caterina Palmieri, the Pirro's - Matteo, Antonietta, Erminia, Lucia and Giuseppe and finally their aunt Rosetta Pirro.

But why was Rosetta there? How did she fit into the equation? Her face was familiar, but who was she? I was perplexed.

I asked *M*. "What was she doing here? Just along for the fun?" But *M* had no such problems.

"Rosetta is here as a vital signatory," she revealed. She inherited part of the estate before Midew bought the lion's share some 20 years earlier. She subsequently gifted it to the five Pirro nieces and nephews but nothing was in writing - a very common practice here.

In fact, it later became clear that I had met Rosetta in the Centro Storico. She was famous in Vico for her *pasticcerie* - pastry making and confectionery. One day when I was doing some house hunting, another friend called Peppe, took me to her house to get a key. She invited us in and insisted on giving me some of her biscuits. What a small world indeed.

So, there we all were, gathered round the *Notaio*'s conference table; the signatories plus assorted family members who deemed that they should be present. Midew, sat next to the *Notaio* dressed in his Sunday best, looking every bit the chief protagonist who had brought this event about. His role obviously not finished yet.

The *Notaio* began to read out the *atti*, word for word. There were five of them so it was going to take some time. It was repetitious stuff - each person's name read out, along with their place and year of birth, the parcels of land and rights they possessed. All seemed to be going well for the first hour with only the odd stoppage for minor clarifications.

Basically we were buying the largest share of the house from Midew along with about 3 hectares of his ground. Then we were buying one parcel of land from Francesco Palmieri along with a water storage tank and some vague rights to the house. From the Pirro's we were buying all their shares in the house along with three parcels of ground from Antonietta, Lucia and Giuseppe. Matteo, Erminia and Caterina were selling their shares in the house but keeping their olives.

We appeared to be reaching the point where the signing

ceremony was imminent when Antonietta, the daughter accompanying the elderly Caterina, asked on her mother's behalf how they would get to their land if we fenced off our ground, particularly parcel 111 that we were buying from Francesco.

Good question and what a time to raise it!

"There's no problem," *M* said immediately. "We have no plans to fence the track and we will sign any amendments to the *atto* accordingly."

All and sundry used the track and surely Caterina's workers had always used it. But either no one heard us or simply this was bread and butter for Italians at an *atto* signing. They would have to slog it out.

For over an hour, they managed to discuss the intricacies: history, terrain, family ties, disputes - whatever, with little sign of agreement. One thing that was apparent was that Midew and Matteo didn't see eye to eye. The *Notaio* kept the whole thing ticking over. Was she looking for an extra couple of hours pay?

The tension was too much. Could we possibly lose the house simply over a right of way? Would Caterina fail to understand the issues and not sign?

I left the room for a break and joined Francesco; he had also had enough and needed a cigarette. It was striking that he didn't seem at all concerned. He seemed a completely different person to the one we had met at San Menaio a few weeks earlier. The tough façade had gone, so had the Hawaiian shirt. He was more interested in giving me some sound fatherly advice on how to look after the olives, handle workers and so on. It passed the time.

When the protracted debate ended, the *Notaio* called the scattered parties together. There was no doubt that many of them had little interest in the proceedings and just wanted to get on with it, but at least they hadn't left the building, gone off to do the shopping or take a coffee at the Pizzicato!

She, Midew and Matteo had settled the details. Everyone agreed, and Antonietta and her mother Caterina had been convinced. All we had to do was sign an amendment saying that we would not fence off the track going through parcel 111. Now hadn't we said that over an hour ago?

There were smiles all round, but we were drained and couldn't help feeling that we had been put through some kind of initiation ceremony.

The *Notaio* circled the table with the document and everyone duly signed.

M and I then went around the table handing out the cheques, exchanging handshakes and *bacini*, the Italian embrace, and receiving congratulations. We had bought their land, their liabilities and their annual olive worries. The relief was apparent on each face. Sadly, we had nothing to give to Rosetta Pirro. She had come along to sign for nothing, she seemed left out but she was smiling. We would have to thank her somehow later.

We assembled for a photograph. Of course, members of various families had to join in and there was no way that we would get a picture of just the 12 of us. The party began to break up. Again congratulations and *bacini* were offered all round as we retreated to the *Notaio*'s office to fill in the figures.

As we sat there without the *confusione,* it began to sink in. What had we done? We'd achieved what seemed the impossible and now we were the owners of a derelict house and lots and lots of giant olive trees - we had changed our lives forever!

~~~

The next day, Sunday, with the sun shining in a cobalt sky we packed a basket - bread, tomatoes, oil, salami, Parma ham, *caciocavallo,* preserves, a bottle of champagne and some Puglian red - a Primitivo from the heel of Italy - and headed for 'our house'. It really was ours at last.

Before leaving Vico, we went to the *Notaio*'s office at the appointed hour to thank Francesco's wife who had travelled all the way from Rome on a bus. We were too late. She had been, signed and gone!

We drove on to the house, this time taking the Volvo all the way up through the S-bends to the terrace in front of the house. The back wheels spun, stones flew and tyres burnt, but we made it.

We cleared a little patch on the lower terrace and prepared for a picnic before splitting up to do a little work.

For an hour or so I attempted to cut a way through to the staircase that led up to the terrace in front of the house - I made little impression.

M re-surveyed the house, making plans for its restoration, designing the living space and taking stock of the contents.

Over the many visits we had made before the purchase, we had left everything as it was. Curious stones, remnants from some violent geological period littered the land. There were perfect spheres, in size and weight some like cannonballs, others distorted like curiosities in a horticultural show vegetable display. My favourite was a large ball with a knob on top, very like a *cash'e-cavadd*. Before we owned the land we couldn't help picking them up, but rather than take them away, like squirrels we superstitiously stored them in specific places - they were all still there.

Now that we owned them, we collected up a choice few to take back to Vico to display in a sort of basket sculpture.

In the upper rooms, there were very few windows left. Someone had taken most of them out and they were leaning up against the walls as if ready for transportation. Most were past restoration. We sorted out the best of them, again to take them to Vico. *M* was in her element. "Their carved frames will make lovely mirrors," she suggested

In the master bedroom, we found *noo' troccoluh* - a mousetrap. A curious looking wooden construction consisting of a shallow rectangular tray with two uprights pinned to the middle of the longer sides and joined by a cross-member. Inside the tray there is a block of wood connected to a shaft, rather like a plunger, that runs through a hole in the centre of the cross-member.

To bait the trap you pull up the shaft, which releases a pivot from its centre. This pivot has a piece of string attached to it with a small loop at the other end, which you thread though an eyehook in the centre of the base tray and secure it by pinning the loop with some bait - a nut, piece of hard cheese or bread - so leaving the block in suspense. When the unsuspecting creature takes the bait, it frees the string and thump, the plunger drops.

We were pleased to see the mouse trap undisturbed. It too was earmarked for transport to Vico to be restored by the carpenter Michele *Kappa da For'*.

In the roof, we found an old mallet. A block of roughly shaped olive wood with a simple short carved handle - it would have been used for all manner of things, especially cracking almond nuts.

After we had collected everything we wanted to preserve, we started lunch.

As we sat sipping M's favourite champagne, Veuve Cliquot, a purchase from our many visits to France, we pondered what to call the house and made further plans for its restoration. We had taken 30 months to arrive at this new period in our lives and we savoured it; how we would manage the project was for now a minor detail.

After mulling over the house name for some time, we eventually settled on Villa Oleandro - the only flower we could find in this sea of olive trees.

In the sunshine of the last day of November, *pan' e pomodor* had never tasted better.

To Work

The euphoria did not last. The next day Midew had me meet him at Villa Oleandro to work and *M* was to follow later with Filomena. We had to harvest our olives before we left for a Christmas break in the UK.

Our olives! Our life certainly had changed.

I arrived at 7am. Midew and Damiano were already there. They had unloaded the working nets from the *treruote* and now they were arming themselves with their equipment. Midew, whose broken arm now seemed completely mended, threaded a leather holster containing his secateurs onto his string belt.

Damiano, similarly clad, removed a studded leather cover from his axe and sharpened its glistening blade. He tested the edge with the hardened skin of his thumb and, satisfied, slipped its handle into his string belt behind the secateurs' holster with the sharp end pointing to his rear.

They said little as we set the working nets; a "pull here" or a "pull there" for my benefit but the work was routine. At the first tree, we laid a patchwork of four nets overlapping the split net we had placed the week before.

On the approach to our property, the olives start in the bed of a former river valley. They are our giants, with huge girths and all more than 12 metres high - hopefully they will be our most productive. We bought one large parcel of land here from Midew and another smaller one from Antonia Pirro. Midew and she had reserved their crops, so there was nothing to harvest on the comfortable flat.

At the edge of the flat, a steep bank climbs up towards the house, some 30 metres above. Beyond the house, there is a further climb, gradual in places and then steep until we reach the summit of the hill flanking the valley at about 300 metres. Fortunately, most of the very steep land is pinewood.

That morning we started harvesting at the foot of the bank and the plan was to work upwards past the house. The terrain was difficult, almost scree-like. A thin layer of soil covering rock littered with stones from broken retaining walls. Midew and Damiano didn't seem to find it in anyway uncomfortable but I slipped around losing my footing and generally found the going tough. They seemed aware of my discomfort and with every slip or trip I heard *"K'yahn, k'yahn -* Slowly, slowly" or *"Stat' attent', attent'* - Be careful, careful."

Of course I was familiar with the routine of setting up the nets, as I had done it with Zio Mimi in November a year earlier; but this time they were our olives and I really had to work. Midew barked out orders in Vicaiolo.

"Bring that net here, hold this, pull here and there, watch out you don't snag that net." Damiano helpfully translated his tirade.

With ladders in place, Midew and Damiano set off with sticks in hand up the first tree and began working their way to the top.

As soon as they reached obstacles, non-productive male suckers that hindered their progress, out came the axes. I had expected olives to drop, but instead *frasca* rained down from the tree. Damiano explained that the trees hadn't been cleaned for a while and this was necessary work and would pay dividends in the coming years.

Frasca is one of the few Italian words they use. It's the generic term for anything cut from the trees that has to be burnt, in some cases not simply suckers but large branches and anything that is determined to be unsafe or diseased, no matter how big, is lopped off with a chainsaw.

Eventually, they arrived at the top of the tree and began the harvest. Midew, having stamped his authority on the day's work, was by now in fine form as he burst into song. From a neighbouring parcel of land, one still belonging to Matteo Pirro, other men were harvesting; their Vicaiolo calls boomed out to us, their tenor voices competed.

Having received no orders, I took a stick, stepped inside the circumference of the tree and chose a spot where I wouldn't be impaled by a falling axe and, with my back to the bole, I began brushing down the drooping branches.

It didn't take Midew long to notice this initiative and a machine gun burst of unintelligible orders rained down. Damiano translated - I was to collect the *frasca* and make a bonfire at a central point between the trees, a position that would not burn the other trees.

"And mind you don't step on the olives!" balled out Midew as if he were a sergeant major who had already decided his new recruit wouldn't make the grade. I nervously picked my way out of the net, took a quick look at the bottom of my boots and sure enough I had already pulped some olives.

Well, at least he had given me something that I was able to do, and it would keep me clear of the olives and out of range of his tirade, or so I thought. But when he surveyed my work from above a few minutes later, he started off again "*Noon, noon* - No, no not like that - do I have to show you everything?"

Midew descended the tree and to add to his ill-humour a rung on the ladder snapped under his weight. He cursed whilst he removed the broken pieces.

He came over to the unlit bonfire and began to pull it apart. "You're putting all the wood on the fire - that's wrong," he began.

"There's *frasca* here with olives on, you see - you have to brush them off onto the nets," he continued, showing me how to do it with a stick. Then he drew his axe from his belt and continued the lesson

"This piece is good for firewood, hold it like this."

He held the branch at the thick end and sliced away the small tributary branches with single clean cuts, until he reached a point where the wood was new growth and he deftly chopped the head off.

"Like this you see, chop away from your body - keep your fingers well away," he concluded.

I didn't understand a word he said, but I got the gist. He left me with a spare axe to get on with it. Before he climbed back up the tree, he disappeared into a neighbouring spinney and re-emerged a few minutes later with a short piece of wood. With his axe, he trimmed it until he was satisfied and making sure that his new student saw everything. He climbed the ladder and deftly inserted the new rung as he went.

I struggled with the *frasca* on the rough stony ground; it was surprisingly tough going and now with the hindrance of a razor-sharp axe I was making heavy work of a menial task.

By the time I had a bonfire in place, Midew and Damiano had moved on with the working nets to the next tree. They had emptied the catch of three of the nets surrounding the first tree onto the split net. All the time Midew was barking at Damiano

"Get that net there. No, the other one - the smaller one. Lay it over there. Pull, pull. Put a stone there. Put a stone there."

I was expecting Damiano to lose his cool, after all he had been doing this work for years, and surely he knew what to do. But he just took it all in his stride, occasionally looking at me with a slight grin and a shrug.

As *M* and Filomena arrived, the sun was coming up over the hills behind the house and was rapidly heating the chilly dawn air. We were soon down to T-shirts. Their arrival sparked a brief break as the neighbouring workers came over to introduce themselves and warmly congratulate us on our purchase.

With the break over, Midew instructed me to light the first, well overdue, fire. He told the women what they had to do in his unrestrained soldierly fashion and then he and Damiano returned to the trees. The women were to get the sacks from the *treruote* and begin collecting the olives from the split nets. Did they really need telling?

My first fire failed to ignite. There was a lot of smoke and then nothing. I was busy putting the situation right when Filomena broke off from the collection of olives to show me how to light it. I insisted that it was no problem, that I knew how to light a fire, but she continued to embarrass me for my apparent lack of basic country skills. Eventually she got it going ... so I was chauvinistically pleased when it went out!

We progressed steadily. *Frasca* and olives rained down. I succeeded in lighting the first fire and as time passed fire after fire. The women went about their business, sifting out bits of *frasca* and debris especially bits of wood and bark that can make the oil bitter, sorting the best olives for preserving into separate baskets. When satisfied with each net they poured the harvest into the sacks.

We stopped harvesting each day at about two in the afternoon, but there was still much to do. The day's harvest was dotted around in the grove in unwieldy 50 kg sacks. I would help Damiano and Midew in turn to lift each sack to their shoulder, and then with one arm pivoted into their lumbar for support they would move slowly down the bank to the *treruote*. I couldn't help admiring the work that Midew and Damiano had put in.

Each afternoon we delivered the olives to the mill. There we unloaded the sacks into large plastic crates each capable of holding about two and a half *quintali* of olives (the *quintale*, a 100kg in weight is the accepted standard of measurement for most things here) and then the mill staff shifted the crates using forklifts to the weighing machine, labelled them and drove them to a storage location.

We weren't alone. From all over the territory of Vico, growers were arriving with their harvest in all manner of transport: donkeys, mules, pick-ups, tractors and trailers, 4x4 vehicles or the family saloon car.

Inside, the mill was a-buzz with the frenzy of production and the whirr of heavy machinery; the atmosphere thick with the heady smell of crushed olives.

By Thursday evening, we had collected about 12 *quintali* of olives and there was one more day to harvest. But we needed to start the milling process. Apart from anything else, the olives shouldn't be left too long in the crates - the longer they wait the more acidic the resulting oil. But we had another reason. We wanted to take some of our first oil to the UK and we were planning to leave on Saturday. We had pressing business about the house to sort out and we would not have time to go to the mill on Friday evening. Midew said that he would take care of Friday's harvest for us.

~~~

We met at the mill at about six on Thursday evening and Midew showed us the process as we patiently waited our turn. As with all Italian practices we couldn't really tell whether it was orderly or not - all sorts of people passed through the mill, watched the milling process and left with their oil.

Many at the mill who knew of us, stopped to congratulate us on our purchase. As had happened to me every evening that week in Vico when I went out to San Francesco; total strangers stopped me in the street and introduced themselves.

Some were neighbours, they would tell me where their ground was, but I couldn't follow them well enough to work out how close they were to us. Others were relations of neighbours who couldn't help getting in on the act. Some had merely picked up the news on the rapid-transit Vico grapevine. Whoever they were, the message was the same, a warm handshake and the words "*Auguri, auguri!*"

It was all very kind but it struck me as strange in a place where most people apparently couldn't wait to get rid of their land.

All were curious. What exactly were we going to do? Were we really going to farm olives? Were we going to build a hotel? Were we going to do *agriturismo*?

When we reiterated, "we're going to restore the house and live there," most seemed astonished.

"What live there?" was their usual disbelieving riposte.

"Ah just for the summer months?" they would add to make sure that they had the full picture.

"No, all year round," we always assured them in harmony.

"All year round! You won't be living in Vico?" they would ask incredulously.

They were all clearly having trouble with the concept.

"Won't you be cold there in winter?" they queried, as if to cast seeds of doubt in our minds.

"Why on earth should we be? It's about 400 metres below Vico. Why should it be cold? And anyway we'll have fires and central heating just like you," we would assert.

We concluded that the Vichesi must draw some warmth from living in numbers together in Vico. For it's a bitterly cold place in winter and we were already feeling it at the start of December. Although the ambient temperature was about 10°C, the combined altitude and humidity chilled to the bone.

We were lighting the fire at Vicolo Sancarlo each night and thanking Midew for his dry wood. Or was the wood ours in the first place?

~~~

Eventually our turn came at the mill. The operators brought our crates on a forklift truck, identified by the numbers painted on them. M took out the camera and photographed every step, much to the amusement of everyone present. We had turned the mundane grind of milling olives into an entertainment.

After about a couple of hours, our oil was flowing into the stainless steel containers we had borrowed from Midew for the purpose of transporting the oil away.

One of the mill workers took a sample and after analysis, held up three fingers - our oil had 3 degrees (.3 percent) of acidity and anything under five fingers is excellent.

We left the mill with 280 litres of Extra Virgin Olive Oil. The first 35 litres went straight into a container that we would transport back to the UK and distribute among relatives and friends as Christmas gifts.

~~~

The next day we completed the harvest. In total that week, we had collected 1724 kilos of olives. The last day was the best; we collected 10 sacks of olives and had to carry the remainder in a cloth (*oo' coolaato'or* - a device laid across the split of the net to stop olives falling into the crevices and hollows of the trees). It was hard to believe the day's work, as we had only harvested four trees realising more than 500 kilos of olives.

We were very proud of ourselves, and Midew for whatever reason was very proud of himself. I was tired, but *M* was beyond consolation, her body aching from head to toe, her carefully manicured hands ripped and pricked by brambles, *frasca*, thistles and the spiny bushes of seeded wild asparagus.

"Never again," she declared. "Next year you'll have to do it yourselves!"

Well, we will be pushed to do the work without the quality control of the ladies I thought, so Damiano and I will have to get to work on this ground over the next year and clean it up.

~~~

Throughout the week, we had been arranging the rebuilding of Villa Oleandro. Each evening we met at the engineer's studio. He was to make applications to repair the roof as a priority - we found it strange that we had to ask for permission to repair something, but we had a lot to learn about planning in Italy. Then he was to draw up plans and apply for permission to renovate and extend the property, request electricity and arrange for permission to drill a well.

Michele the builder was present at these meetings, as was cousin Mimmo. They were to be left in no doubt that this was a project that we were serious about and when we returned from the Christmas break, we would like to see things started. Everyone agreed that the sooner we get on with the roof, the better!

They all assured us that while we were away we could relax; they would take care of everything. We exchanged email addresses and telephone numbers. If there were any problems or hitches, then they were to contact us.

The next day we left for the UK but our hearts and thoughts were with Villa Oleandro, our giants and future harvests of Extra Virgin Olive Oil.

Vico from the road to Canneto

Terraces opposite the Centro Storico

Centro Storico - cupola of the Mother Church on the left and the tower of the Della Bella castle on the right

Centro Storico - a labyrinth of narrow alleys, archways and staircases

140

A typical house in the Centro Storico of Vico

Impressive doorway of a house abandoned before 1981

A Cucina Monacesca built into the Centro Storico walls

Part of the cemetery ("pauper's" graves in the foreground)

Tittino with Rosina

Antonietta plaiting garlic

Franco the baker delivers
Pugliese loaves

Michele d'Aprile making a
basket for M

Midew

Mastro Michele

Rodi from "our beach" at San Menaio

View of Calenella Bay and Rodi from Monte Pucci

Trabucco

Saracen look-out tower

Villa Oleandro - first view and first photo

Walking with Giants - our olive trees in the valley below Villa
Oleandro

Villa Oleandro - view of the house from the front terrace

Villa Oleandro - rear view showing the partially caved in roof

Villa Oleandro - the defunct bread oven

Villa Oleandro - stable with manger and tie rings

Villa Oleandro - the remains of the front door

Villa Oleandro - the kitchen with broken wall to stable

Villa Oleandro - rubble staircase up to cross-vault half-landing

Villa Oleandro - dereliction in the bedroom
(mousetrap in the foreground on the right)

Noo' troccoluh
The Mousetrap found in the bedroom, now restored

Roadside boat builder at Peschici

Part II - Margheri' fah oo Pan'

Wood smoke

My eyes smarting, I squinted through the smoke towards the blinding sunshine up on the horizon. I thought I had noticed movement on the road bordering the wood. As I cast around through the many smouldering fires I caught sight of a flashing blue light. A Land Rover stopped.

I wiped my eyes with a handkerchief and mopped my brow. With clearer vision I spotted three menacing figures silhouetted against the deep blue sky. When they dropped below the bright horizon I could make out their khaki uniforms. Two were tall and bulky, the third short and thin. All wore sunshades. All had guns. They meant business!

I called to Andrea, the nearest worker and pointed in the direction of the three figures. He glanced at them, smiled wickedly and crossed his wrists, one over the other - the handcuff sign. The feared Corpo Forestale had arrived and they were about to arrest me.

Andrea called to the others, Damiano, Mario *Gatt'ohn* - Big Cat and Giovanni *il Vino*. They spotted the Forestale and, with that same smile, gestured to me - the handcuff sign. They carried on with their work - cleaning the woods.

Andrea and Mario were working the chainsaws; Damiano and Giovanni, their assistants, pulled away the cut brushwood as it fell and, with improvised hooks cut from the base of young trees earlier in the day, tensioned brambles for cutting. I was in charge of the fires.

How could I be in trouble? I had papers. I had permission. I waited anxiously.

The three men from the Forestale arrived; there was a brief lull as the chainsaws idled. The bulkiest of them was an officer - I scanned his uniform - three stars and a label bearing the name Di

Maria-Vittoria tacked onto his chest.

"Who's in charge here?" demanded Di Maria-Vittoria with an intense air of authority. Andrea pointed to me.

"Well, what's going on?" he demanded.

"We have permission to clean the wood," I replied, "I have the papers in the Jeep."

"Let me see them," he barked, impatiently.

I obediently turned and headed down the steep slope to the olive groves and retrieved the papers from the Jeep. "It's okay," I assured myself, "we've done everything correctly, in *regola*. We have permission."

I struggled back up the stony slope, drawing heavy breaths as I tried to deliver the papers to Di Maria-Vittoria as quickly as possible. I handed them to him and mopped my brow a second time with the soaked handkerchief.

Di Maria-Vittoria studied them carefully, the workers carried on chain sawing and burning as if nothing was up. Eventually, Di Maria-Vittoria handed back the papers. I felt a flush of relief.

"You're not allowed to do this," he suddenly declared.

"But, I have the papers, you've seen them" I pleaded. "Why can't we do it?"

"It's the wrong time of year," he announced.

"What? It can't be, we've only just received the papers," I argued.

He took the papers from me again, found the relevant section, and pointed to some dates. The permission states 1st April. Fine, that's today. But then he pointed out two other dates - the work could only be done between October and March! We had a year to do it, but we weren't allowed to start for another six months.

The other large officer stopped the workers. They were having a chat. It seemed they all knew each other and maybe he was explaining the situation. Andrea silenced his chainsaw and came over to speak to Di Maria-Vittoria.

As they conversed in Vicaiolo - a language that still paralyses my comprehension at the best of times - they seemed to contest each other's every word and I could only envisage them falling out, my mind drifted to the scene we had been creating since dawn. Behind us towards the house lay a trail of smoking fires, small trees felled and billeted. Around us, some five or six fires were still burning furiously. As we approached midday, the winds were beginning to whip up off the sea and now the Forestale were here.

155

No wonder they had come to see. The smoke would have been visible for miles all morning. If the workers were right, they would handcuff me soon.

Andrea and Di Maria-Vittoria seemed to be at loggerheads. I intervened.

"The man from the Agro Forestale, Nino, gave me the papers this week. He didn't say that we couldn't do the work. Look at the state of this wood. Even Nino said it was *pericoloso* - dangerous, a tinderbox. If we don't do something it could go up in smoke at any time this summer."

"We are only cleaning," Andrea backed me up. "Nino said that we can clean, we are not felling big trees."

Di Maria-Vittoria listened to the arguments with more patience than I had been led to expect from the notorious Forestale. I was still a free man.

"How much more work is there to do?" asked Di Maria-Vittoria.

"About 6 days," answered Andrea.

"All right then. You can continue, but you're only to clean. And be careful! Don't burn if the wind gets up." Di Maria-Vittoria directed his final remarks towards me, "if you burn any trees you'll be in trouble, you'll be fined."

With that the three Forestale bid fairly friendly goodbyes to the workers, turned and left.

My relief was palpable and I hoped that the team had not noticed just how worried I'd been. We returned to the job at hand - we had another hour to go today.

"Who was that?" I asked.

"That's the Maresciallo," replied Damiano. He's the big boss around here.

I gazed at the big man as he climbed into the passenger seat of the Land Rover and my thoughts turned to Villa Oleandro.

"The JCB!" I shuddered. "What if they see or hear the digger? They're bound to interfere there too."

I left the workers and ran towards the house. It's not as if we're doing anything wrong, I reminded myself. We have the permissions. But such was the grip, the legend of the Corpo Forestale, that I was sure they'd find fault there too.

The Corpo Forestale has jurisdiction over land and the movement of earth. You cannot excavate anything in the Gargano, even the foundations for new buildings, without their say so. We had

156

obtained the papers from the council to fix the road and clean around the house, but the engineer and project leader had failed to notify the Corpo Forestale. He was, apparently, concerned that they would say "No"!

We were moving large amounts of rock, and when rock is de-compacted its volume increases three-fold. We were dumping this huge quantity of material at the base of the 12-foot wall that retains the terrace on which Villa Oleandro stands. It was now a glaring white pyramid and they surely couldn't miss it.

As I arrived at the house, I tensed. The JCB was silent. I could feel the cold kiss of the handcuffs already. The silence was eerie. Then I realised - it was lunchtime. Another huge sigh of relief, this time at full volume as there was no one around to witness my anxiety.

The builders stopped habitually at midday and Michele *Dent' D'Or* (Teeth of Gold) the JCB driver had silenced his engine and joined them. The Forestale had passed by - it was their lunchtime too. I scanned the road below and after a short while I noticed the Land Rover across the valley moving slowly up the road towards Vico. I hoped they wouldn't look back and see our white mountain.

~~~

Applying for permission to clean the woods was one of the first things we did when we returned to Vico in late January after our 6-week break in the UK.

Although I had walked the boundaries of the property before the purchase, I had not really paid much attention to the state of the woods. With time, I had taken a walk and done a survey where I could penetrate the bramble-covered trees. What I found was a scene of utter neglect. Someone had chopped down trees for logs but had left branches and everywhere dry brushwood littered the floor.

In places, especially near the roadside where dry grass and cast-off cigarette ends were a recipe for disaster, many trees were scorched at the base of their boles indicating that ground fires had swept through under the trees,.

I consulted Damiano. He said I should visit the Agro Forestale and "*fah ah demand*" to clear the woods. Again, Italian bureaucracy bemused me. Here we have a few acres of woods in extremely dangerous condition and we have to ask permission to clean it up.

"And then what do we do?" I asked Damiano. "There's a lot of work and I'm no expert at felling trees."

157

"You should get someone to do the work. There are *boscaioli*, woodsmen, who specialise in this sort of work. They have tractors, big chainsaws - all the equipment needed to do the job," he explained.

"That sounds expensive to me," a stock phrase we used whenever discussing money with locals. With the purchase of our house in Vico and now the land and Villa Oleandro, the locals had pigeonholed us as rich. No one could understand that we had spent relatively little money, money that would buy little in the UK.

"You don't need to pay," said Damiano, "they will take the wood."

"But what if they take more wood than it's worth for the work?" I asked.

"You need them to go and see the wood, then they'll tell you what they can do. Make arrangements, negotiate and keep some of the wood for yourselves," he added helpfully.

"Fine. Who shall we ask? I once met a guy called Munno, Tommaso Munno, he's a lumberjack. He showed me a house in the Centro Storico. Shall I ask him?"

"No, no, he's no good. Hasn't got a tractor. No, you need to talk to Mario *oo' Brout*," came the response from Damiano. It was almost too quick. Did he have a vested interest?

~~~

Over the Christmas period, we had not heard anything from Aldo the engineer or cousin Mimmo. They were supposed to be doing the applications for rebuilding Villa Oleandro and making requests for electricity and water. We were confident that they were all in hand.

We were to be disappointed. When we returned in late January nothing had been done.

Aldo, the engineer, looked at us as if to say "Well when you said immediately, I didn't think you meant it. What's the rush?" He didn't apologise for his broken promises. He simply said they were busy with the *condono* - a cyclical ritual in Italy where the government declares an amnesty on *abusivo* building. The perpetrators of the illegal building employ engineers, surveyors, geologists and so on; they draw up the papers, the owner pays the fines to the government and whatever monstrosity they have built becomes legal. All concerned, especially, the government are on a good little earner.

Mimmo looked at us with that resigned air. He had warned us

many times that this was how things worked in Vico.

"Well could we get back on track Aldo? It has been a terrible winter; there's been a lot of rain and we're really worried about getting the roof sorted out," *M* urged him to commit.

He agreed to get on with it. He would make a special request on the basis that the roof was now unsafe, even dangerous. It was a start, but we left the meeting, frustrated and very disappointed. We now knew that it was a mistake to return to the UK. We should have stayed and pushed.

As a precaution we decided to visit Michele the Builder. He was at home with wife, Rosetta. We had the regulation coffee and Michele got out a bottle of grappa. The purpose of our visit was to assure Michele we were serious. That we had asked Aldo to get on with the permissions and we didn't want him to start other work as we would get the go-ahead soon. He could go and start clearing up around the house, we assured him. Surely we didn't need permission for that!

Michele was cool. "Have another grappa he insisted. *Non ti preoccupare* - don't you worry, everything will be fine".

~~~

M and I visited the Agro Forestale office and made the request for permission to clean the woods. The officer in charge turned out to be a civilian, Nino, and he explained what was involved.

First he would have to come and inspect the wood to see if it merited the work; then if it did, he would make a request to the Corpo Forestale in the provincial capital of Foggia and they would come to inspect. If all went well, then Nino would mark the trees that we could cut down and we could get on with it.

"How long will all this take?" I asked as I was impatient to get the work out of the way before the Spring.

"Not long," Nino assured us. We signed the papers, which for some curious reason required our *Codice Fiscale*, and we left. He would be in touch.

A few days later Nino and I went to the wood to do a cursory inspection.

"It certainly is dirty," he said, as we penetrated the perimeter of the wood. Brambles and brushwood enveloped us and the natural light faded. Nino occasionally took out a spray can and painted the bole of a tree with a red circle. If the tree was large, he took out a double-headed axe. With the sharp blade, he trimmed away some bark at the base of the tree, and then he stamped the exposed flesh with the other head.

"You can only cut down the trees I have marked," he said. "Those smaller ones don't need the stamp, you can cut them. But you must leave the stamp visible on the bigger ones."

This, he went on to explain, stopped people from deforesting whole zones.

We moved deeper and deeper into the wood. Both of us by now bearing cuts and scratches from snagging on prickly ivy and brambles.

The going became tougher as we negotiated the steep rocky banks that led to the tinderbox area. "Ssssss," he expelled air between his teeth. "This is *pericoloso* - we should do something about it right away". We didn't go any further. He would make the request to Foggia immediately.

Several weeks passed and we heard nothing. I called in on Nino often; the response was always the same, he shrugged his shoulders and said that we had to wait for Foggia.

Meantime, I decided that we should be ready to start work when the permission finally arrived. I arranged to meet Damiano at *Mezz' Cavoot*, where we could speak to Mario *oo' Brout*. Now, I was not looking forward to meeting this Mario 'The Ugly'. What family misfortune could have given this poor soul such a terrible nickname?

Mario turned out to be congenial and certainly not ugly. He was stocky, tanned even in winter, with thick curly black hair and intense blue eyes. He was huddled inside the *Vecchia Cantina* with a friend, Valentino - a Vichese with Greek heritage.

"Had we got permission?" he asked.

"It's on its way," I shrugged, "the inevitable delay at Foggia," I added.

"What name was the request made under?" asked Valentino. He wrote down *M*'s maiden name, which she uses for all official matters here. "I'm off to Foggia tomorrow," he said, "I'll make sure your request goes from the bottom of the pile to the top."

Ah, that's how it works. Not at all reassuring. I had images of other people doing the same for their friends and our papers never coming to light. No wonder it was taking so long.

We made an appointment with Mario to go and see the wood the following day.

The inspection didn't go to plan. Mario was a lumberjack. An expert. He worked in the Foresta Umbra where there were real trees. He took one experienced look at the wood and said there wasn't enough timber to make it worth his while.

However, he didn't dismiss the work out of hand; he would wait and see what Nino marked. We might have to pay after all.

~~~

At the end of January we saw our first snow at Vico. From our roof terrace at Vicolo Sancarlo we had a picture postcard view of the Centro Storico.

It was a crystal clear day and we could see distant Apennine peaks. Nearest to Vico there was the dormant volcano of the Maiella, half of one side blown away, then further to the north at Pescara the Gran Sasso; beyond the Sibillini range near Ancona over 200 kilometres away.

Had it snowed at Villa Oleandro? It had rained almost constantly while we were away in the UK and, with the snow, we were increasingly worried about the roof at Villa Oleandro and water penetration. We bumped into our neighbour Raffaele on our slushy way to market.

"No," he answered to our inquiry, "the snow line is 100 metres below Vico - it never snows down there."

Harvest Banquet

Due to the bad weather, the olive harvest was well behind and when we went down to Villa Oleandro we found Midew, Damiano and Filomena hard at work.

They had completed the trees in the valley and were slowly working their way through the sloping groves behind the house. They had many days to go, so we offered to help.

The format was similar to our own harvest back in December. I went down at dawn to meet Midew and Damiano; *M* and Filomena followed on later in the morning when there would be work waiting for them in the nets.

Although it had rained throughout the winter, there had been little wind, especially in the protected valley behind the house. The crop was still sticking stubbornly to the trees.

But by the end of the first week in February the harvest was complete and a timetable was set for the banquet.

~~~

Midew had arranged everything. The pruners would start work on our trees and afterwards we would have a feast.

The squad that day was Damiano, Andrea and Donatello - Matteo *da Pecora* was not available. Donatello was the youngest member of the team, but this was to be his last day.

He had had enough of the olive life and would be leaving for Modena shortly to start a job in a factory. Coincidentally, as we talked, I discovered that he was the son of the people who tried to sell us the historical house with film set potential. No, they hadn't sold yet!

The squad pruned the neglected olives that used to belong to the

Pirro family on the steep bank leading up from the valley to the terraces in front of Villa Oleandro. I burned the *frasca*.

Midew lit the oven. He started the fire with bundles of dry *frasca* that he had stored up earlier for the purpose - they burned like petroleum, fierce flames and black smoke pouring from the mouth of the oven.

As the fire took hold he built a pyramid with dry wood. To the pyramid he added long branches that trailed out of the oven door. Every now and then he checked the oven and poked the burning branches further through the entrance and when appropriate he added another branch.

Late in the morning, *M* turned up with Filomena, her brother Francesco and the banquet. By this time the oven was well heated and a fierce fire was whitening the terracotta interior dome.

At midday we stopped work. Midew drove the *treruote* ceremoniously onto the terrace at the front of the house. He dropped its pick-up sides, swept the load bed clean and covered it with a tablecloth. *M* and Filomena spread the banquet.

We men began with beer - workman's water - to wash away the smoke and quench the thirst. The ladies took soft drinks. We toasted our efforts.

Midew pushed the embers into a heap on one side of the oven and cleaned the base with a makeshift brush - a long stout stick with a head of leafy brush cuttings. The stick re-emerged with its head on fire. The oven was ready. Filomena delivered a large dish of *pasta al forno*, which he spooned into the oven using an old builder's long-handled shovel. The feast could begin.

Filomena and *M* laid out homemade preserves on the *treruote* table along with starters of sliced salami, Parma ham and *mortadella*. Midew held a half-round of a 5 kilo Pugliese loaf to his chest and, sawing towards his chest with a serrated knife, he deftly cut it into slices.

The women had forgotten the basket of cutlery - it was in the car down below the S-bend leading up to the house. I went off to fetch the basket but before I returned the boys, who were hungry and wanted to get on, had made forks from olive cuttings in the same manner that Tittino had many years earlier. Here old skills never die.

The banquet progressed. Bottle after bottle of Midew's homemade *benzina*, his affectionate name for his homemade red, were emptied as the squad had helping after helping of the delicious lasagne from the *forno*.

~~~

I chatted to Francesco. Although he was not one of the squad, he helped Midew out with the harvest. He worked for Apulia Water and asked me what we were going to do for water. I told him we wanted to apply to drill a well.

He suggested that there was water in the area - the main was 1500 metres down the road towards Calenella and a pumping station up on the summit behind the house. He would look into it and let us know whether we could get connected to the mains.

~~~

Under the azure blue skies, the banquet rolled on as we moved to the sweet and cheese courses. Everyone, including the girls, by now well oiled. In the background, Filomena was baking biscuits in the oven. Midew was observing that smoke was coming from under the terracotta tiles of the oven - the assembled sages declared that the oven was kaput.

As the party drew to a close they urged *M* and myself to go to the first floor balcony for a toast. We made our way up the rubble of the staircase, through the master bedroom into the study where plaster was falling off the walls revealing roots of the trees on the roof, and appeared on the balcony inebriated enough to forget about the rebuild that lay ahead and to take the salute of the banqueters.

The squad was now ours. The handover was complete. From now on, for what it was worth, we were in charge.

As we packed up in the twilight, I arranged with Damiano and Andrea for the squad to start work the following week. We wished Donatello luck in his venture up north and assured him he could return if things didn't work out.

~~~

The next day, Sunday, we went down to Villa Oleandro and found Michele at work clearing the terrace in front of the house. He introduced us to his son, Leonardo, who would be building with him.

Michele was wearing what looked to us like a baker's hat - a snug fitting white hat with a band around the base. We'd never seen Michele with a hat before. He had always been bare-headed, a flap of hair partially covering his whiter than white scalp - the curious white band round his forehead was a mystery no more.

Leonardo was slightly taller than Michele, dark skinned with thick black curly hair and a strip of beard under his lower lip. He was then 25 and had been building with his father since he left school at 15 years of age.

One fire, placed where the *treruote* had served as the banqueting-table the day before, was smouldering to a finish. There were neat piles of bric-a-brac dotted around the freshly strimmed terrace leading up to the front door. Piles of broken terracotta tiles, cut stones, saggy spring bedsteads, a sink, bits of old iron, twisted gutters and rusty drainpipes, wire, barrel hoops, saucepans, bottles and cast-off tools.

Michele was heading into the dense undergrowth beyond the door with a rigid blade strimmer. As he went, Leonardo pulled the felled brush away and laid it on a newly started fire. The smoke plume drifted towards the sea.

He rejected our offer of help. We were, perhaps, too genteel, his 'clients', we couldn't possibly sully ourselves with such work. He pointed to his strimmer and said he wanted us well away.

With access to the house now eased, we decided to go in and sort the chaos in the room we had christened the Hall.

By mid-afternoon, Michele and Leonardo had cleared around the north side of the house to get access to the stable and the grotto behind. The fires were out. The work had laid bare three sides of Villa Oleandro.

M & I had removed defunct furniture, made stacks of useful wood, burnt the remainder, and generally tidied up. We saved whatever we thought might be useful: doors and windows that were beyond repair but we would strip them of their antique furniture.

Outside on the terrace we gathered to admire our work.

Villa Oleandro uncovered looked impressive but there on the front to the side of the main entrance, we gazed at a stark bright yellow "VG38" sign - Midew had paid the *Vigili Gargano* to guard property number 38. Was it an omen?

~~~

On the trip back from the UK, we called in at Bologna. Apart from visiting relatives, we wanted to find a work vehicle. Many people advised us to do this - much better to look up north where second hand cars were plentiful. In Vico, and the south generally, people buy cars and drive them into the ground.

We envisaged a 4-wheel drive, a pick-up for helping with the building work, hauling wood and as a donkey for our olive work. There was only one choice - the Mitsubishi L200 with a 4-seater cab.

We had no luck in Bologna, despite help from our relatives. So we decided to call in on the coastal towns south of Ancona and try the local dealers. We had little luck, until we found a dealer at Porto San Giorgio. He had nothing second hand, but a couple were due to arrive. He would call us.

We got the call a couple of days later and immediately made the 3-hour journey to view two examples. We liked the first one we saw - 6 years old, but tidy. The other was newer, had twice the mileage and smelt of stale cigarettes. We bought the first and arranged to pick it up in early February.

When we returned to Vico with the vehicle, you'd have thought that we'd bought a Ferrari. It seemed everyone wanted to know where we got the Jeep (the Italian name for pick-ups in these parts). How much did we pay? Did we buy it new? As usual, their curiosity and directness surprised us.

~~~

Another visit to Aldo, the engineer revealed that he had finally requested permission to repair the derelict roof and that he should get a reply within fourteen days. But he had done nothing more about general planning or the application for electricity.

We took things into our own hands and rang the electric company ENEL. It turned out that the engineer couldn't make the application anyway - we had to do it personally.

Within days ENEL called us to the office where we had to complete the contract and provide them with documents - they wanted everything, identification, *Codice Fiscale* and even a copy of the deed of sale for the purchase of the property.

Things seemed to be moving fast. Out came the maps and they surveyed the possibilities. In quick time they agreed that they would connect us from a property down in the valley. Five or six poles should do it, but we needed permission from two people. One of the technicians said he knew one of them; he was called Vittorio, a very fair person who was sure to agree. The technician would get the necessary permission from him; the other, someone called Peppino, they told us had a Pizza restaurant. We had to visit him and get his agreement ourselves.

We visited Peppino and he was as helpful as could be. "Yes," we could put poles over a certain part of his ground, but not other parts as these had irrigation systems buried underground. The route he suggested was ideal; it wouldn't affect his underground systems and the parcel of land bordered Vittorio's.

However, Vittorio (or as we found out later his wife) would not agree. The technician told him that they would run the electric across his land anyway, which probably didn't help. It seems that in Italy, ENEL have the right to take electric where they want but, having made a request, if a landowner who is affected says 'no' they must wait for a period of 2 years, then they can go ahead whatever the owners objection.

Perhaps the process is more complicated, involving court judgements and so on. We were too horrified to think of this option. There would be no electric for the builders and we would have to live with a generator for years!

We pressed the technician for another route. After much resistance, he gave in and suggested two other possibilities; two pieces of ground adjacent to Vittorio's. A second Peppino owned one! A third Peppino owned the other!

Great, we were playing a name game. He couldn't tell us who Peppino 'Two' was, but Peppino 'Three' was Peppino *Dent' D'Or* - the uncle of our JCB driver.

Back in Vico I collared Midew in the Gran Caffe, playing cards as usual, and explained the situation. He knew all the Peppinos, of course, and assured us he would sort it out.

The next day, as we passed the parcels of ground owned by the two Peppinos, we noticed a car. We stopped and found a pruner, high up in one of his trees. It was Peppino 'Two'. We introduced ourselves and he came down the tree in a flash.

How could he help? We explained the situation and he was only too happy to have electric go underground, but as he explained, his trees were giants too, even taller than ours. If he had electric cables running through them then there would always be a danger that he, or the wind, would lop a branch and bring the line down. Perhaps with disastrous consequences!

He was right. With his help, we looked at Peppino *Dent D'Or's* parcel. Much lower trees and certainly a possible route. He also showed us the original route over Vittorio's ground - it was the best with large open spaces and gaps between the lower trees. We both considered the same prospect - perhaps we need to grease the owner's palms?

~~~

Saint Valentine is patron saint of Vico, the protector of the orange harvest, which starts around February.

Vico dresses up for the occasion. The locals adorn lamp posts, doorways, gateways and balconies with branches of bay (for orange branches are busy at this time of year) dressed with oranges.

There is a procession; all the brethren from Vico's twelve churches assemble to escort the statue of Saint Valentine, from his shrine in the Chiesa Madre, through the streets.

The Carabinieri accompany the statue dressed in ceremonial uniform: white-gloved hands, dress swords, cross-belts, lanyards and fringed epaulettes - the whole topped by hats resembling Nelson's, but sporting tall red plumes.

Behind follow the other forces, the town *Vigili, Corpo Forestale, Guardia di Finanza*, assorted dignitaries and a military band - the whole effect being slightly spoilt by the youths carrying Saint Valentine, dressed in denim jeans or working clothes.

The first *festa* of the year is, thankfully, short in the cold of February at 500 metres.

After the procession they fire off a *batteria* in the street at Fuori Porta (the Outside Gate) - the entrance to the Casale and Civita zones of the Centro Storico.

We met Michele 'The Builder' at the *batteria* and popped into a bar for a warming brandy. He assured us he was on course to start when the permission arrived.

A week after Saint Valentine's Day, the permission arrived. We notified Michele and to our surprise, he turned up to start work on the last day of the month.

~~~

With the olive harvest barely finished, we began the process of pruning the trees. Damiano, Andrea and Matteo *da Pecora* turned up on the appointed day.

Just after dawn we assembled in the upper groves. In Vico it was a bitterly cold start; down in the groves there was a chill, but with the rising sun it felt much warmer.

The team were sharpening their axes and secateurs and deciding where to begin. Andrea, explained that the trees were in need of drastic treatment - Midew had eaten for years, taken the fat, now the trees would need to be re-invigorated.

Da Pecora inspected my chainsaw. "Too big, too clumsy," he said. He produced a miniature chainsaw from the back of his Jeep. "You need to buy one of these." He walked off to begin work, his chainsaw nonchalantly dangling from a loop of rope over his shoulder.

I always feel helpless under these circumstances. I had taken advice from Michele *oo Noyrr'* and we went together to buy the chainsaw from Michele *oo' Brout* (the father of the lumberjack Mario). Michele first showed me the miniature chainsaw used by pruners, but I had wanted a tool that would cut all sorts of wood - a general purpose chainsaw. We eventually agreed that the miniature was not right. For some reason it had not dawned on me that they climbed up the giants with these machines.

Now it seemed that I had made my first mistake with the workers.

With the chattering over at 7 a.m. we started work. The three of them selected one of the main arteries of the first tree. *Da Pecora* fired up his chainsaw; Andrea and Damiano shared mine.

Thud, thud, crash. Large branches tumbled to the ground around the tree. It was too dangerous to get near, so I watched and waited for them to finish the tree before I started the clear up.

As they warmed to their work, they chattered away. They could have been chimpanzees babbling for all I understood. I could detect small differences in their accents. Damiano was the clearest, Andrea was very difficult to understand but *Da Pecora* spoke raw Vicaiolo. He was impossible to understand.

"John, John," they would call out to me. "You must learn Vicaiolo."

"No, no. My name is Ian," I insisted. "John is English, Giovanni in Italian. Ian is the Scottish equivalent of John, maybe the Italian would be Gianni.

"Ooh, Gianni, Gianni, what are the girls like in Scotland? Next time you go, we'll come with you."

The chatter continued as they laid bare the first tree. *Da Pecora* seemed amused by the Scottish element; I could hear him muttering "*oo' Scozzese*" from time to time.

They eventually reached ground level and waded around in the *frasca* at the base of the tree, tenderly pruning off the trailing branches that had borne last year's olives.

I set to work cleaning up the *frasca*. By now I was stripped down to a T-shirt as the early morning sun rose above the hill. When we had picked the olives shortly after buying the ground I had done the same work, but this was much heavier. Large branches tangled up with small ones and it was evident that untangling them was going to take a lot more effort.

I strode in with my axe, reducing branches to manageable units before dragging them out to cut up at the point where I would build the fire.

The team moved on. By the time I had started the first fire they were four trees ahead of me and with the relentless onslaught of the two chainsaws the *frasca* was mounting up.

Andrea came down to see how I was doing. Not very well it seemed. He waded into the *frasca* with my chainsaw like a man possessed; lopping off branches and reducing the whole to a morass of manageable sticks in minutes, while simultaneously hurling out billets of olive wood for the home fire as he went.

"How do you say *motosega* in English?" he asked.

"Chainsaw," I replied. "Chain … Saw," I emphasised.

"Chen … soh," he repeated over and over. He moved to the next tree and set about the *frasca* there. "Chen … soh, Chen-soh."

When he finished he took a breather. "Io sono grande *boscaiolo*," he declared. "What's *boscaiolo* in English?" he wanted to know more.

"Lumberjack," I replied. "Me *grande* lumberjack," he announced surprisingly well.

"Gianni, Gianni," he repeated. "*Ti piace come abbiamo fatto gli ulivi* - do you like how we have done the olives?"

I looked around me at the skeleton trees, not knowing what to say. "Yes, yes they look fine," I eventually said with little conviction. At least I could see lots of firewood for future winters.

"Gianni, what did you do in Scotland?" his thirst for information was insatiable.

"I was a computer programmer," I answered.

With that piece of information and having shown me how to handle the *frasca* he headed back to join the others taking the chainsaw with him. I set about the work again with my axe, wishing he had left the chainsaw but then realising that I would probably slice

170

off my leg if I copied him.

Some time passed and then *Da Pecora* summoned me. He called out "*Joo'wah, Joo'wah, ven ah doh*". I didn't realise he was speaking to me. He called out again and beckoned me from the top of a tree as I looked over to see what was going on. "*Joo'wah, Joo'wah, ven ah doh - Giovanni, Giovanni, vieni qui*". He wanted me to join them.

I pulled my tired body up the slope and looked at the work ahead in dismay. When I arrived, *Da Pecora* asked some equally unintelligible question. Damiano translated - he had learnt that I was a computer programmer and he wanted me to pirate a SKY card.

"I don't know how to do that," I answered truthfully, for I really hadn't got a clue. "Anyway, it's illegal," I added.

Da Pecora found it difficult to believe and insisted that I had to produce the card, or he would not work for me, or something like that. I tried to change the subject, talked about anything - chensoh, lumberjack and so on.

I left them to it. Chattering away in the trees, occasionally shouting out with their booming voices to other teams of pruners across the valley or calling out to me to bring them oil and fuel for their chainsaws. I was beginning to wonder who the boss was.

As I lit fire after fire I contemplated what I had taken on. Heavy work, not so much the making of the fires but scrambling about on these stony slopes; dealing with these pruners - were they working well for their money or just chatting their way through the day doing a bit here, a bit there? The language, Vicaiolo! Were they sending me up?

By lunchtime I was all in. I had cleaned up five trees and was staring at another 15 or so up the bank ahead of me. The team bounced down the slope, swooped on the *frasca* of the trees surrounding my last fire and in minutes it was cleared up and burnt.

As *Da Pecora* put his chainsaw away, not a bead of sweat on him, he beckoned me towards him "*Joo'wah, Joo'wah oo' Scozzese*".

And that's how it happens. "*Oo Scozz'ese*" was to be my *sopranome*.

I joined him at the Jeep where he observed my sweaty state and gave me some advice. I couldn't make out what he was saying, but I understood what he meant - that I didn't know how to work efficiently. By the time he finishes with me I would be a worker.

Emergency Work

With the renovation work about to start I took Damiano and the new chainsaw to Villa Oleandro one Sunday and we set about clearing behind the South and East walls of the house. Michele had cleaned the others, what remained was a challenge.

We began behind the bread oven; the zone was heavily fortified by rock fall, brambles, brush, fig and an assortment of other wild trees. One, a large tree called locally '*leggra'marr'*', looked like it would easily crush the bread oven if it fell wrongly.

To watch Damiano work with a chainsaw in difficult conditions was a revelation; at the same time I was comforted by the knowledge that we were officially employing him so that if anything should go wrong we were covered. He was quick and progressed relentlessly through the obstacles, chainsaw in one hand while the other despatched cut material behind him for me to gather and move to the fire. It seemed highly probable that he could have a very nasty accident if he made a mistake.

All went well. By the end of the day we had cleared the remaining sides of the house, burnt all the *frasca* and billeted the wood. The *leggra'marr'* had come down sweetly just where we had planned and the bole had been cut up into manageable pieces.

We had revealed a high rock face running parallel to the rear of the house; to the south the rock joined the house at a height of about one metre and then ran down to ground level at the north. There we found a sort of filter arrangement - a bed of gravel. Rainwater fell from the roof to the rock and the natural slope coursed the water to the filter from where, some kind of channel underground directed the water to the store on Francesco Palmieri's parcel of ground.

Some stone walling still retained soil on top of the rock face, the rest had collapsed many years earlier onto the rock watercourse. The

172

root of a massive carob tree lay pole-axed and precarious on top of the rock face.

There was still a lot of work to do, but having cleared the way we could at least see what lay ahead.

~~~

On the penultimate day of February the builders began work. A week earlier we had received the permission to carry out emergency work on the roof. Michele, true to his word turned up to make a start.

It was not a moment too soon. Snow was blanketing most of Italy; in the Gargano we were lucky, only catching the back end of weather systems. The roof was sodden and the damp was tangible on the upper floor.

Michele brought his son Leonardo, Pierino (his uncle) and Pierino's son Nicola - it was to be a family affair. They set about laying a concrete base in front of the house to support the scaffolding. By the end of the third day the scaffolding at the front of the house was in place. Until a JCB digger could come to clear the rock and debris behind the house, this limited scaffolding would have to do. The builders installed an old metal door in the entrance to the grotto behind the house, which would serve as a lock-up to store their tools.

Cold north-westerlies off the Adriatic and cobalt skies dominated the first few days. For lunch, the builders erected a makeshift table out of trestles and scaffolding planks in a sunny spot sheltered from the wind by the house. They sat on the cylindrical blocks of the *leggra'marr'* we had cut earlier.

Lunch was at noon. *Pan e' Pomodor* with assorted bottles of home-made preserves, cut meats or salami and whatever raw vegetables that were on offer - usually broad beans or chicory hearts - washed down with a plastic cup of Pierino's home-made wine. After they'd eaten they would clear everything up and get back to work as soon as Michele allowed. He insisted that they must digest lunch properly before exerting themselves. One o'clock was the designated time. Pierino was keen to warm up and everyday he pushed to start earlier, but to no avail.

They only endured a few days outside - their bodies cooled too quickly - within a few days we arrived with our own lunch and found them in the kitchen. They'd lit the fire, swept up, shuttered the gaping hole in the wall to the stable, set up a table and were much happier.

We took lunch up the track behind the house - a spot under an olive tree where we could sit on an outcrop of rock that absorbed the midday sun; it was comfortable, sunny and surprisingly sheltered from the relentless winds.

~~~

With the scaffolding in place the work on the roof began in earnest. The crew carefully rescued the unbroken terracotta tiles, lowered them to the ground and stored them among some bushes.

"Better that they are not seen," explained Michele, "otherwise they will be whisked away!"

He made a sign with his hands, rotating the wrist and fingers clockwise as if he were bowling an off-break in cricket. The sign that there are *ladri* - thieves about.

This was not a welcome comment - we'd been warned by *M*'s father, Michele *oo Noyrr'* and just about everyone else who knew about our purchase that we would have problems living out in *campagna* - was this a sign of things to come?

The clear up continued – the builders cut huge wooden beams now penetrated with rot and woodworm from the walls. Rubble was shovelled into wheelbarrows, adaptable ones whose handles could be switched into a vertical position to attach to a pulley, lowered to the ground and, with handles repositioned, the contents were swiftly despatched over the terrace wall. Things were beginning to move.

One day after lunch on the rock outcrop I went to inspect the works. As I threaded my way up the broken staircase there was a loud crash from the floor above. I raced up the remaining stairs and peered into the bedroom just as a wheelbarrow smashed onto a fresh pile of rubble on the floor. Through the dust I could see Leonardo dangling through a hole above - Michele had hold of his arm and just saved him from falling 4 metres on to the barrow and rubble.

One side of the vault had collapsed. Disaster! Well it could have been worse. Leonardo could have been seriously injured. He was smiling. Michele pulled him to safety and then peered through the gap. I looked at Michele with that 'now what on earth are we going to do?' look.

"*Non ti preoccupare* - don't worry, Signor Giovanni."

I called *M*, who was still sitting up on the rock taking in the sun and engrossed in a book. She was as anxious as I was on seeing the damage but more worried about Leonardo. We really had no idea what was going to happen next but Michele assured us not to be concerned.

That afternoon we popped off to Vico to do some errands. We wanted to collect some of our olive oil from the store in Midew's garage and try it out. When we returned late in the afternoon, to our great relief Michele and Leonardo had patched up the vault. It looked rough, but Michele assured us that once it had dried it would be as strong as it ever was.

So why did it collapse? "Water," he said. That area of the roof was particularly exposed and covered with soil and weeds over the years. It was a very weak point. Michele assured us that he had checked the other vaults and there was no danger of further collapses.

That evening we poured clear green olive oil onto a plate added a little salt and black pepper and wiped the plate clean with Pugliese bread. Our oil was delicious, if still a little hot on the throat - it would soften with age. As we helped ourselves to seconds we reflected that Michele really was the '*mastro*' we had been told about. Villa Oleandro was in safe hands.

~~~

Bureaucracy is a way of life in Italy and we had prepared ourselves for the worst. We desperately wanted to clear the rock around the house to enable further scaffolding to go up. We also wanted to widen the driveway for delivery vehicles, particularly so that cement lorries could reach the house.

As is the custom, we had to obtain permission first. Our engineer had been to the Council with photographs and plans for this and eventually he managed to get the necessary papers. Then he should have taken the papers to the Corpo Forestale, who would, hopefully, give the go-ahead. For some reason, our engineer was reluctant to do this and eventually the day came when the JCB could come and we just decided to go ahead.

But Michele didn't need it anymore. He wouldn't wait for the road or the clearing of rock around the house to mount a full scaffold. Work had gone ahead at a pace. He had cleared the roof, strengthened the vaults and wasn't going to leave his work exposed to the weather so he constructed a floating perimeter safety fence using wood braced to either side of the wall and bound using thick wire. With this safety net in place he was ready to go ahead using only scaffolding at the front of the house.

As the time approached to complete the roof we had a visit from a surveyor who represented the cement company. We looked at every possible way to get cement lorries up the drive and eventually decided that they could reverse up to the S-bend. But that was it. Still 50 metres from the house and even using pumps they could only manage to get within thirty. We would have to make concrete for the roof and floors by hand.

Despite this setback Michele was optimistic. According to him the concrete they delivered was no good anyway, only he knew how to make it.

We wanted to reconstruct the roof with wooden beams, but the engineer and Michele wouldn't have it. There are rules, regulations concerning earthquakes and we would have to abide by them.

So, the tops of the walls were reconstructed and then belted with reinforced concrete cordon to hold the walls together in the event of a seismic shift. Before we knew it the roof was constructed and they were ready to cover it.

This turned out to be a mammoth operation. Michele and Pierino were laying the concrete. Nicola operated the pulley and that left Leonardo alone in charge of the cement mixer. This was my cue – for the first time Michele had reluctantly decided that I would be useful and he handed me a shovel. By now we had become firm friends and Michele was no longer treating me as a client. I was now Gianni although *M* was still La Signora. For two days, I laboured as I have never done before. The pace at which they worked was breathtaking; I wolfed my *pan e' pomodor* huddled with them in front of the kitchen fire and in the evenings I collapsed into bed.

The work had begun one month earlier, and the roof was now complete, waterproofed and we could breathe a sigh of relief. All around us Italy had experienced one of the wettest, snowiest months of March anyone could remember and we had managed to work through it and save the house.

Things didn't go completely smoothly though. We arrived one day to find Pierino's son sporting a bandage on his forehead. He had been to Vico for several stitches. What had happened? Apparently, he'd failed to secure the pulley motor in its sliding rack and on the very first lift that day the pulley flew out of its tracks and hit him on the head. We didn't dare ask how close he came to falling off the roof. He worked for a while and then Leonardo took him home - we didn't see him again that week.

We were elated with the work, though, and when the roof was dry we all clambered up, sat on the apex and toasted its completion with large bottles of Peroni beer. *M* was nervous of the climb going up, but took it in her stride coming down.

~~~

Meanwhile the JCB driver, Michele *Dent D'Or*, had demolished the bread oven, powered his way to the back of the house and was hammering away at the rock face and the watercourse.

He regularly consulted the *mastro* (we had come to realise that our builder was referred to as "mastro" by everybody who visited the site) as he went about his job. They agreed how close he could get to the house, bearing in mind that the lower walls were carved out of the surrounding rock; he had to be careful not to crack them.

Every so often the JCB emerged from the work face, turned around, went in bucket first to retrieve the rubble, and despatched it over the 4-metre terrace walls.

Within a couple of days two mountains of white rock announced to the world that we were moving earth and that was the territory of the Corpo Forestale.

We had avoided their scrutiny a week or so earlier when Di Maria-Vittoria passed to check on the wood clearance, but something had come to their attention - maybe two mountains of rock that could be seen for miles? Leonardo came to find me in the woods with the news that we'd had a visit from the Forestale. They wanted all documents delivered to their office. Immediately!

That afternoon we dutifully delivered copies of our deeds, planning permissions and the all-important documentation giving us authorisation to clean the area around the house and fix the road.

Our engineer's decision not to inform the Forestale had backfired and now all we could hope for was mercy.

~~~

The noise of the builder's generator was getting on everybody's nerves and *mastro* Michele urged us to chase up the electricity.

He was also worried about the water supply. It was the same water that they had used to mix concrete for the roof, drawn from the storage tank on Francesco Palmieri's ground. Now with warmer weather it was beginning to smell and rightly needed sorting out. We needed to get the well drilled as soon as possible.

With a lengthening list of things to manage we headed back to Vico.

First we rang a drilling company in distant Manfredonia. We had decided to by-pass the engineer's office, as we did with the request for electricity, and discover from the experts what we had to do. The drilling company said it was straightforward. We had to see a geologist - he gave us the details of one in Vico - who would fill out the necessary forms for us. It was as simple as that. He ended his advice by recommending that we do it quickly as he had a number of other wells to drill in the area soon and he could give his best price if they he did them all at the same time.

That evening we called in on the geologist. He filled out the forms and said he would be in touch about a site survey.

"How long would it take to get the necessary papers?" *M* asked.

"Two months," he replied, then sensing our urgency he added, "maybe I can get them through in one, I know someone at the office."

In the meantime I made a mental note - must find a way of getting fresh water on-site.

Walking away from the geologist's office we met *Dent D'Or* and he took us to visit his uncle, the third Peppino, to ask his permission to pass the electric over his ground. Peppino was very accommodating. We had expected to have to negotiate, maybe to pay something, but no. He agreed immediately and then with a kind of an afterthought he suggested that while his nephew was down with us he could use the JCB to dig up an old olive tree. Naturally, we would pay the expenses. We agreed.

Peppino, like the other two we had met, showed the same typical hospitality we had received wherever we went in Vico. Apart from one or two exceptions the population seemed to fall over themselves to help.

The next day we had a call, coincidentally, from ENEL who wanted to survey the site. We telephoned Peppino *Dent D'Or* and he agreed to come down. Together we met the surveyors, planned the route and popped the question.

"How long?"

"Ten days," came the unexpected reply.

~~~

Another little job we had to sort out was residency. We began with *M*'s as it ought to be straightforward. She has dual-nationality, so all we had to do was go to the Council. Her father Vincenzo, who has an aversion to bureaucracy, many things Italian and anything Vichese, had, rather surprisingly, had the foresight to register all his daughters' births in his home town.

Armed with all the necessary documents and photographs we went to the Council's *Ufficio dell' Anagrafe* - register of births, deaths and marriages. They checked *M*'s birth registration records, filled out the forms, charged her 26 cents stamp duty and told her she would receive her ID card within ten days. Like our earlier visit to San Severo to obtain our *Codice Fiscale*, we were witnessing that rare thing in Italy - turbo-charged bureaucracy!

"When it arrives you must change your driving licence to an Italian one immediately," was the official's final instruction.

This last remark slowed us a little. Did we really need to change our licences?

M's ID arrived without delay. In the meantime, we had discovered that we needed to go to the local driving school to discuss her licence.

At the driving school, they confirmed that *M* must change her licence. It was not automatic and certainly not cheap. *M* would have to have a medical, we had to pay 200 Euros and she would have to renew the licence every five years. They took her existing licence, gave her a slip of paper that enabled her to drive temporarily and made an appointment for her to see the doctor on his next visit from Foggia.

So much for Europe, I thought - surely her UK licence was valid here? So I decided to do some long overdue research on the Internet, wading through page after page of euro-blurb and 'legalese' until I eventually found and deciphered a page that seemed to indicate I was right.

Back at the driving school we presented the evidence and asked for her licence back. The licence couldn't be returned. It had gone to Foggia or somewhere, and we would never see it again. And anyway we were wrong.

"No, no," they insisted. "She is now a national and a resident and the information that I had found didn't apply to her."

So what will happen to me? Will I have to change my licence when I become resident? "Yes," they insisted.

The day came for *M*'s medical. We attended the driving school at the appointed hour and, like any doctor's waiting room, we waited patiently while the visiting doctor processed the queue. *M*'s turn came.

Ten minutes later she reappeared from the classroom that was being used for the medicals. All was well, she had passed. The Italian licence would be on its way. We left.

"So what happened in there?" I asked as we walked away.

"Oh, not much," replied *M*. "The doctor gave me a quick examination and tested my eyesight - I was fine."

"That was it?"

"Yes, except he also gave me a colour-blind test," she added.

I froze. "What?" I couldn't believe what I was hearing. *M* had been given a colour-blind test and she had thought nothing of it.

I am colour-blind - not just red-green colour-blind. I cannot properly distinguish between any colours. I can, of course, see Red especially if it's in the mass of a London bus. I can also see the Red, Amber and Green sequence of traffic lights and have negotiated them safely for 35 years. Even if I couldn't really tell the difference, it's easy to learn the sequence and I had no problem adapting to the US horizontal format, where red appears to the left.

Colour for me is a matter of association learnt as a child. Buses are usually red; grass is green; sky is blue and so on. If there's been a dry summer and the grass is brown, I am unlikely to detect it though and it's easy for me to make mistakes.

As a boy I lived in a little town in England that had two bus services: the Midland Red and the Bristol Blue. One day someone asked me which bus went to Gloucester - I replied, "the blue one."

The person stared at me blankly, cursed and walked off. It turned out that the Bristol Blue buses were actually green. I had never associated them with grass!

There's no colour-blind test for driving in the UK, so why one here? And what happens if I fail it? *M* had no answers so we immediately returned to the office hoping that the doctor was still there. We needed to resolve this before I made a potentially catastrophic application for residency.

The doctor was there, testing the last patient. I asked the driving school people the consequences of failing the test. No licence, they assured me.

Alarmed by this, I explained that I needed to know whether I would be allowed a licence before making an application for residency. Could I take the test now and see what the outcome would be? There is a simple colour-blind test that I always pass for some reason, perhaps that's all that I would have to take.

The doctor agreed to see me. He presented me with the first slide of coloured dots in a circle. I picked out the '?' in red with ease - it was the slide I always got right, but then he continued. I failed the rest.

"You're definitely colour-blind," he declared.

Great, what now? He rummaged through his briefcase and produced five reels of coloured cotton.

"Which one is Red?" he asked. I imagined a bus and obliged.

He continued and, on demand, I correctly identified Yellow, Green and Blue. How could I see them? It's a mystery to many people and difficult for them to understand that in isolation the colours are clear and can easily be associated with buses, submarines, grass or the sky. But if the colours are blended together in some way as they are in the test slides, their uniqueness disappears in my eyes.

I was doing well. He changed tack. This time there would be no lead. He picked up the remaining roll and asked me what colour it was. I wasn't sure. It looked like an orange, but it could have been yellow, green or even grey. Was this the real test?

"Is it Orange?" I asked.

"Yes," he said, "you can have a licence."

I was relieved, but still a little concerned.

"Yes, but would I pass the same test with another doctor?" I asked pessimistically.

He assured me that I should be optimistic!

~~~

The water situation at the house was getting serious. The builders were being repelled by each bucket of foul smelling liquid that they pulled up from the water store. I had to act.

Asking around, Damiano suggested that I buy a pump, put a tank on the Jeep and collect water from *Aq'wuh d' Koivuh'chuh*, a spring not far from the house.

He had a cousin who sold pumps and he put me in touch with him. Giovanni quickly sold me a powerful pump, a 5000-litre water tank and gave me a second hand 1000 litre tank to go on the Jeep.

With the water collection system in place, we set off to find

Aq'wuh d' Koivuh'chuh following Damiano's instructions. We missed the turn off twice as he had said it was a good road. We eventually took the plunge, quite literally, down a steep single track road praying that we would be able to turn around. The concrete road became a stone track within a few metres. We followed its twists and turns, its dips and rises through olive groves for a few hundred metres until we came to a clearing and the spring - a long stone trough once used by local women to do the washing. It was obvious that nobody had done any washing there for years.

We primed the pump, set the tubes in position. *M* held one end in the water, the other I placed in the tank. I started the pump and, after a few teething troubles getting it to draw, water was pouring into the tank at over three litres/second. We relaxed and looked around - a mistake. The tubes weren't anchored properly in the tank. Before we knew it, water was spraying all over the place and I couldn't stop the pump. I managed to grab the flaying tube, got soaked to the skin in the process and inserted it back in the tank. After five minutes, the tank was full and M managed to stop the pump as water poured out of the tank all over the Jeep.

Our first trip to the spring had not been very professional. We were just packing away the pump and tubes, when a *treruote* pulled up. Two elderly men got out and seemed not take very little notice of my bedraggled state.

"You're the people who bought the house from Midew," one of them said.

"Yes," *M* confirmed.

"It used to belong to my aunt. It was a lovely house once," he said. "And now you're restoring it? Are you going to live there in the summer?"

"No, no - all year long," came our stock reply.

He looked at us oddly and then decided to wish us the very best of luck.

We shook hands and left.

We made four more journeys that day to fill the tank.

In the coming months the builders consumed water as if they were watering a desert to ward off a drought. With regular visits we had the system tuned and normally came away as dry as we arrived.

The road was always tricky, especially with 1000 litres on board, but *Aq'wuh d' Koivuh'chuh* was a very remote place where few people passed. The completion of each journey was a relief and kept us focussed on the need for a well.

~~~

Meanwhile *M* started to find suppliers and get quotes for materials. We needed doors, windows, ironwork and gutters. In the Gargano, if not everywhere in Italy, it's not like going to the local DIY store and picking a dozen doors.

No, they all have to be hand-made by local carpenters and we are presented with a whole range of woods to choose from - oak, chestnut, nut, deal, pine and even olive. They each have to come and measure, talk about design, door surrounds, shutters and accessories.

"Well, these are the door sizes approximately. Can you just give us an estimate for, say, oak on the external doors and chestnut for the internal ones? Simple design, nothing too fancy. We'd like the front door to be traditional, that's all," *M* always pleaded in order to shortlist the suppliers.

They all answer in the negative. No, they need to come on-site and size up the job.

Eventually we give in and choose two, maybe three people who we like the most to come and go through the same routine at the house. They all know the builders and stop them from getting on with their work and at the end of it all they all give us the same rounded up figures.

Before the Euro, they would make a traditional front door for say 3 million lira (that would be 1500 Euros). Not 2,750,000 or 2.9 million it would always be in round millions. Now they will make the door for 3000 Euros, not 1500 or so as it ought to be, or even an outrageous 2,900. Interesting how the introduction of the Euro has given the economy a boost.

It's not just the tradesmen. The whole process begins in the vegetable market. Before the Euro, a bunch of parsley would cost 500 lira (or 25 cents) - just about the smallest denomination that anyone was prepared to deal with in either currency. Since the Euro, the bunch of parsley has cost 50 cents!

We had to go through a similar sort of non-bargaining process with electricians, plumbers, ironmongers and gutter manufacturers (yes, even they make gutters to measure).

M had spent hours drawing plans on the computer specifying electric and telephone points, radiator locations, bathroom layouts and so on. They all admired her work but none would give us a firm quote. In their cases, we had to choose the supplier based on estimates. After all, they reasoned, we were bound to change our minds about lots of things as the job progressed.

~~~

Meanwhile life in Vico carried on as before. Since our return in January, all manner of people had accosted us in the street, shops or café's. They had heard that we had bought olives; discussed the project, warned us of the dangers and many would tell us that they were our neighbours, explained where they had ground and so on.

Naturally, we knew all of our direct neighbours because of the research that we had done when buying Villa Oleandro. So where all these neighbours actually had land would remain a mystery until we bumped into them on their ground. As time passed, we did encounter them on the roadside anywhere between us and Vico and learnt that 'neighbour' here means that we can maybe watch each other across the valley, drive a mile or so to see them or for the very few who were that close we might even be able to shout to each other.

Giuseppe, Francesco and Michele

Throughout my working life I had to attend innumerable meetings, very often being introduced to new people especially foreign ones.

Each meeting went the same way for me. I would be introduced to strangers and would instantly forget their names; forenames and surnames.

It was a dreadful affliction. Depending on the circumstances I would, if pen and paper were to hand, write down the name as I heard it, or if I knew who was going to be attending I would make notes in advance. But these opportunities were rare. In most cases I would, maybe, know one or two people in advance, walk into the room only to find a whole swathe of further people to remember.

It should have been easy. After all, the names were distinct enough, but I spent most of my time in a panic once I realised that I couldn't remember whom I might have to address. I tried all kinds of memory enhancement techniques - word association, mnemonics to name just two - but with no success. As a result, I came out of the meetings often without really having a complete grasp of what went on, because I spent more time thinking about their names and avoiding embarrassment.

So it became a complete surprise to me when we moved to Vico, that I would be introduced, or more likely someone would come up to me in the street and introduce themselves, and I always remembered their names. Perhaps it was the air?

Even more surprising when considering that there are only about 10 men's names used in the town and the most common are Giuseppe, Francesco and Michele. Of course, I may be using inaccurate statistics for I'm sure there are no reliable ones. The other popular names, as far as I can make out, are Antonio, Giovanni,

Domenico, Matteo, Nicola, Pasquale, Tommaso, and Vincenzo but I'm sure most Vichesi would agree with my top three, just as their top choice of women's names would be Maria, Antonietta and Caterina.

I didn't have to remember their surnames for they are rarely, if ever, offered - it would only be necessary to remember their *sopranome*. In the case of Michele there is Michele *ah Nerr*, Michele *oo' Noyrr*, Michele *Dent D'Or*, Michele *oo' Coo'reyr* (the courier), Michele *Manya Poc'* (eats little), Michele *Many'Assah* (eats a lot), Michele *Tramp ah Tramp* (I have had heard so many explanations for this, but the one that suits him is that he tramps about from place to place getting up to no good), Michele *N'Calacapost'* (Horse Shoe Nailer), Michele *duh Stronz'uh* (Turd), Michele *duh Strozzal'uh* (Bric-à-brac) and Michele *Mantoin'u'muh Kwoist* (Hold this for me!) - the list seems endless, the meanings occasionally lost over the years.

But remembering the forename and *sopranome* isn't the end of the story, because often the forenames have many derivatives - Giuseppe becomes Peppino, Francesco becomes Franco and so on. Peppino in turn has many variations: Pepp', Peppi, Beppi, Pino, Nino, Pinuccio or Ninnucio. That's just the Italian, in the dialect Pinuccio becomes *Pinooch'*.

Imagine the typical Vichese family, often composed of at least four living generations and each generation nearly as reproductive as the previous. In each branch of the family the parents traditionally christen newborn sons after their elder male relatives, newborn girls the same. Say, the grandfather is Giuseppe, then each of his male sons' eldest son will likely also be christened Giuseppe then at the many family gatherings there's a good chance that there will be a litter of Giuseppes of all ages and somehow the family has to establish a code for each one - so the diminutives begin. But if the grandfather has always been known as Peppi, then at least one of the grandsons could be referred to as Giuseppe proper.

The rest of us, outside the family, just have to follow suit! How schoolteachers manage is a miracle. But to my surprise, despite my utter failure to remember people's names in my former life, here in Vico something made it easy.

~~~

By May the builders were well on inside the house. They'd stripped the walls of all the old plaster. Upstairs this took no time at all as the plaster was literally falling off the walls with the damp anyway.

Downstairs was another matter. The plaster was dry and very stubborn indeed - at the end of the day their physical tiredness was apparent for the first time.

After they had stripped the walls and given them a coat of watery cement they literally uprooted what remained of the old flagstone floors, removed the soil base and a tangle of roots, laid a base for the new floors, replaced the rotting wooden lintels above the doors, repaired or replaced window stone mullions where necessary and inserted stainless steel chimney tubes where the wood-burning stoves would go.

Progress was almost too good to believe ... we were still on course to be in the house by our target date of August. Then the builders could get on with the extensions, but we were still awaiting the plans for these from the engineer, let alone the permissions.

The woods were now clean and the firewood that the cleaning yielded was lying about in piles on the border of the olive groves and reasonably well away from prying eyes (and sticky fingers) up on the road.

The pruners were coming one day a week to complete the transformation of the 100 or so trees that run down from the woods to the back of the house. So, for me the pace of work was slowing, but I remained busy. There was still a backlog of clearing up to do after the pruners and I was slowly stockpiling firewood up behind the house.

~~~

Most evenings I went to the hub of Vico, the roundabout at San Francesco, to catch up with friends and make new ones. Saturday night is obligatory - it's '*cazz' di padrohn*' - the master's penis or '*cazz' di Sabat' serr'* - Saturday night business. The Italians use the derogatory word *cazzo* throughout their slang, in this case to describe the purgatory of pay day.

The workers hang about the roundabout waiting for their various bosses to appear or they comb the card tables for their prey. When they've collected they meet up with other members of their squad and square up. Everywhere you look cash is changing hands.

One evening in the Caffe Crème I bumped into the operatic pruner, Antonio whom we met on our first harvest day the year before. He was with a group of friends and introduced me to Vincenzo who was a director of an extra-curricular school that gave

187

courses, including English, to aid tourism in the Gargano.

They were drinking beer and eating salted lemon - a strange combination but it works. At first Vincenzo was interested in my English, presumably as a teacher, but he soon recognised my thirst for the dialect and as we became firm friends at these regular meetings he helped me a lot with the language, in particular providing me with one of the few printed books in Vicaiolo.

Nonetheless it came as a surprise when one day he invited *M* and I to go with him and some students on a tour of the Gargano, he called it a safari.

Really we were too busy to take time off, but it was a great opportunity for a break from the building work and pruning. After all, we had been ignoring the Gargano since well before we bought the house. We accepted and he gave me instructions to meet him at the school the next morning at 9 am prompt.

The next day we made sure we were early, but we needn't have bothered. There was the usual Italian slack approach, hardly any of the students were there, the transport hadn't arrived and we considered the possibility that this could be a wasted day.

Vincenzo welcomed us, showed us around the facility, which would have looked dated if it had been my infant school. After the tour he gave a few orders to the gathering students and then he beckoned us to his car. Where were we going? For coffee of course.

We drove the short distance to San Francesco roundabout where cafes are abundant, negotiated it, and headed down the main street. Vincenzo sensed our curiosity.

"We're going to Il Ritrovo bar, they make the best espresso in town and delicious homemade *cornetti*" (croissants filled with cream or jam) "they serve Illy coffee and it's the only place to go."

The Il Ritrovo bar is near the daily market and when we entered we could tell it was well run. It was full of clients snatching some caffeine, the mixed aromas of coffee and freshly made *cornetti* dominated the atmosphere.

The owner, another Michele, welcomed us warmly. He seemed to know who we were. How were we getting on with the builders? Did we like Vico, the countryside and olives? He was casually, unobtrusively going about his business, while picking up snippets of information.

We finished our second breakfast and with some uncharacteristic urgency, Vincenzo said we'd better get back.

We arrived at the school to find two long-wheelbase safari-style Land Rover 100s parked under the shade of a Scots pine. The drivers were smoking with the students.

Vincenzo introduced us to Michele *ah Vretyuh'* - the Ear, knowing by now that I was an *appassionato* of *sopranomi*. Michele was the owner of the safari company and he welcomed us aboard.

We left Vico and headed off for Peschici, stopping at the viewpoint of Monte Pucci with its Saracen lookout tower and *trabucco* jutting out to sea on the rocks far below. It may have been educational, but the only thing I noticed was that we had made the first stop for a smoke.

We continued on to Peschici. En route, the students who had been relegated to the rear compartment of the Land Rover to make way for we guests in the middle negotiated with Vincenzo for the first coffee. We stopped in Peschici and had another hit of caffeine.

Having prepared themselves fully for the studying in hand we set off again in the general direction of Vieste using the coast road. We pulled off the main road a few kilometres out and stopped at a sanctuary. A few educational tips were passed on to the smoking students and then we headed off.

Michele drove with one hand on the wheel, the other lazily perched on the back of the front bench seat as this made it easier for him to turn round and speak to us all. He told jokes - very funny ones, although *M* had to translate all of them for me. The students in the back obviously liked Michele. Vincenzo did as well - it was great to be out and about in the Gargano instead of in his dreary office.

In between jokes we discussed lunch. Where were we going? What would we eat? It was all very educational.

Suddenly, Michele swung the Land Rover across the road as we took a track towards the sea. There was a sign saying private road. He ignored it. We pursued the tree-lined track passing a villa that used to belong to a famous TV star - I didn't get the name or whether it was part of their education - and soon after we drove out of the pines onto a barren piece of ground. The Land Rovers pulled up about 50 metres from the sea and we all clambered out.

The view was breathtaking, the sea air refreshing. The two drivers lent on their vehicles and lit up as we made our way to the cliff edge. This was the *Sfinale* - the end of the world. The most northern point of the Gargano, a rugged stretch of rock slowly being eroded by the sea. The cliffs were not that high, perhaps a 20 metre drop to the sea, but nonetheless impressive as the next wave thundered into the underbelly and spray shot up out of the many blow holes drilled through the soft limestone.

We walked around this barren but beautiful stretch of coast until we came upon a Saracen lookout tower. The Land Rovers followed as if we were on a political walkabout. The tower was collapsing and certainly too dangerous to enter, so the students all went in, but the holes in its outer walls which could easily have been made by shell hits in some past war did reveal the immensity of the walls from a safe distance.

The lesson over, we clambered back into the Land Rover and headed off for the coastal town of Vieste and lunch.

Instead of instilling sleep into Michele, the five-course lunch seemed to bring out the mischief in him. Driving back along the windy road to Peschici he had managed to persuade one of the female students to sit between him and Vincenzo. As he took each right hand bend he managed to manoeuvre the Land Rover in such a fashion that the hapless girl was forced centrifugally into his arm, which was, as ever, hanging limply on the back of the seat so that he could turn to us and tell us even more jokes.

At Peschici, he left the main road and headed up a valley towards the forest. The tarmac roads turned to rough tracks of stone, dust bellowed in our wake obscuring the trailing Land Rover. The ride became erratic as Michele negotiated the potholes.

Soon we were deep into the trees, sunshine flickering through the canopy. The road became rock, then just as suddenly turned to mud, which the Land Rover took in its stride throwing out waves of water, which had accumulated in hollows from the Spring rains.

Michele was certainly an ace off-roader but with every bump, every slide, every sudden turn the girls would scream for freedom. Vincenzo was calm, turning to us and smiling - no doubt he'd had the post lunch trip with Michele before.

We came to a clearing where the Land Rovers stopped to provide us with a respite and of course a smoke. Everyone clambered out with relief.

On the edge of the clearing some large dogs appeared - Abbruzese sheep dogs. They barked fiercely until their owner appeared and ordered them back to their work guarding a herd of goats and sheep.

The shepherd was Angelo - we had met him in the Autumn with

a herd of cows and pigs while picking chestnuts with Midew. It was a brief encounter and all I could remember was him appearing carrying an axe, which he used to free animals from the undergrowth. On this occasion he was without an axe and seemed far less formidable. He remembered me - we shook hands then he fell into amicable conversation with Michele. They probably meet often on his safaris and had plenty to catch up on.

After the smoke, we bid Angelo farewell and drove the final leg to Vico. Michele didn't let up on the way as he put the Land Rover through its paces. We all climbed out at Vico a little shaken and bruised.

I couldn't really make out what the students had picked up, but we had certainly discovered more of the Gargano.

As we parted, I asked Michele what he did when he was not shaking tourists to pieces in his Land Rover.

"I have an olive mill at Ischitella," he replied. "I'm busy there all winter and the safaris are just fun to do in the summer."

"Ah, we have olives. Perhaps we should talk more?" I suggested.

"Really, how many trees?" he asked.

"About two hundred and eighty trees at Calenella," I informed him proudly.

He seemed taken aback or was that the 'are you mad?' look.

"Oh well, you must come and see me then," he said as he gave me his card.

I promised we would do that.

Spring of Surprises

With summer on the way, everything seemed to be coming together. We had cleaned the woods, the fire hazard no longer so great. The pruning of the olive trees was well on its way.

The electricity company came as agreed, they spent a day digging holes and erecting the poles. When they left they promised to return the next day.

The Geologist turned up with the owner of the drilling company. They did a minimal inspection of the site and decided that the best place to drill the well would be on the car park below the three terraces that front the house. The car park was a new creation, built from the mountain of excavated rubble that the JCB had dumped over the main terrace wall.

I asked them whether they could consider drilling up on the hill behind the house; that way we could have a water deposit that would feed the house by gravity in the event of power cuts. They didn't reject the possibility out of hand; we did a short survey of the road above the house and then they dismissed the idea.

"No," said the driller, "the road's too steep. We'd never get the compressor up here". He reconfirmed. "We will have to do it on the car park."

"Okay, but what about water? Aren't you going to do some sort of scientific survey? Sonic tests, something of that kind?"

"Oh, no," said the driller. "There's water there."

I looked to the Geologist and he nodded in agreement.

"What not even a diviner?"

No, not even a diviner.

"Well what if you don't find water?" I asked the driller.

"We'll give you a discount," was his assurance, "but don't worry we'll find water there".

"What depth do you think you will need to go?"

"One hundred metres," he said.

At 40 Euros a metre this could be an expensive exercise, especially if it were to fail.

We had no choice; we'd already looked into the possibility of bringing water from the mains some 1.5 kilometres away as Midew's brother-in-law, Francesco, had suggested. But we had ruled that out - too expensive, too many potential pitfalls and bureaucratic delays with every agency possible involved in obtaining the permissions.

We agreed to speculate on the well.

"What about the papers?" *M* asked the Geologist.

"They'll be with me within a week," he replied confidently.

~~~

I went alone to see the engineer to talk about water storage tanks and to enquire about the status of the planning for the extensions. After all he had been working on them now for months. Surely he had something to show us. *M* was doing a little shopping and would join me later.

He seemed wound up. Something was bothering him as he rummaged through the pile of documents on his desk. Eventually he laid out the plans. Indeed he had sketched some ideas for the extensions that we wanted to build on either side of the house.

They would be set back, not intrusive to the original frontage. Two L-shaped double storey extensions both providing guest apartments upstairs. Downstairs, one would provide a workshop, storage space for olive oil, olive nets and equipment, a dry wood store and my shower room so that I could strip off working gear and clean up before entering the house. The other would be *M*'s domain - a utility room for doing the washing, making preserves and general housekeeping storage and most important of all her pottery and crafts studio.

Aldo seemed to have grasped the idea, although his roof pitches were all wrong but we could sort that out.

As I perused the drawings he seemed to become more agitated. He began to shuffle files and documents, muttering something about regulations.

"But we've already asked you about regulations," I reminded him. "We have the necessary land and planning indices to build up to 400 sq metres. Our plans are nowhere near that big".

In fact, before we bought Villa Oleandro, we'd asked everyone and anyone about planning and what we would require. They had all asked the same question "How much land will you have?" We have 4 hectares and each person confirmed. "You can build four hundred square metres".

Now Aldo was about to spring a surprise.

"Yes, but it's the volume you see," he said dismissively.

"Volume? What do you mean volume?" I asked, stomach muscles beginning to tense as I sensed something not very pleasant was coming.

"There are regulations about volumes," he continued. "You can only construct a maximum of 1000 cubic metres on a parcel of ground".

It didn't really sink in. "So what?" I pressed.

"Well you already have 1080 cubic metres," he finally blurted out. "All your allowance has already been used".

I was stunned. In my mind I was doing a mental calculation - it was pretty simple - the existing structure was about 10 metres high, 12 metres long and maybe 8 metres deep. He was right the building was, if not over, certainly about 1000 cubic metres.

"But what about the 400 square metres?" I asked as if it was some sort of get out of jail question.

He shook his head.

I wanted to throttle him. Here we were 6 months on into a project with plans that we had discussed from the beginning and the man in charge of all the planning had failed to make a mental calculation at the outset, the result of which would certainly have made us think again. He must have been familiar with the regulations and such a rule would be very difficult to fail to remember - surely he couldn't have simply forgotten them?

"It's a disaster!" I declared. I could imagine the tears welling up in *M*'s eyes when I told her.

"Disaster?" Aldo enquired as if nothing had changed.

"Yes, a bloody disaster!" I reiterated. "Where are we going to store olive oil, olive nets, all of the paraphernalia that goes with looking after the land? Where are we going to keep wood in the dry?

"But you've got 150 square metres of house," Aldo intervened.

It was true we had. Although the house is very imposing and about 1000 cubic metres in volume the thick walls, some approaching a metre, and the impressive staircase take up a lot of square metres.

"What about the thickness of the walls? Does that count as volume? What about the vaults and the ceiling space? Can we deduct some volume there?" I grasped at straws.

He shook his head.

"But 150 square metres is nothing! It simply isn't enough. Where will guests sleep?" I pleaded.

"Look," he said patronisingly, "people here in Vico live in far less space. One hundred and fifty square metres would be a palace for most of them," he said piling insult on injury.

"We don't care about the people in Vico," I retorted rather selfishly. "Why couldn't we have known about this before?"

No answer.

I sat in stunned silence. All of our plans in ruins.

"You could, of course, utilise the roof space," he interrupted the silence.

"But how? The roof space is full of vaults and anyway where would we have access to them?" Was he suggesting a corridor in our bedroom? I dismissed the option with incredulity. There are five vaults protruding into the roof space. Each one a different size, ranging from the huge one topping our bedroom to the tiny coffin-sized one covering the entry into the Cucina Monacesca. The vaults had already been restored and reinforced; we couldn't demolish them to make space. Anyway that was unthinkable - we wanted the house restored to its former glory; not some hotchpotch of flat ceilings and corridors leading to the roof.

No, it was simply a disaster and we were too far into the project to do anything about it.

The arrival of M and her cousin Mimmo broke the silence. He inhaled the atmosphere. Aldo explained the situation. Mimmo rolled his eyes - a look that said it all - he had warned us about bureaucracy on many occasions. M was speechless but contained the tears.

"What about underground?" Mimmo suggested.

He was proposing that we could maybe build extensions underground behind the house - there was the 4 metre rock face running the length of the rear of the house, a corridor about 3 metres wide. The regulations specify that space underground is not included in the 1000 cubic metres, but generally it applies to space directly under the house, not at the back of it.

It was an idea; but a far cry from our plans. It could solve some storage problems but that's all. If it ran the whole length of the house it would take away light from the main hall.

No, it was a tacky solution.

While we thought through the pros and cons Mimmo was still formulating.

"Maybe there's another solution," he continued.

"If we put the profile of the land behind the house against the cross-section, then technically part of the existing structure is already underground," he added.

"If we calculate the volume that is technically underground then, maybe, we could deduct it from the overall volume and provide space for the extensions," he explained. "They too would also be partially underground," he threw in for good measure.

Aldo didn't take to the idea immediately, but slowly he came round to Mimmo's thinking.

We all mulled it over and agreed it was at least a way forward. We had nothing to lose. Even so, for us it would be a compromise. The space that we would recoup would only allow for single-storey extensions.

Guests would have to make do!

We agreed the next step forward. Aldo was to speak to the planning officers and get their opinion. We begged him to get on with it and left.

Despite the glimmer of hope, we felt completely deflated. Why didn't Aldo tell us months ago? Would he be able to pull it off? After all it was not the only thing he had delayed to our cost. He had failed to apply for electricity. He had done nothing about the well. He had avoided delivering documents to the *Forestale*. We were disappointed.

~~~

The next day we went down to the building site to talk about progress and to think through our new plans.

When we arrived *mastro* Michele met us with a concerned expression.

"They've broken into the grotto," he complained.

"What, we've been burgled?" we questioned in unison.

"Yes, he's done it." Michele declared.

"Who, who's done it?" *M* interrogated.

"*Oo' Pes'keh'chyah'n* - the one from Peschici" he confirmed as if we should know who it was. We asked him to clarify.

"It was Ruggero," he pointed up the hill behind us. "Roger's

196

responsible for everything that happens around here. He's a regular tearaway".

"But then all *Peschiciani* are rogues," he added as if to cover his original accusation. "They'll steal everything, you'll see". Michele should know - he is a *Peschiciano*.

"Well what have they taken?" *M* asked.

"The beer!" Michele began, and in order of priority "a can of diesel, a sack of cement - that's all we can tell for now".

We examined the door to the grotto. The perpetrator had forced it open rather easily. Michele demonstrated how Roger had twisted the barrel lock with a pair of pliers until the frame holding the lock inside the door broke. There was a simple solution and he suggested we take the door off and take it up to the blacksmith at Vico for an immediate modification.

Inside I searched for my valuables. The water pump was still there - the most valuable item in the grotto. I removed it.

While driving to Vico with the door for repair I pondered our problems. First the builders had started drinking beer. It was a subtle start. At the outset, they had always had a beer at lunchtime and Pierino his wine. Now they were bringing beer down by the crate.

When we questioned them about the viability of drinking on the job and suggested that water would be better, they had laughed it off. "Water makes us sweat, beer doesn't," they argued.

Then there were the *Peschiciani*. If we believed everything that we had been told then nothing was safe. Vincenzo had warned us. Michele *oo Noyrr* had too - all those people in Vico who had raised their eyebrows at the thought of us living out in *campagna* - as if it were bandit territory.

The pruners had warned me too. Ruggero had stopped his battered *treruote* to talk to them when we were cleaning the woods. They all seemed very friendly. He was unusually tall and blond. He looked a little rough and was very muscular. He certainly passed for a rogue. When he left, Andrea immediately said, "You watch out for him - he's a bad man!"

As I drove I became preoccupied with my woodpile, now about 10 tons of prime olive wood and clearly visible from the valley road. If thieves came in the night, there would be no one to stop them stealing the lot. Now I wished that I'd left it sprawled around the groves - at least they would have to work for it.

In Vico, the blacksmith made an immediate modification to the lock so that I could return with the door that afternoon. He already knew about the burglary and was very uncomplimentary about the *Peschiciani* in general and one in particular.

~~~

When I returned with the door that afternoon, Aldo was visiting. He had some good news. He had spoken with the regional superintendent of building and he had agreed to consider the proposal regarding the calculation on volume.

While not plain sailing, things were looking up.

The builders replaced the door, while *mastro* Michele, Aldo and I surveyed the site.

Aldo admired the neat piles of flagstones and terracotta tiles then said "Are you going to leave those here - they'll be gone before you know it!"

Before I went home that evening I set about camouflaging the stones, the tiles and the wood pile as best I could in the vain hope that if they came at night they would miss them.

As I left I checked that everything was secure. Then I noticed piles of sand scattered around the place, which seemed a little odd for our tidy builders.

~~~

The electric company hadn't turned up again as promised. We still had a couple of poles lying around on the car park and we were beginning to wonder what they were if they would finish the job. Michele pestered us daily as the noise of the generator was beginning to get on everyone's nerves.

Out of the blue they turned up, two weeks after they'd promised, erected the remaining poles, attached the cable and wished us farewell with the news that we would have power the next day.

It was near the end of May and we still hadn't received permission to drill the well. We paid a visit to the Geologist.

"Where had we been?" he asked. He had been trying to call us for a week.

"You need to sign another declaration," he explained. "You need to declare that you will not water the olives".

"What? But we've already declared that we will only use the water for domestic use," M complained as we contemplated further delay.

"It's just a formality," he assured us. "They saw from your deeds that you have olives and it's necessary to add this declaration."

Once again we were left feeling "well why didn't we do it in the first place?" Surely it was his job to know that they would need it. He was the one who supplied them with a copy of our *atto*, which would clearly state that we had 6 acres of olives.

Here we have another professional, just like Alberto at the Notaio's office and Aldo the engineer. We asked them to do their job and they all come back with some kind of lame duck excuse or a bureaucratic nightmare. They all shrug their shoulders as if to say "it's the way it works". Cousin Mimmo had warned us. They are all Vichesi and, hard as we try, we find it impossible to hold a grudge against them - after all they can't help it, can they?

~~~

With Spring rolling into Summer, our run of luck seemed to be fading.

A few days after the grotto incident, we had another visit in the night. This time they stole the engine and the wheels from the cement mixer. The grotto door though was untouched.

Michele pointed to the large footprint in the sand. After the first burglary, every evening before they left the site, Michele and Leonardo would lay white sand at strategic points in the hope of catching the culprit.

"It could only be Ruggero!" he cursed.

It seemed that it was now clear we had let ourselves in for a roller-coaster time of petty crime and the prospect of never feeling safe at Villa Oleandro.

To top this we still had no idea when we could drill for water and of course the electricity didn't get connected the next day.

Michele decided that there was no other course than to go down at night and check things out. I pondered the wisdom of this, especially when he suggested that I accompany him.

I had little choice. I couldn't let him go on his own.

So when dusk came we would set off brandishing only torches.

The first night I was in for a surprise. As we made our way on to the terrace there seemed to be movement everywhere. But not the human kind. The floor of the terrace was a teaming mass of *scroffoli* - wood lice. They covered the walls of the house and we couldn't walk without crushing scores to death with each step.

Even Michele seemed bemused.

We sat and gazed at the stars. All about us pitch black - the only light being far away at Vico.

Ruggero, or for that matter any other *Peschiciano,* never came on any evening when we were standing guard or if they did we didn't see them.

Fizz

The first day of summer we went south to visit Ostuni - a picturesque town at the top of the heel of Italy; partly for a break and partly business.

In May we had ordered most of the fittings for Villa Oleandro locally. We had commissioned a stone *portale* for the front door and replacement stone mullions for some of the windows from the mason; external doors in chestnut from the carpenter; windows in oak from a specialist manufacturer; copper gutters from the gutter maker.

The one thing that we couldn't find locally was suitable flooring, but we knew what we wanted. In the Centro Storico we had kept our eye on a restoration project each time we passed it.

It's a huge building that at one time had been an olive mill - the builders were gutting the whole place and when we enquired they said it was going to be a bar.

When '*Il Trapetto* - The Mill' opened we were among the first to visit. Inside the cavernous building we found a treasure of antiquity: vast forms carved in the rocks at the rear that once held the screw presses. Deep troughs where freshly pressed olive oil would be allowed to settle and separate from water, little alcoves decorated with antique tools, a huge crushing bed and stones converted into table tops.

And on the floor, flagstones that looked like they could have always been there. It was Ostuni stone.

We eventually managed to contact the firm who cut the stone and the owner, Pietro, paid Villa Oleandro a visit. We decided that we would lay the stone throughout the original house and Pietro prepared a quote. As he departed, he invited us to visit his factory and promised to take us for a meal.

We took him up on his offer and arrived to view the factory just before lunch. We chose our stone and ordered it.

Lunch was splendid. Even though we agreed it would be a light lunch as we wanted to spend the afternoon looking around Alberobello, it was not to be.

The courses flowed: antipasti, risotto alla marinara, a whole grilled Sea Bass, cheese and tiramisu. It was difficult to refuse washed down with a crisp bottle of local Chardonnay.

After recovering from lunch, we set off late afternoon for Alberobello - the home of the *Trulli*. The small circular houses with conical roofs made entirely of stone resembled the Bories we had seen in the region of Gordes in Provence while house hunting there. The honey-coloured stone walls reminded us of the Cotswolds, our former home in the UK. But for us there were too many tourists in this region of Puglia. We preferred the relative obscurity of the Gargano.

~~~

Back in Vico, we decided to start another bureaucratic chain of events. We would need a telephone at Villa Oleandro especially as the reception for mobiles was very poor. Inside the house it was non-existent.

We dialled 187. Went through the usual rigmarole pushing keys until we eventually got to speak to a person. They were very helpful until we couldn't give them an address. Our Vicolo Sancarlo address was no good; it had to be the address of Villa Oleandro. But there isn't one. The postman never goes there.

M, who handled virtually all these irritating exchanges, insisted that there had to be a way and talked the operator into finding one. Eventually something clicked.

"Do you have an electricity contract?" the operator asked.

"Yes," replied *M*.

"Can you give me the number?"

"Yes, of course," *M* found the number and gave it to the, by now, patient operator.

"OK, that's fine. You should get your phone within six weeks!" came the unlikely conclusion to the call.

~~~

In the second week of June we headed up to Pescara to collect M's parents Vincenzo and Emilia, who were arriving for their now traditional 3-month stay in Vico. For us it was a day off from the builders and in the car we had time to catch up on things, but Villa Oleandro was never mentioned - Vincenzo was still very anti and the subject was never raised.

The following day we went down to Villa Oleandro and arrived to an eerie silence. We heard voices and eventually found the builders round the back of the house.

"It's arrived," declared *mastro* Michele when he saw us.

"What, what's arrived?" I implored, wondering what on earth had turned up now.

"The electricity - they connected it yesterday" and before we could say anything, he added, "and the *Pastora Vacca* came as well".

The generator had fallen silent after 3 months and we knew that the builders were pleased, but Michele seemed more pleased and was very excited by the appearance of the *Pastora Vacca*.

He had been telling us for months that we needed one. "No house in the country should be without one," was his opinion.

Villa Oleandro had been abandoned for scores of years - we don't yet know how many - and in that time all forms of animal life had taken over, as our encounter with the *scroffoli* had shown. Falcons and buzzards regularly circle overhead in the knowledge that there is an abundance of prey. Then there are lizards by the thousand and sticking miraculously to walls and ceilings the *scroofadyohn* - the dialect name for geckos.

But the *Pastora Vacca* is the guardian. According to Michele, it eats mice rats and snakes.

"You won't kill it will you?" said Michele, half an order, half an enquiry. "You'll tell the pruners not to kill it!"

"Yes, yes, don't worry Michele," we assured him not really knowing what we would do as the *Pastora Vacca* is a snake. A very big snake!

The *Pastora Vacca* that came with the electricity was, apparently, curled up on the drive underneath the meter box. When it uncoiled and made its way off it was fully two metres long according to the builders, with a girth as big as their wrists.

"You must feed it," insisted Michele, "it won't hurt you, and they're not dangerous. It likes to eat eggs. They're especially good for keeping the vipers away".

We had still not seen a *Pastora Vacca*, although I saw something disappear into the roadside hedge one day at speed. They are a beige colour - but when *M* saw one later on the road going up to Vico she described it as resembling the colour of a dried stick - with bright streaks of various colours. Many people had told us about the *Pastora Vacca*.

They said they were friendly to humans, non-aggressive. They certainly weren't poisonous but they could give you a nasty hug. They get their name 'Cowherd' because, according to legend, they coil themselves around the legs of unsuspecting grazing cows and suckle the milk from their udders. Others have said that they can be a danger to women suckling babies. According to folklore they will take the women's milk without them even being aware.

Naturally most people don't like them and will kill them on sight and unfortunately for the snake, their skin makes a lovely belt.

Although we had not seen it, we were pleased that it had passed by but we did wonder what our reaction would be to seeing one in the flesh.

When we told the good news to Vincenzo that evening he responded, without hesitation, "did you kill it?" justifying Michele's fears for the beast.

~~~

The next day we were woken early. At about ten minutes to six there was a deep resonating bang and then the whole house vibrated for a few seconds - it even woke *M* whose capacity for sleep is legendary! I don't know why, but we were quite calm about the whole thing. While the house shuddered we were glued to the bed unable to stir. When it was over we got up and dressed to join everyone else out on his or her balconies to exchange experiences.

The earthquake was small - about five on the Mercalli scale. Definition: almost everyone feels movement. Sleeping people are awakened. Doors swing open or close. Dishes are broken. Pictures on the wall move. Small objects move or are turned over. Trees might shake. Liquids might spill out of open containers.

We spent the day chasing up the artisans who had promised to make our fittings.

First we delivered the *scarpe* - shoes or pedestals of the front door mullions. They were the only pieces of the stone door surround that had not been stolen for some curious reason.

Well, stolen is probably not the correct term as we had heard that our *portale* had gone to France and the most likely suspect was Midew himself. It was typical of the way things worked here - the logic being that the house was going to fall down anyway and none of the other owners would have a need for them, so if someone comes along and offers good money then what is there to lose?

Midew, of course, would deny it vehemently. No they stole it, making a reference to the *Peschiciani*, whoever they were.

The mason looked at the *scarpe* as if to say, 'what am I supposed to do with those?'

A *portale* consists on each side of a pedestal, a column, a capital (a plinth that sits on top of the column) and an arch. The whole is then locked in place with a keystone.

"Well, we want you to make the *portale* to the same design and then clean up the pedestals so that we can use them," explained *M*.

He looked at her as if she were mad. "You want to put those back?" he spluttered.

"Yes, we do," answered *M* unswervingly.

"They'll look terrible against new marble," he announced.

"Well can't you make the new marble look old? Sort of antiquate it," suggested *M*.

The answer was undecipherable, but we took it as a yes.

We also gave him *M*'s design for the keystone. At least he seemed to approve of that, although he was amused. The design depicted two olive branches, below them the letters VO and below the letters a thistle, the Flower of Scotland.

We explained the reason for the thistle and left with a promise that the materials were on order and the *portale* would be ready by the middle of the month.

The carpenter and the gutter maker all assured us that the work was in hand.

~~~

True to his word, the mason called us mid-month to say we could pick up the stone - there were 14 pieces in all.

We arranged for the lorry driver who delivers the builder's sand, Rocco *Meyh'n Mazz'* - Rocco 'The Beater' (literally Throw Sticks), to meet us at the yard where we loaded the stones onto his lorry with a fork-lift truck, carefully wedging the pieces with wood.

With the load secured, we set off in convoy down to Villa

Oleandro. Half way down the mountain road the Guardia di Finanza - a sort of Corpo Forestale version of the UK's Customs and Excise (except that they drive armoured vehicles, carry guns and dress in military style uniforms) – stopped Rocco. We pulled up behind as there was no way to pass.

The Guardia di Finanza, like the Forestale, also have extraordinary powers of stop and demand. Whenever we were travelling back to the UK from our summer holidays we always used to take 50 litres or so of Tittino's olive oil and maybe a *damigiane* of red wine. Tittino would always insist on giving us a receipt just in case the Guardia di Finanza stopped us.

Carrying of goods however was a more serious matter and I realised immediately that we didn't have any documentation for the stone. No delivery note, no invoice.

They didn't bother getting out of their vehicle. They just waved down the lorry and an officer talked to Rocco through the window. The conversation seemed heated and lasted a few minutes. But then the Guardia di Finanza drove off passing me by without so much as a look.

When we arrived at Villa Oleandro, Rocco was unconcerned.

"They told me I shouldn't be on that road with my lorry, I should use the main road," he said, and then went on, "so I told them where to get off," or words to that effect.

"What, they didn't want documents or anything?" I asked.

"No, they just wanted their lunch," came the reply.

After lunch, we all helped to unload the stones and laid them in the main hall on planks of wood.

While we were doing so, M was admiring the cleaned pedestals and looking at the pristine un-antiquated columns when she noticed something strange about the design.

"Let's just check that the pedestal and columns match," she suggested.

They didn't. The design was more or less the same but the concave bevels of the columns were a different size to those of the original pedestal. There was no way they could go together - they were like a square peg in a round hole.

It was obvious that the mason had made no attempt to match them up, just as he had made no attempt to antiquate the stone.

We called him seeking a solution - he didn't have one other than making new pedestals. We had no choice. He would have them ready in a fortnight.

~~~

That evening I joined the builders for a drink at *Mezz' Cavoot*. Unloading the stone had been a heavy and exacting task. We had managed it without breaking anything and I wanted to celebrate.

Mastro Michele was on good form, the work was going well especially without the generator and with the good omen of the *Pastora Vacca*.

But there was some bad news to come. Nicola, Pierino's son, had to leave for his summer job. He and Pierino always went to a farm in June to help with the harvest. It was good regular work, although it paid less than we were paying them, and it guaranteed 3 months of National Insurance Contributions.

NIC's in Italy are very important as up until very recently once someone had paid 35 years of contributions they could retire on a full pension irrespective of their age. So many people in Vico were able to retire in their late forties, early fifties.

Pierino explained that they had held off their farm employer as long as they could. Nicola now had to go and he would have to follow shortly.

"Well let's hope you can hang on for as long as possible, Pierino," I said with another chink of the glasses. In truth we would be sorry to see him go as he was a very good worker.

"What about replacements?" I asked Michele.

"Ah, we'll have to see Gianni," he said wistfully. I was still Gianni to Michele. He couldn't utter "*Joo'wah*" like all the other commoners, but he had dropped the Signor.

As I entered Vicolo Sancarlo at dusk *M* was stood in the lit up staircase by the front door with a little bundle in her hands.

It was a puppy.

"Oh, do please let's keep her," *M* pleaded, knowing that I didn't want a dog until we were settled in at Villa Oleandro and the builders were long gone.

"Well where did you get her?" I asked, already contemplating the litter of puppies in 6 month's time that is de rigueur for Vico dogs.

"I found her in the street," she replied.

"Well, why didn't you leave her there? There's probably someone looking for her right now," I argued.

"Well these children were playing with her, kicking her around

207

like a football. Then she tried to hide under an old woman's skirt and she shooed her away for more punishment. I asked whom she belonged to and they all said nobody. She's only little!" came the defence.

Before I could say anymore, she added "I told them I'd take her and that if anyone came looking for her they should send them to me."

She did look a poor thing, her ribcage only too visible. *M* fed her and she ate like a gannet.

"She has got big ears," I remarked. "Some kind of terrier, but ears that big!" She also had lovely markings, her body was mainly black and white but with streaks of tan. Her eyes were circled in tan, with a white streak running between them and enveloping her nose, except for her black nostrils. Her ears tan at the front and back.

We watched her have her fill. Then she turned and pricked up her ears, a sparkle in her eye.

I caved in, "well what shall we call her?"

"Fizz," said *M*.

~~~

I spent the last few days of June up on the road next to the wood. We had decided to fence it, to keep animals away and hopefully people out.

Ruggero had a herd of goats and he was always wandering around up there. Goats do a lot of damage, especially to saplings and if they stray into the olives they eat the tender new growth as high as they can stretch up the trees. Ruggero was always losing his goats and it gave him an excuse to come around looking for them - we wanted him as far away as possible.

I enlisted the help of Andrea, Damiano and Matteo *Da Pecora*. The end of June is a quiet period for them. They had finished pruning and now they were waiting for their summer work. Andrea and Matteo would join the Corpo Forestale in August as fire lookouts while Damiano had nothing else on until we started the next session cleaning the trees. So they were grateful for a few days work.

I bought chestnut poles, reels of barbed wire and staples. Damiano suggested we would need some concrete as well, which the builders could make up for us and we could carry up on the Jeep.

On the first day, Andrea and Damiano helped me fill the Jeep with poles, wire and tools before we set off up the hill to meet

Matteo.

He was leaning nonchalantly on his Jeep whittling a stick. "Having fun?" I asked him, implying that he might be digging a hole.

"*Quist y'eh ah mesow'r*! - this is the measure," he said, justifying his stance. He held up a stick with a V-prong on its end and continued, "this is a measure of twenty five centimetres - you'll see how it works soon *Joo'wah*."

He took a ratchet winch out of the back of his Jeep and headed off up the hill. I drove my Jeep slowly up the hill while Damiano and Andrea unloaded the poles at 2-metre intervals. As we returned to the bottom of the hill to start the first hole, we passed Matteo who had attached the winch to a stout tree about 25 metres from where we were due to start.

They had divided the work. Damiano and Andrea would dig the holes; Matteo and I would attach the barbed wire.

It was 7 am and the temperatures were already in the mid-twenties. We had a long hot day ahead of us especially where there was no shade.

The work progressed quickly and with ten poles in place, Matteo and I began attaching the first strip of wire and using "*ah mesow'r*". I held the measure on the ground while Matteo placed the wire in the V and then secured the wire to the post with a staple.

"Very clever," I congratulated Matteo on his invention.

"*Joo'wah*, you have to use your brain to work in the country," he never tired of telling me. For in truth Matteo never stopped talking at all. He was the biggest chatterbox I had ever come across. But his Vicaiolo lilt more than made up for it. Of course our conversations were not that easy as I had to ask him continuously to repeat whatever it was he'd said and more often than not had to refer to Damiano to get a translation.

After we'd stapled the wire to a few poles, he went on ahead with the reel, attached it to the winch and pulled the wire taut before we stapled the remaining poles.

Back at the start we commenced on the second row. This time placing "*ah mesow'r*" with the V on top of the first row of wire. It was a perfect 25 cm measure.

"*Ha voist, Joo'wah?* - you see *Joo'wah*?" he complimented his own ingenuity.

Just for good measure, every time the wire passed close to a tree Matteo would staple to the tree for strength. If the tree was a large pine, he would chip off the bark with his axe.

"Now, should we be doing that?" I asked.

"Not really," came his reply as resin oozed from the wound.

"Well won't the Corpo Forestale have something to say about it?" I suggested.

He shrugged his shoulders and dismissed the Corpo Forestale out of hand.

"We are supposed to be concreting in the poles for strength," I added, but in truth the poles had gone in well. The ground was very stony and it was easy to wedge the poles firm.

"Are we going to concrete them?" I asked the others.

"No need, the fence is strong enough," came the reply in unison.

We spent three days completing the 300 metres or so of fence. As we did so, all of the neighbours above us passed by on their way to and from Vico. They complimented me on cleaning and opening up the wood. "It was really dark and so dry," most of them said, and for good measure, they would state the obvious, "if there had been a fire it would have been a disaster?"

They all said the fence was a good idea too - even Ruggero - it would keep people and animals out.

~~~

Back at the house, the builders had finished the work inside. They had replaced all the broken window mullions, given all the doors new lintels, wired and concreted all the floors on the upper floors to reinforce them and rendered all walls and ceilings.

Only the front door *portale* was missing, but the mason had told us the stone pedestals were ready to collect.

The inside looked pristine.

"You can call the electricians and plumbers," announced Michele with some pride.

That evening we contacted the electricians and plumbers.

Both predictably said that they couldn't come. We had been warming them up to the idea in the preceding weeks, but apparently to no effect.

Perhaps they hadn't believed that Michele would be ready on time.

The Keystone

Whenever I had the chance I put Fizz in the Jeep and drove her down to Villa Oleandro. She enjoyed the Jeep and from the back seat she always had her head out of the window, one paw perched on the rear of my seat, the other on the lip of the window frame.

Down at the house, I transferred her into the pick-up section where she took up position with front paws up on the side of the load bed, ears pricked listening to every noise as if she had advanced radar and was collecting a database of sounds. If it was a new sound she barked at it.

If I was working on the land, safely away from the building site, I took her with me and she settled into the routine following me around ears always alert. Every now and then she would rush off barking at something invisible to me. She was a territory dog.

When *M* arrived with lunch, Fizz would sit around us twitching her nose for a piece of *caciocavallo* rind, which she adored. We promised ourselves that we would keep her well away from the builders at lunchtime. They would spoil her very quickly.

~~~

It was the first day of July. I picked up the new pedestals from the mason and headed down to the site at 7.30 am.

Mastro Michele, Leonardo and Pierino were ready. Nicola had long gone to his tomato-picking job.

Today we would mount the front door *portale* and I really had no idea what was about to happen. I was there as the official photographer. *M* had taken pictures of every detail of the work to-date for future reference. Today she had charged me with the task until she arrived.

211

Since our trouble with the grotto I had been very worried about the stone *portale*. They'd been lying where we unloaded them in the house for some two weeks and, based upon all the dire warnings we had received, it would not have surprised me to arrive one morning to find them gone, probably following the original ones to France!

Now I was relieved that we could finally start the installation. Michele began by making a mock up of the *portale* flat on the ground to check that the pedestal design matched the columns. They did. He then checked a few measurements and, satisfied, he began to reel off instructions to Pierino and Leonardo.

They offered up the pedestals only to discover that they would have to knock some stone out of the walls for them to fit - the stonemason had cut new ones perfectly whereas the originals were probably rough-hewn on the inside and the stonework would have been built around them. Once we had overcome this little hurdle, Michele fixed the pedestals in place using fast-drying cement.

Just as they were beginning to move the first column a car hurtled up the drive and came to a dusty halt on the terrace in front of us. Another vehicle followed.

It was the electricians.

All work came to a stop and we had the first beer of the day - Michele's favourite, Moretti, fresh from the grotto. The electricians chatted through a few things with Michele, how deep to excavate and other dos and don'ts.

Having given the quick drying cement ample time to go off, the installation of the *portale* recommenced. Michele applied a further layer of cement to a pedestal and as they offered up a column, *M* arrived - she couldn't bear to miss it.

By 9.30 the two columns were in place with wedges of wood between the pedestals and columns ensuring that the stones were vertical and aligned.

M arrived to mayhem in the house as the electricians, having marked where they were going to place control boxes and tubing, started up their pneumatic drills.

Michele and team had swept the house - it had been spotless. Within minutes it resembled a bomb site, rubble strewn across the floors and dust flying out of the windows and doors. Generator-less silence had been shattered.

We stopped for the builder's breakfast, naturally with beer. Another two vehicles drove up onto the terrace. The plumbers had arrived.

What followed could have been a debate in the Italian parliament, except of course for the punch up.

It was all really very amicable, but somehow we had to accommodate four electricians and four plumbers in the house at the same time. *M* and I certainly didn't want any of them to go away - we couldn't believe our luck that they'd arrived. So we helped to broker a deal where the plumbers worked upstairs, the electricians downstairs until they needed to swap over.

Once settled and having taken counsel from Michele about the dos and don'ts more mayhem ensued. It really was devastating to see all the newly laid floors ripped up, the walls gouged. But Michele had been right about doing it this way.

The original stone walls were thick, but they were also extremely dry and, when uncovered, fragile. Even as it was with a thick layer of render on them, gouging out a neat channel, proved difficult. Some stone was soft and crumbled at a touch, but most of the stone was rock hard and stubborn. We agreed he was right about the walls, but surely they could have made some provision in the cementing of the floors? Having to dig up new floors seemed to be criminal, but apparently this is how it was done and anyway it was too late.

Whilst brokering the deal, we had taken our eye off the ball. When we returned our attention to the *portale* it looked odd. They had placed the first *capitale* and it looked completely wrong - it was upside down! Luckily the fast drying cement hadn't set and they could remove it without any trouble.

Written clearly on the bottom was the word '*sotto* - bottom'; put there by the mason, who presumably had seen this mistake before.

Michele laughed it off - we were more inclined to think they'd had too much beer. As I surveyed the terrace around me there were bottle cap after bottle cap ground into the earth - they were drinking too much and I had missed an opportunity.

It came to me in a flash - it would be a piece of art suitable for the Tate Gallery. A 54 litre *damigiane* full of Italian beer bottle caps.

With a few stern words to Michele, I informed them that the next day I would bring the bottle and I didn't want any more caps thrown on the ground - after all this was our environment. And a little less beer may keep the head clear!

"*Non ti preoccupare* - don't you worry," said Michele.

With the *capitale* mounted the correct way up, the builders erected a scaffold, half of it outside the house, the other half inside, using two trestles bridged with planks of wood. Off this platform other planks were placed at right angles spanning from the platform to the main scaffold surrounding the house. The builders needed plenty of room to manoeuvre and place their feet.

They lifted the keystone onto the main scaffold, then the first arch onto the platform. Leonardo and Pierino positioned the first arch, while Michele placed the levelling wedges. *M* watched the alignment - such precise work needed her eagle eye and natural ability to see an out-of-plumb.

When the arch was in position, Michele supported it with a thin plank of wood, placed roughly in the centre of the platform and angled into the arch.

"Now, Gianni are you ready?" asked Michele.

"Ready?" I must admit that apart from the photos and some carrying I had not done much, but then what was I supposed to do?

"Come up here on the platform," he ordered. "That's it, now kneel down and make yourself comfortable. You must support the arch here," he said, placing my hand where his had been and continued "against the supporting plank with fingers pointing up and just touching the arch."

"Now rest the other hand around the other side just to make sure the plank can't move. Don't push, just hold it," were his parting words as he left the platform.

They fetched the other arch and lifted it up. Space was becoming a problem and it was a difficult manoeuvre. Both I and the plank were in the way. I was already tired of the position. My nose was itching. The planks were pressing into my uncovered knees. How long would this take?

With much more difficulty, due to the lack of room, the three of them mounted the second arch; once levelled Michele placed another plank from the centre of the platform to the underside of the arch. Pierino held this from an equally uncomfortable angle. By now the sun had come round to be full on the front of the house.

Michele checked the alignment of all the stones and adjusted the wedges to get them perfect. We were ready for the final act.

"Are you alright Gianni?" asked Michele. I felt like saying just get on with it for heaven's sake. I'd been there maybe fifteen minutes but it seemed a lot longer.

He and Leonardo picked up the keystone and offered it up. It didn't fit! There was room right and left, but something was blocking it at the back. They'd have to work on the hole. Leonardo ran for a chisel and hammer and Michele banged away at the offending rock. Inside the house the electricians and plumbers were in full flow demolishing the walls and floors. The sun was beating down.

Michele and Leonardo offered up the keystone again. It was not quite there. More hammering. Eventually Michele was satisfied. He placed a small amount of cement on the butts of the arches and inserted the keystone.

"You can let go now," Michele said with a knowing smile. I tentatively took my hands away from the plank. Nothing moved.

Michele removed the supporting planks, rechecked levels and alignments with the wedges and said, "there you are Gianni - nothing to it."

I mopped my brow, rubbed my knees back to life, flexed my fingers and suggested we all have a beer! They never refused.

The rest of the day was spent making good the surrounds and preparing for further work on the roof the next day.

The fitting of the *portale* had transformed the front of Villa Oleandro. Where, only months before, there had been a gaping wound where the original stones had been wrenched out; now there was a beautiful facade, if a little over-pristine for our taste. It really felt like we had made some progress.

The electricians and plumbers emerged at the end of the day to admire the work. They gazed at the keystone and asked about the thistle.

~~~

The next day Michele started putting more layers of protection on the roof. He already assured us that water would never get in, but according to him you could never put enough on a roof. The smell of burnt tar surrounded the house all day.

At the end of the day, Michele came to us with unwelcome news. Pierino had to leave for his summer job. He would not be coming anymore.

"Well, he can come back after," M suggested.

Michele didn't respond.

"I want to talk about the tiles," he changed the subject.

"Yes, what about them?" From his tone I could tell we were'nt going to like what we were about to hear.

"Well it won't be safe to lay them in the traditional way. The roof is quite steep and will be difficult and dangerous to maintain," he stated authoritatively and after a pause he added, "and anyway there aren't enough good ones."

"What are you suggesting?" asked *M*.

"Well, they've got a new system of interlocking tiles," and sensing our immediate disbelief he went on, "they're not that bad, they have them now in an antiquated style."

"Yes, we've seen them on the restored Hunting Lodge at San Nicola - they really don't look very good," *M* insisted.

"Well that's just one type, there are lots to choose from," he argued.

We decided to do him the favour of having a look at samples, but after having carefully removed the originals from the roof, stacked them and protected them from prying eyes for months we weren't going to give up easily. We wanted to see the originals back on the house.

That evening we called in on the various builders' merchants to do Michele the courtesy of looking at the systems. Our principle merchant to-date couldn't believe that we were even considering it, but showed us some samples anyway. It was a non-starter and at the next opportunity we told Michele so.

~~~

On the Saturday, we sat down to lunch with Michele and Leonardo, as had become the custom but lunch was not so good without Pierino's wine.

After lunch we broached the subject of the roof. We told Michele the tiling system was out of the question and insisted that we find a solution using the original tiles. It was a laboured conversation - I still couldn't understand Michele's Peschici dialect after 6 months - but eventually *M* and he came up with a compromise.

We would lay new terracotta tiles on the underside and cap them with the originals - he argued that the new tiles were stronger and once the old ones were in place we wouldn't notice them. The only condition being that we would have to lay them "*pieno* - full."

"What, cement each and every one of them?" I couldn't believe what I was hearing.

"Yes, it's the only way - lots of cement and they'll never move and we can walk about on them in safety."

It was his final word on the matter.

"That will take ages, surely?" *M* quizzed him.

"*Non ti preoccupare*" was his stock and increasingly irritating reply whenever we asked a question that he wasn't going to answer.

The *mastro* had made the decision. We called the builders yard and ordered the tiles for Monday.

~~~

On Sunday we had kittens!

We went up the hill behind Villa Oleandro to visit our nearest neighbours Stefania and Gaetano (known to everyone as "*oo Milanaiz*" as he was from Milan).

Stefania had promised *M* the kittens when they were born. Since then they had lived in a basket on the back of her bicycle and they were still there now - perhaps 5 weeks old and looking very thin and scraggy. Their eyes closed by conjunctivitis. There was no sign of a caring mother.

Life for cats and dogs here is and always was a lottery. Nobody has them spayed, so they reproduce like rabbits. Their offspring have to take their chances. Stefania had many cats and she always tried to find a home for the kittens, but rarely succeeded.

Earlier in the year she'd promised us some from another litter, but they didn't make it. Perhaps they fell prey to the fox or even the *Pastora Vacca*?

We had coffee and chatted under the shade of their vine. They wanted to know about our progress and were amazed that we'd managed to get electricity so quickly. They had waited three years! And, ominously, even longer for the phone.

On hearing about the *Pastora Vacca*, Gaetano told us how one had got into his dovecote - a very posh word for a collection of bedsteads and corrugated iron held together with bits of string and wire.

"What happened?" *M* enquired.

"I opened the door and there it was - bloated beyond belief - it had eaten all the birds."

Gaetano continued the tale, "I went back to the house, got my gun and shot it to pieces," he said without a shadow of sympathy.

Stefania and Gaetano kept chickens and rabbits and had once had goats but they caused too much trouble. But rabbits, chickens and doves were a good source of food and the *Pastora Vacca* had received its rightful punishment.

We must raise chickens and rabbits of our own they insisted.

"Well, later on maybe; when we're settled; as long as Gaetano will do the slaughtering." They seemed bemused by our unfamiliarity with the art of butchering.

The bloodthirsty conversation continued as Gaetano quizzed me about my gun. "What, you haven't got one? You'll need one here in *campagna* - all sorts of shenanigans go on here - you'll need to protect yourselves," he warned.

"You've met Ruggero," added Stefania as if guns and he went together.

"Yes, seems OK to me but others have told me different," I said, trying not to offer an opinion either way.

"You be careful of him," she warned, "but don't tell anyone I told you so."

It was time to go. We collected the kittens, put them in a cat box, and loaded with freshly picked lemons and a plastic bag of free-range eggs we set off.

As we bid farewell, Stefania mentioned that more kittens would arrive in August.

"Oh, thanks but I'm sure these two will do," I replied.

I looked for confirmation from *M*. She didn't give it.

Back at Vicolo Sancarlo, we rigged up a run inside the house and *M* went to work on Tosh (a ginger tom) and Bonnie (his black and tan sister with partially white toes).

M de-flea'd them, de-ticked them and bathed their eyes with cold tea. They were not very happy, but too weak to do anything about it.

"If they survive, we'd better hope that Villa Oleandro is ready by the end of August otherwise they'll be climbing up the walls," I remarked as I left the house to go to the bar.

Outside Fizz was on ultra-alert. She had sensed something new.

~~~

I was watching Michele and Leonardo laboriously laying tiles and thinking that any hope we had of moving in for August was vanishing in front of my eyes. Progress was becoming a word of the past.

"Surely, he could bring in some labourers to help?" I muttered.

And then there was the inside to get on with - couldn't the tiles wait? We had tried to persuade Michele that he could leave the tiling as the roof was absolutely water proof - his words not ours. But no, once he'd started a job he would finish it.

Fizz was watching them intently, whether she shared my anguish is anyone's guess, and then suddenly she barked. Her ears were rigid and pointing to the driveway.

There was a groan, a violent crack and sudden movement followed by a loud crash. The main branch of a carob tree had split away and plunged down the bank into the olives.

Carob trees are dotted about here and there among the olives, but this tree was special. It had the most remarkable twisted trunk - it was a specimen in a million that stood in a prominent position at the top of the drive and now it was in trouble.

The tree was loaded with carob beans and they presumably had caused this branch to fail. Carob beans are our other paying crop but often the locals neglect the trees in favour of the olives. After all they don't attract an EU subsidy; we harvest them late August early September for a paltry sum of money. The stricken branch was a mess and needed cleaning up but Michele suggested that I prune the tree immediately as it is a species prone to collapse - the branches and bole of the carob hollow out over time and Midew had not tended this tree for many years. We would have to sacrifice the crop and do it soon.

The next day I arrived with the chainsaw. Before starting work I took Fizz for a walk up behind the house into the upper olive groves, checking that the wood pile was still there as usual. Fizz was taking to her puppy training well.

When I returned there were voices and a Land Rover by the Jeep. It was Maresciallo Di Maria-Vittoria and burly sidekick he had with him when he visited the wood clearing. His sidekick was making a note of the Jeep's registration number.

Fizz went into a defensive stance. Ears communicating with her database; no data found. She ran towards them barking furiously, but didn't get too close.

"What now?" I thought.

By the time I'd arrived they'd climbed back into the Land Rover and were just about to depart.

"What's up?" I asked.

"Oh, everything's okay," replied Di Maria-Vittoria, "we spotted the Jeep and didn't know whose it was. It's yours, is it? It hasn't got English number plates."

"Ah, yes it's ours," I confirmed. "Only the Volvo has English plates."

"Just checking" said Di Maria-Vittoria. "We don't want anything happening to you here. Nice dog - extraordinary ears!"

"Were our papers all right?" I asked him. We had handed them in what now seemed months ago and had heard nothing.

"Oh, yes. Fine. You've done everything *in regola* - a rarity here."

They bid me "*Buongiorno*" and started to leave.

"And will it be alright if I burn on Sunday? There's a fire ready to burn at the bottom of the drive."

He nodded approval and added, "just be careful. Do it early in the morning when there's no wind."

"Well, that's really something," I pondered. Now we had protection from the Corpo Forestale. Perhaps things wouldn't turn out so terribly with all these 'bad' people about.

Michele and Leonardo arrived and headed for the roof. I gazed at progress and groaned.

I reached for the chainsaw but it was too late. There was an almighty crack and thunderous crashes. The carob tree had simply disintegrated before my eyes, the bole gyrating and splitting into many pieces.

Our beautiful carob tree was gone.

~~~

As the heat of summer built up, I turned my mind to jobs that Michele was never going to do. The foul smell from the water storage tank below the terrace walls was the first task.

I arranged for Damiano and Mario *Gatt'ohn* (Big Cat), who had helped with the wood clearance, to come one Sunday.

First we dealt with the fire. It was a collection of *frasca* that had built up over the Spring and I'd failed to burn. It was down in a pit; a big fire that was very dry. I left them to it and went to sort out buckets, ropes and tools with which to clean the *cisterna*.

I returned within a few minutes to see huge flames leaping into the air.

"Bring some water and the chainsaw," shouted out Damiano. I brought them at great speed.

Damiano and Mario were beating the sides of the fire with leafy branches. They took the buckets of water and walked around the fire spraying it out with their hands as if they were sowing seeds. It

220

seemed to be stemming the spread, when suddenly a dead branch in the canopy of a tree above burst into flames. There was no wind but the fire was generating its own.

We were surrounded by trees; mainly holly oaks, but there were also three olives - one belonging to a neighbour.

"What the hell happened here?" I asked.

"The fire was too dry and too big to move once we saw it was getting out of control," said Damiano.

The fire burned rapidly, the flames swirling around, but luckily did not spread to the canopies of the other trees.

We eventually brought it under control and turned to survey the scene. Next to the fire the boles of some smaller trees were smoking - they were on fire. Mario grabbed the chainsaw, looked at me for approval, and in minutes the burnt trees had been downed and billeted into one metre lengths. Damiano heaped the extra green *frasca* on the fire creating massive plumes of smoke.

I was sure that the Forestale were going to pay us a visit, for even though I'd asked permission, the firewatchers scattered around the countryside couldn't have missed it. If Di Maria-Vittoria wasn't on duty then who would know that I'd asked? After all we'd got permission to burn, not to cut down trees.

Damiano despatched me to get the Jeep and we loaded up the billets as quickly as possible.

"No, not that one," interrupted Damiano, taking a billet off me. "Look it's smouldering. Never put burning wood on a vehicle." He doused the wood with water.

We worked quickly. The fire was spent; we covered the cut stumps with dirt and leaf mould; within a short time the scene looked normal. There had been a normal *frasca* fire and only close inspection would reveal otherwise.

We moved on to the main job of the day. As we headed towards the *cisterna* I asked them why they burnt the fire if it was so dangerous.

"Because you said to," came the reply.

"Yes, but you're the experts - shouldn't you have known?" I questioned.

"Ah, well you're the boss," Damiano replied with a smile.

Mario, who drew the short straw, found himself at the bottom of the *cisterna* standing on what appeared to be about 50 cm of mud and rubble. The previous day I had pumped out the sludgy water until the pump would do no more.

First he killed a rat that scurried out of the rubble on his arrival.

Having despatched the vermin and checked for others Mario began to dredge. Damiano pulled up the buckets and I dumped their contents as far away as possible. The stench was sickening.

Within a few hours we had brought the skeletons of three Wild Boar and two dogs to the surface along with piles of rotting wood, various pieces of bric-a-brac: chains, cutlery, the rusted barrel of a gun, and bits of broken pottery. The *cisterna* was spotless and ready for Michele's attention if he ever came off the roof.

~~~

In the middle of July we finally got permission to drill the well.

The drillers arrived in the area a few days later and began to drill for other people. The first was for Giovanni *Tre Mid'yerr* - Johnny Three Wives, who runs the Eurobar in Vico and in our opinion makes the best takeaway Pizza in town.

Johnny Three Wives was building a new house on a piece of land outside Vico and he invited us to go and watch the drilling. There we met Leo and Michele, the drilling team from Manfredonia and asked them when they'd be coming to us.

"Soon," Leo answered.

The drilling was well on its way. They'd already gone 100 metres and no sign of water. It didn't instil confidence. But that evening when I called in at Giovanni's bar he was smiling. They had found water and an abundance of it, but they had gone to 150 metres.

Leo made a visit to our site. He was not in agreement with his boss.

"We'll never get the compressor up here," he said. "We'll need a big tractor".

We didn't know what the implications for this were, but when the day came to start drilling, the compressor arrived towed by a huge red tractor that they had brought from Manfredonia for the purpose.

They placed the drill rig and compressor in position. Then they unloaded their lorry of 3-metre drill-bit extensions and polyethylene tubes and stacked them neatly to the side. And that was that. They went home.

The next day they turned up and drilling began in earnest. At this point a battered old Bedford van came up the drive and the driver got out. He was short, stocky and very scruffy.

I had seen him a few days earlier at Giovanni's site - he brought the drillers food and drink. I assumed he was a member of the team. In the back of his van he had a 3000 litre water tank and he began to pump it out into a tank used for the drilling.

At the house *mastro* Michele asked "What's *Tramp ah Tramp* doing here?"

"Who?" I hadn't understood.

"Michele *Tramp ah Tramp*, the one delivering the water".

It seemed that *Tramp ah Tramp* was not with the drillers at all, he was from Vico and whenever the drillers were in the area he stuck to them like a parasite. Apparently, I would have to pay him for the water.

I went back down to talk to the drillers and *Tramp ah Tramp* only to find out that it was true. He wanted 30 Euros a load.

I looked in the 3000 litre tank on the ground and noticed that it was far from full. When I raised the issue of the level with *Tramp ah Tramp*, he simply shrugged his shoulders. I paid him and said that I wouldn't need his services any longer - I had my own water transport system.

The water was running low by about midday; so much sooner than expected we loaded the tank on the Jeep and I headed off to the spring to bring water.

By mid-afternoon I had refilled the tank and was about to start off for another load when the drilling stopped. I hadn't noticed but all of the drill-bit extensions had been used up.

They had drilled 93 metres and there was no sign of water. The car park was awash with white gritty water, a by-product of the drilling process made from the water we were pumping in and the ground up powder of the borehole. Slowly this water was draining away into the olive groves below, leaving a white scar as it went.

They left for Manfredonia promising to return the next day.

The drill site was 100 metres above sea level and I was beginning to wonder what we would do if they didn't find water. If we had to, where could they drill another borehole? They had already ruled out above the house, which would afford us more altitude.

The next day drilling recommenced and when I wasn't fetching water I looked on anxiously. We finally struck water at 111 metres. For me there was just the faintest hint of something different as they lifted up the rig to add on the 38th drill-bit extension - more water than usual seemed to be released?

But it was not enough. They measure the capacity of the well by the number of litres per second; roughly it is the measure of water that is needed to replenish water as it is drawn from the well. According to the drillers we had less than half a litre a second - quite how they knew I never deduced - but we needed to have at least one litre per second and ideally two.

The drilling resumed, by now the nauseating squealing and screeching of the machinery getting on everybody's nerves. Michele *Tramp ah Tramp* turned up. We had no idea why, he just hung around the place.

At 123 metres they confirmed half a litre a second; at 132 metres one litre per second. The drilling team wanted to stop at this point.

We weren't really sure. What were they concerned about? Sea Water? Surely not we are 2 kilometres from the sea. We telephoned the Geologist.

"Don't worry," he replied to our concern. "Go another ten metres".

We went to 144 metres and still, apparently, had one litre per second. We called him again.

"Go to one hundred and fifty," he said without hesitation.

We did and shortly after we recommenced the water pressure coming out of the borehole seemed to increase dramatically. We stopped at 150 metres and according to the drillers we had our two litres per second.

After they had lifted the 49 drill-bit extensions and the diamond-bit to the surface, Leo dropped a rope down the well with a bottle, then drew it back to the surface, metre by metre, in all 87 metres of rope, indicating that we had an abundant 63 metre head of water in the borehole. The drillers seemed pleased with their work.

Leo ceremoniously poured the milky water into a plastic cup and drank. His face grimaced and he spat it out.

"There's salt," he said.

He gave the cup to *M*. She drank and the look on her face said it all.

I grabbed the cup and took a small sip - it was sweet. They, especially *M* were taking the proverbial water! Everybody laughed at my expense.

Of course work stopped everywhere, including on the roof and we celebrated the birth of the well with beers all round.

The drillers tidied up and headed home saying they would be

back tomorrow to line the well with the polyethylene tubing.

We called the plumber to tell him the good news about the well and asked if we could get on with installing the pump.

"That could be difficult," he said. "Tomorrow's the first of August; everybody's closing down for the holidays."

Now why didn't we think of that?

The pump would certainly have to wait for a month, but at least the well was another keystone in our project.

~~~

We were just about to leave for Vico when Di Maria-Vittoria arrived.

In the intervening weeks since I'd found him jotting down the number of the Jeep, we'd discovered a lot about him from *M*'s father.

Since his arrival, Vincenzo had been taken aback by his encounters with acquaintances in Vico who wanted to congratulate him on our project.

For years now Vincenzo had been keeping himself to himself on holiday and had lost contact with many old friends. Now he was making up for it as he toured old haunts with a new-found enthusiasm, for although he would never admit it, he was probably proud of his daughter achievements.

One of the people he renewed friends with was Di Maria Vittorio's father. Long ago they were neighbours in Vico. Vincenzo had even been present on the day of the Maresciallo's birth. Moreover, *M*'s grandmother and the Maresciallo's mother had been inseparable friends. Back in those days when Vico families lived in each other's pockets, being so close was tantamount to being family.

Mario Di Maria-Vittoria arrived that afternoon with a broad smile on his face. He greeted *M* with the customary Italian cheek kiss and me with a hearty handshake.

He had brought colleagues with him to meet us and to familiarise them with the house and the project as whole.

"Don't you worry," he assured. "We pass by often and we'll keep an eye on things."

"If there's anything you need, anything we can do for you please don't hesitate to ask. After all we are family," he said as they left.

~~~

August was upon us.

Michele had finished the roof and we attempted to turn his attention

225

to the inside. He had to make good the electricians and plumbers work - tubes and pipes were visible and vulnerable everywhere.

Then there were all the materials we had ordered and tradesmen we had bullied to be ready before August.

According to the carpenter, the doors were ready although we'd only seen the wood. The window supplier was ready and eager to come, install and get his money. Our builder's merchant had picked up nine pallets of valuable stone flooring from Ostuni and had nowhere to store them - eventually they had unloaded them in the yard of the local agricultural cooperative, where the general public could admire them, where lorries and forklift trucks could whisk them away in jiffy.

The electricians and plumbers had reserved time before their August break to come and continue their work.

We pleaded with Michele, suggested that it would be so much better for them to be finishing off inside in the torrid heat of Summer.

But, no, Michele had never even contemplated going indoors. "We have to render the outside first; get it ready for bad weather."

"What bad weather, Michele? It's not even August yet!"

The Day of The Dead

Mastro Michele's stubborn approach had one advantage - there were no decisions to make. Rendering was rendering and that was that.

The electricians, plumbers and other tradesmen were winding down towards the 15th of August, the *Ferragosto*, which is a national holiday and the safest day to venture on to the deserted Italian motorways.

Immediately after the *Ferragosto*, Vico celebrates its biggest festival, San Rocco, and by then everyone has laid down tools until September. Michele said he would be working all of August, but we now urged him to take a break. He insisted he would stop on the *Ferragosto* and be back a few days later immediately after the *festa* of San Rocco.

We resigned ourselves to the fact that moving in anytime in August had been too ambitious. We were now more worried about security, but there was nothing we could do about it - at least we had the Corpo Forestale on our side.

We tried to relax. Went to the beach. Reintroduced ourselves to relatives and friends who were all complaining about how little they had seen of us.

This year we had Amelia, our niece from the UK, for the month of August. She was thrilled to be here and took to Fizz, Tosh and Bonnie as any 10 year-old would do. She also had the therapeutic talent of taking our minds off the project, especially *M*'s, as she filled our day with projects that she wanted to do.

Nonetheless, I went down to Villa Oleandro most mornings to give Fizz a run and check things out. There was still work for me; the builders needed the water topping up; the woods we had cleared in April needed some attention with the strimmer to keep them under control, so most days I would do a couple of hours before *M* and Amelia had risen from their beds.

~~~

One morning I had been strimming since dawn, always working from the edge of the olive groves uphill towards the road. As I neared the road, the sun was coming into my eyes and the insects were beginning to bite. It was time to call it a day, but at that moment something unusual caught my eye. I stopped the strimmer, lifted my face mask and gazed at barbed wire hanging from a tree.

The fence was broken.

As I moved up to see what had happened, I wondered whether there had been an accident - maybe a car or a motorcycle had hurtled through the fence.

But, no. There had been no accident. The fence had gone. At least the fence posts had gone. There before me were pieces of barbed wire 2 metres in length. They had spring-coiled themselves to form a tangle of wire one would only expect to see on a battlefield.

Everywhere I looked there were pieces of barbed wire. Someone had stolen the fence. It took my breath away. As I walked on up the hill I began to recover on finding some fence still intact. After I had surveyed the scene, it was evident that they had taken about 50 poles. Somebody had brought a pair of wire cutters, left about 250 pieces of barbed tangle strewn over 100 metres and had, presumably, driven off happily with staple-studded poles.

So this was it, this is what we had to live with. I remember thinking at the time, "Well it was silly really, fancy leaving a fence lying around. Someone was bound to take it."

~~~

Back in Vico, when I told *mastro* Michele and Leonardo they couldn't believe it. We had not had any trouble since the grotto was broken into and now this.

Michele denounced the culprit, Ruggero.

I went to San Francesco just before lunch to find anyone to talk to about it. To take some advice if anyone would give it. Everyone I spoke to was shocked and, in general, they all blamed the *Peschiciani*, but nobody in particular.

One after another they advised that we "*fa la denuncia* - denounce the villains."

So we did. We went to the barracks of the Carabinieri who are responsible for hearing a *denuncia*. We sat waiting for some time while people passed us by without even asking us what we wanted. Eventually someone summoned us into an office.

There was an officer in uniform sitting at a desk. He motioned us to sit down. At an adjacent desk sat someone in plain clothes, in fact just casual clothes.

The officer asked us what we wanted, so *M* explained what had happened.

The man in plain clothes immediately took over the interrogation. He wanted to know the full details of the crime: location, time and the value of what was stolen.

The other officers deferred to him, and whilst the interrogation was going on many other people passed through the office to talk to him - he too was a Maresciallo or Captain of the Carabinieri, the highest rank in Vico.

He listened with great sympathy and then said there was little they could do. They would make the usual enquiries, go through the motions, but in his opinion it could only be one person, but he didn't name him.

We finished by making a formal statement to the initial officer and left with a piece of paper in our hands - the *denuncia*.

That evening we called in on Mario at the office of the Corpo Forestale to give him a copy of the *denuncia* and to seek his advice.

He digested the facts. Said something very derogatory about Ruggero and said, "leave this to me". He promptly closed the office and rounded up his staff and we all went off to the nearby Eurobar for a drink. As we entered, Johnny Three Wives said how sorry he was to hear about our fence.

~~~

One day we had a visit from the Vet, Silvio. He had come to give Fizz her injections.

It was the first time he'd seen her and her ears amazed him too. He said that she was a Volpino a breed of fox-like dogs that come from the mountains in Calabria.

We were chatting generally about the house, the well and the electricity when we brought up the subject of the *Pastora Vacca*. I wanted to know if he could tell us the real name of the snake.

He couldn't; but he was fascinated to hear about the snake,

which we had not seen again, and he had some news. He had been called to a plot of land not a kilometre from Villa Oleandro recently. There they had found a dead *Pastora Vacca* wrapped around an Abbruzese sheep dog, which was also dead. It was a big snake - it would need to be to kill such a dog – so it probably was not ours. Apparently, the other dogs in the compound had killed the snake.

~~~

I continued to maintain a vigil at Villa Oleandro, but it was impossible to be there 24 hours a day.

A week later I found another section of the fence had gone. They had not stopped at 50 poles or perhaps another band of fence robbers was raiding us?

A day or two later, on the evening of the *batteria* of San Rocco, I felt uneasy. I had a hunch and said to *M*, "they're there now, I can feel it in my bones." She urged me to go and see, but I hadn't got the energy and didn't want the confrontation.

The next day I went to Villa Oleandro early to check the fence. My hunch had been right. There was nothing left - hundreds of metres of cut tangled barbed wire. I began the laborious process of cleaning it all up.

Later that day we brought the Carabinieri and the Corpo Forestale up to date, but it was clear they could do little.

~~~

August passed and *mastro* Michele stayed at home. Perhaps we had misunderstood the meaning of 'I'll be back after San Rocco'.

For the most part we had a traditional holiday, except that we had never been pulled off the beach for a barbecue. One day the abundant corpulence of Mario Di Maria-Vittoria appeared on the road above the beach.

"Come on you lot," he beckoned, "we're going to eat!" He invited us to lunch at his summer home. It's extraordinary - in the UK people from the North, for example, have holiday homes in the South and people from London drive hundreds of miles to the West Country for a weekend, but here in Vico people have holiday homes just down the hill.

We went to Mario's holiday home. He disappeared into a pine wood and came back with a collection of brittle firewood and lit the barbecue. Every now and then he was called on his mobile; there was

230

a big forest fire around the coast and, though off duty, he was being kept in touch with developments. We could see the plume of smoke and watched the Canadair as it swooped in and out of the sea near Peschici to take another load of water in an attempt to stem the damage.

While we chewed on a huge mound of barbecued goat and pork, Mario told me that they had not been able to locate our fence; there were no sources of information coming forth.

However, he had been to visit Ruggero's grandfather; he wouldn't waste time on Ruggero because he had "*ah kapa tost'* (a hard head)". No, this was a matter of family honour and he went to the font of the family and made it clear to them that "we belonged to him, were family" and that if anything else happened Ruggero would be the first on the visiting list.

I thanked him. Really I wasn't sure how to react, but this petty pilfering with the threat of worse to come was putting us under pressure and anything that might potentially relieve it felt good.

I drank his health.

"How do you like the wine?" he asked.

"It's good," I answered, "a little on the light side for my taste, but good all the same. I like this really dark wine they make here *Vino Paesano*," I explained.

Without a word, Mario left the table. Got on his scooter and disappeared down the road. Ten minutes later he reappeared with two large bottles of wine and a *caciocavallo*. He had been to his brother's who had a holiday home not far away.

"Now you can taste some real wine and cheese from the forest," he announced breathlessly.

We poured the wine. It was jet black. The aroma was blackberry. He had been right - we had never tasted local wine so honest.

Mario took a large knife and quartered the *caciocavallo*. We could tell by its deep colour, especially the last centimetre of the rind, that it was mature. It was; it was *piccante*; it provoked wine.

We sat, drank and ate until the delights were no more. From time to time I cautioned Vincenzo that perhaps he was overdoing it. "Rubbish," he would reply, "this wine is really special, I'll be alright". The women took little notice, too busy gossiping about something.

Vincenzo eventually excused himself for a smoke. As he wondered away, his feet got into a tangle.

~~~

The first Sunday in September marked the opening of the hunting season. We had been told to expect the worst. We were told that the *cacciatori* had the right to go anywhere and shoot anything. "They will cut fences (or maybe even steal them?) and generally cause mayhem."

In fact, their freedom is not so extensive. They're not allowed in the olives, must not shoot within 100 metres of a road or a dwelling. That was some comfort, but when I spoke to people about it they just dismissed the idea "Pshaw, the *cacciatori* do what they like, especially the *Peschiciani*."

In general the Italians shoot songbirds, especially thrushes. I've never seen a pheasant or partridge here, nor a rabbit come to think about it. *Mastro* Michele say's there are hares, but they are just as elusive. At least they do eat what they shoot, but as the birds are so small I imagine that more of the meat is shot than is edible.

We waited with baited breath, but the expected outbreak of hostilities never seemed to happen. A wild boar shoot passed across a hill opposite Villa Oleandro and managed a kill, but apart from that things were quiet. Perhaps there was nothing left to shoot?

As Autumn drew on we were enjoying a spell of fine weather. Michele and Leonardo were back on the job. At last they were plastering the inside of the house.

"Michele, couldn't you get someone to help, someone to speed things up?" I implored.

"We are *rifinituri* - specialist finishers," came the reply from Leonardo. "Nobody does this work like us."

"Yes, but we're not expecting a finish for a palace," I countered, "surely there was some other way."

"Don't you worry, Gianni," was the only response we got from Michele as usual.

With no decisions to make we headed for long walks on the beach with Fizz. Now the beaches were deserted; as is the case every year, the Italians flock back to the cities in the last weekend of August, usually enduring torrid heat in *traffico critico*.

~~~

By mid-September the plastering was complete - it hadn't taken so long. The plaster was a work of art - a finish resembling marble. Villa Oleandro was clean again and it looked like a palace indoors.

Mastro Michele ordered us to arrange the delivery of the stone flooring and to prepare the electricians, the plumbers and the window fitters to return.

"You have to tell them," referring to the other tradesmen, "to work carefully," ordered the *mastro*.

He started work on the final layer of floor, *oo mass'ette*, a thin levelling layer of screed on to which he would lay the stones. He laid the screed downstairs in one day and when we inspected inside we found small chips in the plasterwork, the coffee machine had spat on the wall in the corner of the kitchen and splashes of cement dotted the walls. Now we could see why the *mastro* had been so anxious!

Michele was not concerned when we confronted him about the amount of mess he had created. He finished the *mass'ette* upstairs, but all the while seemed preoccupied about something else. Eventually he decided to speak. He called us for a conference. It took him a while to get around to the problem.

"These stones are all cut to a different thickness," he finally announced.

Maybe there was a millimetre in it, not more, but according to him that was no good. Memories of the saga of the roof tiles came flooding back. What were we going to have to do, cut the tiles to the same thickness?

"But Michele, we brought you samples of the stone; why are you telling us this now?"

No answer.

Ostuni stone is the nearest thing here to the flagstones found in the UK; it is stone that looks old and has rough edges. We were sure by this stage that this was not to Michele's taste - he has a uniform mind and we think this explains why he was having a last minute fit about laying them.

"Well there is no other option, Michele, you have to lay these stones," urged *M* with authority. "We will just have to find a way to grade them and then you can do batches of the same thickness," was her final word and he seemed to agree. *M* and Michele set about devising the method for grading.

Afterwards we went inside and finalised where he would start, aligning the stones in the centre of the Main Hall to a mythical fireplace that we had yet to build. With all decisions made, we left them grading the stone in preparation for a start the next day.

Over the following days we supervised the laying of the stones and helped with the grading. It seemed to be going well and soon the ground floor was covered. With only the grouting to do we decided we could relax. The weather was perfect so we packed a picnic lunch and headed for the beach. We called in at Villa Oleandro on the way to deliver some materials and admire the flooring. The grouting was well under way, but to our horror Michele was filling the gaps level with the stone tops. He was trying to hide the imperfection of the stone's rough edges, the very thing that attracted us to it.

That was that. *M* rolled up her sleeves and started to clean the excessive grouting from the cracks before it set, revealing the true nature of the stone.

She despatched me back to Vico to get rubber gloves, brushes, cloths, kneepads and various tools to scrape - the beach was not to be. By the end of the day, the downstairs floor had been 'cleaned'. The builders got the idea, but, just to be sure, the next day we were there again.

~~~

Mastro Michele walked into the stable one morning and surprised a viper. It was cool and perhaps the viper had strayed in that morning or the night before. He couldn't be sure how active it was. When the viper coiled into its attack position Michele realised he was in danger and before it could strike a shovel had taken off its head.

"They're very dangerous, Gianni," said Michele for the umpteenth time.

"Yes, yes, Michele I'm aware of that. I will be careful."

That day we went up to visit Stefania. She had three trainee snake catchers to choose from - we had agreed to take two of the kittens. I had argued that it was too soon, Tosh and Bonnie were climbing the walls and dying to get out into the world. We had no idea when Villa Oleandro would be ready. *M* stood her ground, she had promised to take them and she would. I consoled myself to the thought that the more snake catchers we had the better and at least they'd have the winter to grow before they hopefully had to confront one.

These kittens were wilder than Tosh and Bonnie; they were living free in the garden. At the time we arrived they were in a flowerbed under a bush. One was ginger, very much like Tosh; another was a tabby just like *M*'s Whisper who had died the year before; the last one looked like a china kitten with very long whiskers.

Whisper was an old cat, she died aged 20. She had always been *M*'s treasure and when not out catching bats she was always to be found on *M*'s lap. But something happened to her when she was about 12; *M* hadn't noticed but I had seen her bump into things quite often. She was going blind.

By the time we went to Switzerland she had been totally blind for many years, but she still went with us. She toured France on our house hunt and eventually came to Vico with us.

No matter where we went she always settled in as long as she had a lap to curl up on. While we were waiting to buy Villa Oleandro, we used to take her for walks on the beach. She took it in her stride; seemingly having no fear of the waves lapping on the seashore. She followed her well trained nose honing in on every new scent and using her finely tuned whiskers to detect hazards.

I didn't expect *M* to take the tabby, but she did immediately. Stefania assumed we would take the other ginger tom too, but we decided to leave him with his mother. I had really taken to the 'china' cat; she was the boldest of the three and seemed to have no fear as she came out to greet us even though she wouldn't let us get too close.

Deciding which ones to take was the easiest part, catching them was another. Gaetano and I resorting to all kinds of diversions until we eventually managed to trap them.

Back at Vicolo Sancarlo, Tosh and Bonnie were on high alert the moment we walked in. What they would make of Tish the tabby and China (who very quickly became Chin-Chin) we weren't sure.

We reconstructed the cat pound and settled them in as best we could. The larger cats were aggressively defensive for a few days, but once they gauged there was no threat they got on fine.

Fizz, who had adopted Tosh and Bonnie, was on high alert again.

~~~

Having finished laying the Ostuni stone throughout the rooms in the house, *mastro* Michele turned his attention to the entrance hall. Here we wanted to lay the thick flagstones we had uprooted from the Main Hall many months earlier and despite the engineer's dire warnings we still had them.

Obviously this was not to Michele's taste - he now wanted the Ostuni stone everywhere as he gradually realised how good it looked even with the edges rough and grout free. It was in keeping with his uniformity not to want to mix the stone.

M gave him his orders. He was to pick the best old flagstones and lay them as he found them. He agreed, but while we weren't looking he cut them all to similar shape and size and laid them. It looks good, but it wasn't what we wanted.

"You can put the front and back door on now," he declared as he finished.

That reminded us that we had some chasing up to do. That evening we called in on the engineer to hear the news that the planners in Vico had finally agreed our project for the extensions. Now the application had to go to Bari, for what he termed 'rubber stamping'.

The carpenter, when pushed, had to admit that he hadn't even started the doors. We couldn't hide our disappointment. All summer we had been bumping into him and he had assured us that they were as good as ready. We hadn't felt any need to put any pressure on him. Now that we were ready, it was like starting from scratch.

We called in on the window manufacturer just to be sure. He was ready. We inspected the windows in his store. We said it would be another week to two weeks and then hopefully he could work upstairs as well as down. He was not too happy - he had been ready at the beginning of August as promised; so we gave him a cheque to be going on with.

~~~

The fine weather continued into October but rain at the beginning then rising temperatures brought out the fungi hunters.

What seemed like the whole of Vico was alive before dawn and everywhere one drove in the forest and around the country lanes there were cars parked and folks shuffling around with their baskets and sticks.

It turned out to be a particularly good year for *porcini* and those who invested a day collecting usually came back with about 10 kilos. Sellers appeared at San Francesco at midday where eager buyers instantly engulfed them to choose the best.

The Vichese enthusiasm is unbridled as they gorge the fruits of the forest; what they don't eat immediately they preserve under oil. If there are still any to spare, as in this abundant year, they sell them for a handsome profit for a day's healthy exercise.

We, of course, could not find the time to hunt mushrooms seriously, but we had some UK visitors for a few days and I was able to take them for a tour in the forest (*M* was cleaning grouting!). I took them to an area I knew from last year when we picked chestnuts with Midew. For about an hour we hunted the precious fungi and we didn't do too badly. We found some very good porcini, a '*mazza tambour*' (drumstick), more commonly known in the UK as the Parasol Mushroom 'Lepiota Procera' - I used to collect them, and various other specimens, on The Malvern Hills when I went to fetch spring water. When we got back to the house Michele dismissed many of the 'various other specimens' as either inedible or downright poisonous but on the whole we had done quite well, especially with the *porcini*.

~~~

While the mushroom crop was booming, the olive crop was not going so well. It was not a serious problem for us as olive crops are biennial. Midew had taken the major crop from our trees the year before and this year was a rest for all but, perhaps, 50 trees.

However, up and down the valley things were not looking good. Other proprietors had sprayed their crops repeatedly to combat the destructive olive fly, but now the olives all around were looking bad. Men were shaking their heads in despair at San Francesco and around the card tables.

"It's too hot," some would say. Others said the fly had done the damage in the summer. But all of them asked me, "have you put the nets down?"

"No, we have very few olives and it's not worth the trouble and expense," was my well rehearsed reply.

"Ah, but you should," they would all respond, "you will lose a lot of olives; what will happen if strong winds come or even a *tromba d'aria* - tornado!"

We, of course, hadn't sprayed our trees. We wanted to be organic, or as organic as we possibly could be. Our ideals had been met with general derision from nearly all, but their methods had not saved their crops this year - we were all in the same boat and the weather would sink us if it could.

Many began to harvest in October before the fruits were ripe; normally the mills do not open until early November. We decided to wait and anyway we were too busy.

~~~

It seemed that day after day we had to exert more and more pressure on *mastro* Michele to finish off essential jobs so that we could fit the doors and windows. But our badgering and cajoling finally paid off and in the last week of October we managed to close the house.

There was no electricity, other than an extension from the meter box, no water, no sanitation. But the evening they fitted the doors I moved in. *M* would have to wait - we still had to do some treatment to the floors before we could let the kittens run riot.

That evening, after dinner, I took Fizz, a mattress, a pillow, a duvet, a torch, a bottle of Malt Whisky and a bottle of water and went to live at Villa Oleandro.

The first job was to sweep the house clean of *scroffoli* and eject any other undesirables; spray for mosquitoes, although we don't think there are any at Villa Oleandro, I wanted to be on the safe side.

With the chores complete, I went outside to watch the stars with the bottles of Malt and water.

The experience was not new to me as Michele and I had regularly visited after dark, but that night there was a full Moon; I had no other distractions apart from Fizz whose ears were in overdrive. I sat with a glass and gazed at the stars. With such little light interference - I could see about four lights at Vico - the spectacle was scintillating even with the light of the Moon.

Fizz found a toad. She pursued it from one end of the terrace to the other; barking and snaffling. The toad seemed to take no notice.

Eventually, I chained Fizz to the makeshift kennel that Michele and Leonardo had built with spare bricks before they left that evening. I went in and locked the doors to Villa Oleandro, perhaps the first time she'd been closed for decades.

It was a strange feeling and no doubt for Fizz as well. She barked and howled on and off throughout the night. I had a restless night, wondering if Ruggero was about, wondering which of Fizz's howls I should take notice of.

Dawn came. I had survived the first night.

~~~

Fizz and I went for a walk to the groves behind the house. She became alert and darted forward towards something moving fast along the ground. I stayed her.

The object was now motionless behind a tree. I crept up on it. It was a bird, a Kestrel. It had an injured wing. I moved slowly towards it. It did not flinch, only the eyelids opened and closed.

I forgot my senses and took hold of the bird around the back and wings. I was in luck, the bird for whatever reason did not plunge its talons into my bare arms, nor did it punish me with its beak. When I paused for thought I realised that I should have covered it with my jacket or something before trying to pick it up.

I carefully spread the injured wing. It had been shot.

I took it back to Villa Oleandro and put it in the back of the Jeep, from which I assumed it couldn't escape. I found a box and, with gloves on, I placed the bird in the box and covered it with a plank - there was a slight gap at the top, but I thought it ought to hold the bird while I went to Vico to perform my ablutions. I was by now in a hurry for although I still have a good grip on my constitution, the morning's adventures were stretching it somewhat. At Vico I left a message on the vet's phone.

When I returned, the Kestrel had escaped. Leonardo had seen it fleeing down the hill. It had disappeared.

Silvio, the vet, returned my call that evening and after I told him about the Kestrel, he said that someone had handed a bird in with wing injuries similar to those I described.

~~~

In the final days of October *mastro* Michele moved outside again, while electricians and plumbers went about their work. He was tasked with installing a Pozzo Immof - a biological septic tank.

The plumbers were installing the bathroom and if all came together well, I would at least have a toilet by the end of the month. No water, of course as this was another job that Michele had to turn his skills to, but a toilet that I could flush with a bucket of water. We were already bringing down a supply of water from Vico for the purpose.

It was Halloween and things were going well, until they opened the box with the toilet in it - it was another bidet. That evening I consoled myself with a large Scotch, gazed at the stars and blessed my constitution.

The toilet problem would last many more days, for on November 1st[t] Italy shuts down for *Tutti i Santi* - All Saint's Day. Then on the 2nd they have the *Commemorazione dei Defunti* - more commonly known as the Day of the Dead.

After spending three November's in Vico, we still haven't quite worked out the full nature of these days, but basically it is the festival of the cemetery and everyone goes to tend their dead. The flower shops and temporary stalls do a roaring trade, and I suppose Vico does too as many migrants return home for the commemoration. Everyone dresses in their Sunday best - I scarcely recognised Peppe *Ci'Catt*, the builder, when he appeared at *Mezz' Cavoot* wearing a suit.

In the days leading up to *Tutti Santi* the women go in their hoards to the cemetery, carrying fresh flowers and other paraphernalia. They replace any old flowers, change dead light bulbs, spruce up the marble tombs and sweep the alleyways clean.

On the Day of the Dead, the townspeople follow the route of all funeral processions on foot or by any other means of transport to visit the cemetery, now completely transformed into a sea of flowers.

~~~

After the commemoration, the mills normally open and the olive harvesting begins. This year, they had already been going for 2 weeks as worried harvesters who had not laid nets tried to save their crops before they fell to the ground.

Mastro Michele, like everyone else, has olives and we were expecting him to disappear for a few weeks to harvest them.

Pozzo

Earlier in the Autumn, we met a couple from Iceland. Snaebjorn and Susanne. They came to the Gargano for the first time and spent just a few days here. They looked at an abandoned house near us with some 150 olive trees and bought it. So we are not alone.

They had done no research, had no local knowledge, had only a sprinkling of Italian phrases and they certainly couldn't understand the dialect - they simply took the plunge.

We knew the house at La Chiusa; we had looked at it ourselves. It was a two-storey building with three rooms upstairs and two rooms downstairs, one being originally a stable with a large vaulted arch.

It was in fairly good condition. We didn't buy it because we sensed that there was an issue with a plot of ground below the house; something that you could only sense if you understood Vicaiolo and *M* of course did. Then there were the utilities; not an electric pole in sight and the only source of water, the roof.

We looked for electric and found it about 1 kilometre away as the crow flies; the chances of getting it there across country in two years were minimal. As for drilling a well, not impossible, but certainly a challenge.

Fausto, a local from San Severo, who had taken up letting on the Internet and was fast becoming a property tycoon, had taken them to see the house. They liked it and bought it.

We admired their bravery. The Italian property market is full of pitfalls; the market in the Gargano a pit full of snakes.

They told us it would be a holiday home, so it would be empty for most of the year.

We admired their courage. Empty houses here get broken into

and become empty in another sense.

But most of all we admired their innocence. One day we met them at the house to talk about what they planned and give some advice.

It was a warm October day and their young son was running around on the unkempt terrace at the front of the house. He was about to pick up an old pot.

"Stop him," I shouted. The boy didn't understand but his father quickly took the boy in his arms.

"You know you have to be careful about snakes," I said.

"Snakes?" They looked at me in disbelief.

"Oh, I didn't want to worry you, but surely Fausto told you? There are plenty of them especially around abandoned properties. Our builders have had to kill a few around our house, but it is getting better as we clear up," I explained without wanting to alarm them any further.

"No, he didn't mention them," Snaebjorn admitted rolling his eyes.

"Really, not a word?" I couldn't believe that he would just let them wonder around here without knowing the dangers, but I didn't want to put them off, "well, it's probably fine at the moment - we've made lots of vibration arriving in the cars and walking around. It's warm today, so if there were any they should be long gone."

They seemed relieved.

"But you shouldn't pick things up, like stones or old pots. Always give them a kick first," I advised "especially if it's cool at this time of the year."

I kicked the broken vase; it disintegrated - only *scroffoli* were inside.

"Are the snakes poisonous?" Susanne asked.

"Well the vipers are, certainly, even deadly," I told them what they needed to know.

"There are black ones, they just bite," I added.

I decided not to tell them about the *Pastora Vacca* for the moment. They had heard enough slithery news for one day.

M changed the subject by asking them what they would do about security.

"Security? What sort of security?" They looked at us blankly.

"Well you see, leaving a house here empty is a big risk. Haven't you noticed that most of the houses here are open?" Again, we didn't want to alarm them, but we couldn't believe their naivety.

"No, we've only seen this one and of course Fausto's house". Perhaps it was dawning on them that Fausto had not been so helpful.

"Well let's hope that you'll be OK here, it's far away from the coast where most of the summer houses get broken in to," I tried to reassure them a little.

"What about the olives? Are you going to do them?" I asked moving on.

"We don't have time, Fausto said that there wasn't much here and that he would take care of them this year on a Sunday."

Fausto was arranging everything, for himself at least.

I surveyed the trees, the olives were in better shape than ours, and decided that on the basis of our olive making last year, there would be at least 300 litres and maybe more if the olives hung on. He'd never do that in 3 months if he just did Sundays.

I gave them my opinion and they were taken aback, apparently Fausto had said there would be less than a 100 litres.

"And what about the cleaning up?" I asked, "you can't simply pick the olives. They'll need to remove all the suckers at the foot of the trees before laying the work nets. Then they'll have to cut the suckers as they advance up the trees. There's a lot of work involved. I think Fausto just intends to pop around with a stick and take the easy stuff."

"Well what can we do? We can't be here. It's our busiest time of year at work back in Iceland," Snaebjorn shrugged helplessly.

"Perhaps I can get Damiano, our worker, to do the olives for you. We have very little to harvest this year and we've paid his National Insurance for days that he won't be able to do with us. I could help too."

I had been wondering what we were going to do with Damiano for some time and this would be an ideal solution.

"That would be great," Snaebjorn seemed genuinely pleased with the idea. "I'll pay you of course."

"And what will you want to do with the oil?" I asked.

"Bottle it and ship it to Iceland," he replied, without hesitation.

~~~

With the nights getting cold, we were eager to install a wood-burner in the kitchen. The Main Hall wood-burner would have to wait until *mastro* Michele had built the fireplace, for the moment there were still other priorities outside.

Michele had taken a few days off to do his olives. When he came back he started work on the water storage tank near the wellhead. We were originally going to use the water storage tank that Damiano and Mario had cleaned, but Michele persuaded us to use another location near the wellhead. It would solve many practical issues and we could save the roof water as a reserve in the old *cisterna*. We agreed.

There was already a huge hole in the ground at the location he had chosen, which must have been earmarked to hold water many years ago. We simply had to line the floors and walls and put a roof on.

The installers arrived late one afternoon with the wood-burner for the kitchen. They unpacked it, read the instructions and started to install.

I returned with a load of wood half an hour later and they'd done nothing. They were both outside, one on his mobile phone, the other was scratching his head. *M* revealed, "they've unpacked everything and the feet are missing. Without the feet they can't start. They're talking to the office now trying to find a solution."

They came back into the kitchen and began to pack up. They had no answer; we would have to wait while they got spares from the factory.

M started to clear up. She picked up a piece of the polystyrene packaging and noticed it was remarkably heavy. She turned it over and there were the feet inside the moulding. It didn't inspire confidence.

The fitters looked decidedly disappointed as they unpacked their tools again and set to work.

I returned a little later with another load of wood and went to see if there was any progress. There had been.

The two fitters stepped back to admire their work. The immediate impression was that it looked fine, but then we noticed that the door was crooked. Closer inspection revealed that the whole stove was skew-if. We pointed it out.

"Oh, no that's how it's supposed to be." said the slim assistant fitter who obviously hadn't a clue. By this time we had identified who was really doing the work. We turned to the senior fitter who was completely out of shape himself and told him that it was unacceptable; that he had to fix it. He didn't say a word, just got back on the job while the assistant watched.

He disassembled, then reassembled repeatedly but couldn't get it right. Sweat was pouring off him as he wrestled with the problem - we thought he might stain the, as yet, untreated floor. Eventually he threw his hands in the air and declared, "I know what's wrong - the floor's not level."

Now we knew better. We had watched Michele meticulously laying the stone. We had paid Michele to painstakingly lay the stone!

The fitter placed his spirit-level on the floor; it was a flimsy looking device that could have come out of a Christmas cracker.

"There you are," he said triumphantly, "the floor's not level".

M picked up the toy device, gave it a tap and laid it down again - it showed level!

The fitters were lost for words.

It was approaching 7.30 pm. I decided to call Michele.

"The wood-burner fitters are saying that your floor's not level," was all I had to say. He would be with us in 5 minutes. He arrived an hour later, with his wife Rosetta. We had just managed to keep the fitters from going.

His craftsman's spirit-level showed the floor to be true and the base of the stove to be out by a mile. Within no time he had the base level and watched by the fitters, he put the stove together - it was perfect.

To finish off, we tried to attach the tubes, but they were not right. There had been a mistake in the measurement, but that was our fault. There was nothing left to do that evening. Michele suggested that we keep the tubes they had supplied and that our gutter man would come up with a fix the next day. We reluctantly paid the fitters the full amount.

That evening Michele delivered the tubes to Nicola, the gutter man and gave him instructions for the modification.

The next day, the kitchen fitters came to install. We had to leave them to it as we had business in Vico, but we had confidence in them - they had fitted our kitchen at Vicolo Sancarlo.

We returned in the afternoon. Everything in the kitchen was looking good. Nicola the gutter man had been and fitted the wood-burner tube. Fast work! The weather was turning, so at least I would have a fire that night.

Then we noticed something was not quite right. The stove was completely crooked again. The kitchen fitters came to look. They scratched their heads. We looked closely at the floor and there were the pencil marks where Michele had centred the stove the night before - it had moved 2 centimetres.

The kitchen fitters owned up. Nicola's modified tubes did not quite fit. So, between them they had manhandled the wood-burner to a new position.

The stove had a single piece solid centre with a ceramic casing (one that would break if too much pressure is placed on it, as the instructions pointed out). We pulled Michele off the water tank and lost another afternoon while he disassembled, reassembled and modified the tubes on the spot to cater for the missing centimetres. We were lucky. They had not damaged the stove.

~~~

The second week in November the weather took a turn for the worse. A thunderstorm came in off the Adriatic. The window shutters rattled and the ground shook as the huge claps of thunder rolled in. The fire was a comfort.

I slept lightly, slipping in and out of dreams about crooked stoves. The storm seemed to have passed. Then just after dawn a violent thunder crack jerked me out of my sleep. The windows rattled, the house vibrated. A few seconds later the tectonic plates shifted again, Villa Oleandro shook. It was an earthquake. It was not my first, but it was the first time I registered the deep resonant noise that accompanies it, transmitted through the rock on which the house stands. It was a mere three on the Mercalli scale. Nothing serious and no damage.

The bad weather continued for days, playing havoc with our plans to move in by the 25th November, *M*'s birthday.

We took *mastro* Michele off the water storage project and moved him indoors to build the fireplace in the Main Hall. The electricians were there at the same time inserting cables into tubes.

The internals of Villa Oleandro had become a tip again. We had laid flattened cardboard boxes all over to protect the floors, but brick dust, electrician's cast-offs and mud covered everything.

M had designed the fireplace. The hearth and mantle shelf was to be constructed from some of the stones from the original staircase, the curved pillars and the cross-member in any material Michele decided appropriate, the sloping canopy in firebricks.

Michele set about the task. He laid the base, installed the stone hearth surrounding a firebrick base, then built a timber frame and inserted the moulds for the pillars, which would be made of white reinforced concrete, plastered to match the marble effect of the internal walls. After he'd built the frame, he called *M* for final details and approval. It was a good job he did!

If it were not for *M*'s keen eyes we would have had a fire at the wrong angle, a twisted canopy and a drunken top! Quite where Michele's mind went when doing jobs like this we really still can't figure out. He is a master with a spirit level, with the finishing touches but when it comes to creating something, like a fireplace, in a location where the walls are all out of square he seems to get completely lost.

With patience *M* worked out where he had gone wrong, explained the problem and Michele and Leonardo demolished and rebuilt the frame. The resulting fireplace was worth the agony.

The electricians needed little supervision, just someone to go around after them to pick up all their rubbish. The biggest issue with them was the placing of switches.

Here in Italy they have a way of doing things that we don't like too much and we were having to reform their thinking. Typically, they want to install light switches outside a room so that one can switch the light on before one enters (just in case there's a bogey man in there I guess).

In the house at Vico we had light switches outside the bathroom. In the bedrooms we had switches that turned on the light outside in the hall. Invariably I left the bathroom light on; and knowing I had this problem I was forever checking whether I had left it on or not. Every time I went into a bedroom I would switch on the light in the hall! Okay, so it's my problem and I should be able to learn that the switch nearest the door is for the hall, but I am incurable so they have to do it the way we want at Villa Oleandro.

~~~

We got a call from the property tycoon, Fausto; Snaebjorn had told him that we were going to do his olives. But there was a small problem.

Fausto had promised some of the crop to the original owners. Not all of it, just 7 or 8 trees. It wasn't his to give of course, but he didn't think that Snaebjorn was interested and when the owners approached him, he couldn't see what was wrong with letting them have some olives this year. After all, he argued, they had tended the land for the year.

"Have you told Snaebjorn?" I asked.

"No, I haven't, but I will e-mail him this evening," he replied. "I just rang to let you know that the original owner's workers would be there tomorrow."

I visited La Chiusa the next day. The workers were just finishing. They had done 10 trees - the biggest, the best and the most convenient. They hadn't bothered to remove the suckers at the base of the trees; where they had to cut the suckers higher up they had done so and just left them strewn around instead of collecting them and burning. They hurriedly left; rain was just starting again.

I surveyed the rest of the crop. The high winds and rain had taken their toll, but it still seemed worth doing.

When a break came in the weather a few days later, Damiano and I went to do the olives. We loaded up the Jeep with nets, sacks and sticks and headed to La Chiusa. Fizz rode shotgun in the back; she could now jump clear into the pickup and wouldn't let the Jeep go anywhere without her.

For three days we floundered around on the neglected steep slopes covered in long dead grass and brambles. Each day the harvest was less than the day before. In the end we made a paltry 72 litres of oil. But it was good, especially for the year. It had 0.02% acidity, making it very special Extra Virgin Olive Oil.

~~~

In the wet spell of weather *mastro* Michele sealed the floors and installed another wood-burner in the newly made fireplace. Finally the day had come when we could move in. It was the day before *M*'s birthday.

Back in February our belongings had arrived from the UK. We had arranged with Midew to rent one of his garages and on the day the removal lorry turned up Midew was there to meet us with the key.

We expected him to go away, but he stayed. As box after box was unloaded, we were attempting to organise them for long-term storage. *M* had carefully labelled them: kitchen, bedroom, living room, office, books, potties (she has a collection of chamber pots), garden and so on. We were trying to decide what we would need easy access to in the coming months while we completed restoration of Villa Oleandro.

Midew took this to be his cue; we obviously had no idea what we were doing and he would sort it out. Not able to understand the labels he started stacking boxes in order of size at the back of the garage. Meanwhile other non-box items were coming off and we were distracted as we inspected valuable items.

When we realised what was happening we tried to explain our logic to Midew, but he was like a man on a mission and a man on a mission doesn't listen. The end result was very tidy, but for the next few months we were pulling our hair out trying to find things.

Now it was time to move the lot. How were we going to do it? With the Jeep? It would take ages. No, we needed a neater solution.

We spoke to Rocco, who had brought all the sand and gravel to the house with his 25 year old tipper truck. We wanted to know if there was anyone with a suitable van. He didn't or at least he wasn't letting on, but he would do it with his lorry.

We told him he'd have to be careful, for we had some delicate pieces. He assured us he would. After all he transported the stone *portale* without breaking anything. We couldn't argue. We gave him the go-ahead.

The next day, with the help of two eager visitors from the UK, we met at the garage. This time Rocco took charge. He decided what should go on the lorry and when.

In a remarkable two lorry loads we transferred our worldly possessions to their new home.

That afternoon we unpacked our treasures, things we had not seen for 3 years. It was like Christmas and in the evening we celebrated *M*'s birthday sat on familiar chairs around a familiar table.

We couldn't move in though; not with guests. There was still no water and things were too basic, for them at least.

Four days later with our guests gone, on the anniversary of the day that we bought the house, we moved in. With a suitcase or two of essential possessions, a box full of kittens and Fizz we set off for Villa Oleandro.

The kittens didn't make a sound on the journey. When we let them out of the box, they were very wary at first. As they tentatively felt their way around, we unpacked another box containing their toys; a collection of tubes, baskets and fishing net floats that we had collected from the beach and set up their familiar play area. But they were not interested; they were already exploring the myriad of cardboard boxes containing endless amounts of rustling packing paper.

~~~

In the first week of December, *mastro* Michele finished the water store. The plumbers and electricians completed the pipes and electrics for the water supply. All we had to do now was get the electricians and plumbers together to install the submersible pump in the well - the one ordered in August!

The electricians had almost finished in the house. We had light and power. The plumbers had installed the pipe work and gas, so we could cook. But the bathroom had not yet been finished and the boiler and central heating radiators still needed to be installed.

We arranged a meeting in Vico at the engineer's office to try to sort out the water supply. The electricians agreed that they could come, but the plumbing partners were at loggerheads. Nobody appeared to know why and I was sure that the plumbers Antonio and Matteo were going to fall out and that our water supply wouldn't happen at all.

Eventually Antonio prevailed and they and the electricians said they would see us towards the middle of the month. They would call.

~~~

We kept the kittens inside for 5 days waiting until Sunday when there would not be any builders and we could safely release them - at least from a construction point of view.

It was also our first day alone at the house and we decided to treat ourselves to a special meal with something extra-special to drink that had been in store for 3 years.

First thing in the morning we let the kittens outside and kept them under constant supervision while they prowled around taking in the unfamiliar scents, obstacles and the scattering movements of lizards still basking in the December sunshine. Eventually, we felt they were safe, left them to it and I got on with the important matter of cooking a Sunday dinner as *M* continued unpacking.

It was an idyllic day and as always when cooking I sustained myself with a good bottle of wine - Centare, a favourite from Sicily made from the Nero D'Avola grape. As the afternoon drew on we celebrated our arrival and the new life for the kittens with a bottle of the fabulous vintage 89 Gosset - *M* loves champagne. As the antipasti course drew to a close, the bottle consigned to history, we moved indoors to dine leaving the kittens happily playing outside, the door open should they want to come in.

Indoors, the Main Hall wood-burner was ticking over comfortingly, two bottles of 89 Pichon-Longueville Comtesse de Lalande (a little treat from my wine cellar that was originally destined to return to France) warming nicely in the hearth.

As we dined, we took it in turns to check on the kittens; all seemed well, but just before the cheese course two disappeared. Both Tosh and Chin-Chin were in, rearranging the packing paper in an empty box; Bonnie and Tish were nowhere to be seen.

We called and called and then eventually we heard a pathetic miaow. It came from somewhere in the olive tree on the front terrace. I shone a torch into the thick growth of the tree and there were the unmistakeable golden eyes of Bonnie. She was about 3 metres up. Then I spotted Tish; she was at more than twice that height and seemingly distressed.

I managed to entice Bonnie down, by playing on the branches with a stick. When she came within reach and I grabbed her and delivered her indoors. I went back for Tish.

She was now higher up on a branch that overhung the 4 metre terrace wall. Kitten release day was not going to plan. Out here in the country, we couldn't imagine the fire brigade coming for a fire, let alone to rescue a stranded cat. What was there to do? After the champagne and wine I was certainly not fit to ride a bicycle, let alone climb a tree.

Eventually, I decided to finish the cheese course. After all, another glass wasn't going to make much difference. To say that I'm not very good at heights is an understatement and so I just hoped she would make it down.

She didn't. Eventually, we could not take the pathetic calls any longer. She hadn't moved. I found a ladder and, my knees turning to jelly, I offered it up to the tree. When I was satisfied that it was in a reasonably secure position, I began the slow climb up to Tish.

The ladder came to within 2 metres of her. She attempted to come to me but wouldn't trust her innate feline skills. I descended and re-ascended with a bamboo cane and tried the same inducements that had worked with Bonnie. It didn't work. I would either have to leave the relative security of the ladder or leave her to her own devices.

M urged me to save her.

I eventually plucked up the courage and tentatively worked my way up the branches. I was sweating profusely more from fear than exertion. I was hanging over a 10 metre drop and was still too far away to grab her. She moved away. The branch was swaying; my head was swimming. I couldn't put Midew out of my mind - a branch had snapped under him. Here I was in the thick of night, only the full moon to help me. I persevered and eventually got to within range. I grabbed her by the scruff of the neck and lowered her towards me, her claws splayed, instinctively trying to grasp at anything.

I managed to get her to my shoulder, where she dug her claws in for dear life. Single-handed, I reversed to the ladder blindly feeling for the first rung. Then step by step I edged us both down to safety.

With all the kittens battened down for the night I poured a stiff Scotch and sat watching the dying embers of the fire wondering why I had decided to become an olive oil farmer.

~~~

The day came to install the pump in the well. The plumbers ordered me to meet them at their office in Vico with the Jeep. There they loaded tubing, cables, ropes and the submersible pump into the pick-up.

The pump took me aback. I hadn't known what to expect. It was a 1.5 metre cylinder and only just fitted into the back of the Jeep.

We arrived at Villa Oleandro where the electricians were already at work preparing the control boxes.

There followed a period of apparent mayhem as Antonio organised the work - this was a job that would entail the two teams working together and, of course, the builders.

After the well was bored back in July, *mastro* Michele blocked the wellhead and made a reinforced concrete cover. The cover was heavy and now it was stuck. Michele left his job in hand to lever it open with a pick.

Meanwhile the plumbers and electricians, having finally decided how the work should progress, set about the task. First, the water tube. One hundred and fifty metres of 4 cm diameter black polyethylene tubing. We wheeled the roll from the wellhead down the drive, out of the gate and down the road towards the dry riverbed. Antonio measured out 140 metres - the pump would be suspended 10 metres above the bottom of the well to avoid immersing it in sediment - and after checking and rechecking we cut the tube.

Alongside the tube we laid 140 metres of rope, power cable and level sensor wire.

Antonio tied the thick lowering rope to a handle on the top of the pump and attached the water level sensors; the electricians connected their cables. They carried out some tests to make sure the pump circuitry was working. All was ready to go.

Franco, the head electrician and the plumber's young mate, Tonino, offered the pump to the hole. Antonio himself stood close by, grasping the lowering rope. Next on the tube came plumber Pierino then Angelo the electrician, whose job it was to clip everything together using nylon ties. Behind Antonio, on the lowering rope, there was *mastro* Michele, Leonardo, electricians Piero and Marco, Matteo the plumber's partner and finally myself. *M* was on camera duty.

As we lowered the contraption, we stopped at every metre and Angelo bound the tube and electric cables together with nylon ties. At the beginning it was easy going, but as the pump, tubing and cabling sank into the depths the pauses to fit the nylon ties became more strained. The weight was beginning to tell. I cast my mind back to when we lifted the tubing on to the Jeep - it had taken five people.

The lowering continued, with no end to the tubing yet in sight. It was a cold clear day, with winds coming in from the North. Franco, Tonino and Antonio were perspiring as they took the brunt of the weight at the wellhead. It was clear that Tonino was not coping too well, so we switched Leonardo to the wellhead to take the strain.

The end of the tube appeared 60 metres away at the bottom of the drive - we were supporting 80 metres of tube and the pump.

The last 60 metres tested everybody's strength but finally after about 45 minutes of grunting and groaning the last metre of tube arrived. At this point Antonio had to release his grip on the rope, so we all took more strain. His job was to clasp the tube in a metal bar bracket that would straddle the wellhead hole and support the whole contraption. It seemed to take an age.

Eventually, with the bracket in place and the lowering rope tied to it, we manoeuvred the last metre into position on the wellhead and all breathed a sigh of relief. I couldn't begin to imagine what we would do if the pump did not work.

The plumbers set about connecting a right-angled joint to the top of the tube, while the electricians connected the cables to the control box. With the joint in place we added the 10 metres of tube we had cut off earlier in the morning. We were ready to test.

With the power turned on, *M* directed the crew to hold the 10 metres of external tube for a photograph session. We held the tube and waited, and waited. Where was the water? How long would it take? The ever-jolly Antonio could see the suspense on my face and as usual uttered some completely incomprehensible Vicaiolo about "*Joo'wah*" that made the crew laugh.

Antonio gazed down the tube; he held his ear to it and then shook it a little as if to indicate that the force of the water coming up was making the tube vibrate.

"Here it comes," he said. *M* braced the camera and just at the point when the first water spouted from our well, she pressed the button.

The water flowed, milky with ground up limestone but it was still sweet.

The crew left the tube pumping out the milky water and retired for a well-earned and very late lunch - it was 1.30 pm and Michele had never failed to sit down for his lunch at Midday.

By the time lunch was over clear water was coming out of the tube. They turned off the power and spent most of the afternoon connecting the system to the water storage tank. As dusk came at about 5 pm the storage tank was filling nicely. The crew had worked hard in, by now, very chilly conditions and we were half way to having water in the house.

I joined them with a bottle of malt whisky and a tray of glasses. We toasted the well. Of course Italians don't sip spirits, they hurl them at their delicate stomachs and within seconds I was refilling their glasses.

Then I spotted him.

Just over the wall of the storage tank, perched on the root of an olive tree there was a tiny kitten, hunched up as if cold and frightened - it couldn't have been more than 6 weeks old. But it was very distinctive with black body, white underbelly, white chin and cheeks; its nose, upper face and head were black except for a devilish white inverted U on top of his nose that emphasised his nose as if swollen. He looked like a prizefighter who had just taken a beating.

As the crew demolished their glasses, I climbed over the wall to approach the kitten but it immediately hid round the other side of the olive tree.

I returned to my services as a barman in demand, suggesting that they might want to try adding a little of the well water to the whisky to bring out the flavour. Not a chance was their reply in unison.

The kitten reappeared. *M* came to join us and wondered what all the fuss was. As soon as she saw the kitten she scurried back to the house to get some milk and food, ignoring all my pleas, "we already have four cats."

The crew all agreed that the kitten was good fortune. It had brought water. The builders built it a house from spare bricks at the foot of the olive tree and having emptied the bottle they all went home in the dark and in good cheer. Antonio's parting words were that he would be here first thing in the morning to connect the water supply to the house.

~~~

The next morning Pozzo, we named the kitten after *Pozzo Artesiano* - Artesian Well, was still there under the tree. It looked sad, very wary and very stubborn. Where had it come from? We could only speculate. It looked reasonably well fed, but it wasn't trying to find its way home. Perhaps the commotion of ten men straining on the ropes had attracted its attention from far off.

M coaxed it to eat some breakfast, which it did with a wolf-like appetite but she couldn't get close.

The plumber didn't turn up. After nine o'clock we had given up on him and convinced ourselves that after 6 weeks, one day here or there now wouldn't make much difference. No sooner had we done so than he arrived looking blurry-eyed.

"Too much whisky?" I asked.

"No, no," he insisted, "I've just become a grandfather again. I've been at the hospital since three in the morning."

"*Auguri, auguri,*" we congratulated him on the birth of his grandchild and wondered again at the mystery of Italians. The grandparents go to the birth?

That morning a very happy but tired Antonio installed the pump in the storage tank to take water up to the house and connected the water supply. He adjusted the pressures and checked for leaks.

Before he left we cornered him on the boiler and the central heating. We now had cold running water and flushing loos, but hot water would be nice.

"Ah, I haven't ordered the boiler yet," he admitted apologetically. "We still have to decide whether you want an internal or external boiler," he added as if to deflect the blame.

"But we agreed," said *M*. "We have to have an external boiler until the extensions are built. You said you had one we could use until we needed the internal one."

He looked as if he'd forgotten the conversation, but then his tired eyes flickered and he admitted, "oh, that one. I haven't got that boiler anymore - I had to fit it as a replacement for someone in Vico."

"Antonio?" questioned *M* with disbelief.

"Don't you worry," he said, "I'll order it today". Then as an afterthought, he gave an unlikely promise. "I'll try and get it for Christmas."

Christmas was less than two weeks away!

Margheri' fah oo Pan'

At Christmas we had an unprecedented visit from Vincenzo and Emilia. Normally they would only ever come in the summer and one plane trip a year was about as much as he could stand. Vincenzo is more frightened of going up in a plane than I am of climbing to the top of a 12-metre olive tree.

We picked them up from the airport and brought them for a first visit to the newly restored, if still unfinished Villa Oleandro.

Only 18 months earlier Vincenzo had declared that he would never sleep out here in *campagna* and Emilia had given us dire warnings of having our throats cut in the night.

Now they were here in the dark. They wouldn't be staying of course; they would sleep at their apartment up in Vico.

But for one evening they would have dinner with us and have a look at progress. After all, it was safe in the evening and there had not been the major outbreak of crime that everyone predicted. The Great Fence robbery was well behind us. Ruggero had all but disappeared off the map - perhaps he too feared the Corpo Forestale.

Vincenzo and Emilia had visited the site in the summer when there were no doors, no floors, no plaster and no utilities. They were still sceptical then, although overall they had been impressed with our progress, they still could not imagine the finished article.

We showed them room by room, downstairs first then upstairs. The finish took them aback and they praised the skills of the builders. The heat coming from the wood burning stoves radiated throughout the house. It used to be a shell, now it was a home that just lacked a few finishing touches such as hot water and internal doors.

When Vincenzo reached the library, it was as if we had transported him back 50 years. The room we now use as a library is the *Cucina Monacesca* - Monk's Kitchen on the upper floor. We had kept it as original as possible. *Mastro* Michele had laid old flagstones from the Main Hall on the floor and rebuilt the fireplace from old stone recovered from the house. The two wooden benches, where Vichesi would chat, eat and sleep flanked the fireplace. Above the window was a recessed alcove with a wooden shelf where the Vichesi would store their bread.

~~~

Over dinner Vincenzo could only enthuse, for the *Cucina Monacesca* had brought back so many memories that he wanted to share, especially about the bread.

In the days before you could go to a shop or to a bakers to buy bread, the women of Vico used to make their own. It was a ritual that they usually performed each month; they would decide on the day to make bread and go to the local *forno* - oven, to book a time for the following day.

For most of the evening, perhaps even the night, they would prepare for the next day. They made the dough in a large wooden box called a *fazzatoor*, the size of a garden wheelbarrow, with slanted sides and a handle on each corner. Working in the little space available in their cramped homes, the *fazzatoor* was designed to be moved about easily to make way for the many other tasks in the kitchen; the daily ritual of making pasta and other preparations for the main meal of the day.

As Vincenzo reminisced he reminded us that there was no room for a table in a *Cucina Monacesca* and meals would be served in a single bowl placed on whatever was handy, usually a stool. His mother would make do with whatever available work surface. There was no running water, no sink – they washed up in a bowl using water brought from the fountain in the street.

On the baking day, a runner for the baker would pass by the houses who had booked a spot in the oven and call out to the women to prepare. The time would vary depending on the readiness of the oven, but usually it was about four in the morning when the runner would pass under the balcony and call out *"Margheri' fah oo pah'n."*

M's grandmother, Margherita, would have been up awaiting the call and she would go to work, kneading the dough to make a month's supply of bread. In those days, they used to add mashed potato to the mixture to add moisture to give the bread the necessary consistency to survive for a whole month.

The runner, having finished his rounds would check with the baker as to the state of the oven and when the baker gave the word he would re-run the route with fresh orders.

"*Margheri' fah ee' panett* - Margherita make the loaves."

In the intervening time, Margherita would have attended to the bread with whatever help she could muster from the children. Once made, the dough needed constant attention - if it was growing too fast, she removed the blankets that kept the dough warm; if too slow she added blankets. It was a month's food and she had to get it just right.

When the order came to *fah ee' panett* she would carefully work the dough into flat round loaves, each weighing about 5 kilos and skilfully shaped to a certain size - for all the women had to make loaves that would bake evenly. As a finishing touch, she would add her mark - some little token that would identify her bread. Perhaps just a sign on the surface or underneath; if she was feeling festive a modelled piece of dough would crown the loaf. Finally she wrapped each loaf in a linen cloth and arranged them on the wooden plank that lived above the door.

The runners would pass a third time and take the bread on the plank to the oven. In Winter they would often have to cover the bread against the wet and cold; in Summer it would go as is.

The ovens were enormous enterprises, each a circular dome perhaps a metre and a half high at the centre and probably 4-metres in diameter. There aren't any in use nowadays, but many examples still lie hidden in Vico.

After baking, the runner returned the large wheel-like loaves to the house where with the plank repositioned above the door, supported by two wooden poles, the bread was stacked in a domino fashion to allow air to circulate.

Vincenzo told us in great detail how his mother made the bread, but wanted to know what it was like to eat. After a few weeks how did it taste? Surely it was too dry, even stale?

"We used to wet it to revive it," he recalled, but it was best made as his favourite, *Pan' n'fuss* - layers of thinly sliced stale bread steeped in a vegetable stock or soup.

And there are many Vichesi who still like their bread wet today; they say it tastes better especially if it's been able to age a little. I imagine our neighbours at Vicolo Sancarlo, Raffaele and Angela, must eat it like that as once a month they go off to *campagna* to make a stock of bread in the old-fashioned way.

These day's there are still many bakers in Vico, but they use a modern oven and bake bread to their own recipe. I doubt whether the bread would stand the 30-day test.

~~~

No Italian meal would be complete without discussing another one. Over coffee and liqueurs we arranged the Christmas lunch. Would we have traditional goat or lamb or would we try pork? We couldn't reach a consensus so we decided it would be up to the butcher.

M had been talking with our cousin, the carpenter, and he would take her to the best Christmas meat we could find.

Vincenzo and Emilia passed the evening well in our dangerous residence. So well did the tales flow with the drink that we were unable to drive them to Vico that night.

They passed an untroubled night at Villa Oleandro.

~~~

A few days before Christmas, *M* got a call from the carpenter. The call had nothing to do with the long-awaited doors. It was to do with food.

"It's the day to get the meat. Come to the workshop tonight at six," were his orders. It was typical Vichese; we had to go tonight without warning.

M met up with the carpenter and he took her deep into the Centro Storico. They stopped at a house, which was bordering on the outlying countryside.

Inside, *M* was pleasantly surprised to see a spotless room. In the middle of the room there was an enormous chopping block made from the bole of a tree.

An elderly lady seemed to be in charge as she wished a Buon Natale to a departing customer.

A door in the back of the room opened and in walked Angelino carrying a couple of legs of goat. He was the shepherd we had encountered twice - once in the Foresta Umbra with Midew when we were chestnut picking and the second time on the safari with Michele *ah Vret'yuh*.

According to the carpenter, Angelino butchered the animals

260

outside the premises, which must have been really pleasant for the neighbours we thought.

Angelino remembered *M* and talked her through the various cuts that he had. She settled for freshly butchered legs of goat.

~~~

Italians only celebrate Christmas Day. Boxing Day is simply St Stephen's and many people return to work. Our builders were off till after New Year, though, and had gone up North to visit Michele's daughter. They took a lorry and tools and we could only assume that they would be working up there.

So, after the festivities of Christmas Day we were having a well deserved and peaceful lie-in when the phone rang. It was Antonio, the plumber. The boiler and radiators had arrived. They would be with us in an hour to start installation.

Just in time too. It was getting colder and although we had managed to keep warm with the wood-burners, upstairs was still damp from years of exposure to the elements and the drying plasterwork didn't help. Now the weathermen were forecasting snow.

In two days of frenzied work, the plumbers installed the outdoor boiler, put together the radiators, mounted them on the walls and connected the pipes. While the work was progressing we called the electricians and to our surprise they popped in to fit and test the thermostats.

Hot water was a luxury. Since late October I had been travelling up to Vico daily for a shower. *M* had endured it for a month.

We thanked the plumbers and electricians in typical Christmas spirit and sent them on their way with assurances that we'd need them back in the late Spring to work on the extensions.

We expected the snow to fall at Vico and stocked up accordingly, but the last thing we expected was to wake up on New Year's Eve to a covering at Villa Oleandro. By lunchtime we couldn't see across the valley for the blizzard.

The central heating got a much sooner than expected test. Inside the house, the four original cats Tosh, Bonnie, Tish and Chin-Chin were in a pile on the rug in front of the fire. Fizz lay beside them. Pozzo rarely strayed from *M*'s company.

It had taken a few days to get near Pozzo, but eventually *M* had coaxed him on to her lap by the olive tree and he received a good de-ticking, de-fleaing and a sex inspection - as suspected Pozzo was a

261

boy.

From then the clean and well-fed Pozzo grew in confidence. He edged nearer and nearer the house; he certainly was not going to return to wherever he had come from. He watched the comings and goings, got into near scrapes with all our other pets who were not going to make friends quickly. Then after a couple of days, while no one was looking, he dashed in through the open door and sat on a chair inside.

He can't have been completely wild. Somebody must have taken care of him before they presumably put him out on their patch of land as is the practice here. Much to *M*'s disgust the locals dump kittens and puppies with a plastic bag of scrap food. In the beginning the owner visits regularly with food, perhaps even builds them a shelter. The kittens and puppies don't leave; if they survive they stay on the patch and keep it reasonably clear of vermin or deter stray hunters and mushroom collectors.

Pozzo, like our other cats and dogs, would escape that particular existence.

His first encounters indoors with the other cats were fierce, but he was not afraid and stood his ground. If they came near he would lash out with his paw and Fizz soon got a scratched nose.

Now he was sat on *M*'s lap purring away. For the moment he was not accepted on the rug with the other cats.

~~~

Over New Year's Eve supper we reflected on the year. It had gone well, even if the building had gone slowly since Pierino and Nicola left. In ten months we had rebuilt a shell, something that we had promised ourselves that we would never consider two and a half years earlier. We had moved in and our new home was slowly taking shape. We had electricity, plentiful water from our own well. The wood-burners were burning beautifully and my woodpile was still intact. The only thing that felt strange was the lack of internal doors. Our carpenter was in no rush.

But we knew there could be no let-up. We determined that we would put *mastro* Michele on the spot when he got back. He had been asking us whether he could have some time off in the New Year to do an urgent job in Vico and we had reluctantly agreed to giving him two months off. But, there was still lots to do especially outside - walls to build, the old water cistern to repair and cover, the sewerage dispersal system was a pressing project as the more than adequate biological tank we had installed was now in full use and some kind of dispersal system would soon be needed. The list of jobs seemed endless and he needed to get Pierino back or find some other help!

He was lucky that we had not received the permission for the extensions otherwise we could never have spared him the time, but rubber-stamping in Bari was taking the requisite amount of time.

As we had learnt over the year no matter what the project, all documents appear to go to an office where they sit for 3 months. At the end of the three months 'they' do something, but not necessarily what you might expect.

Our application for a telephone was typical. The Telecom spokesperson had promised it would take an unlikely six weeks. We waited patiently and nothing happened. When we eventually rang Telecom to ask about progress some months later they revealed that the application had expired after three months. We applied again.

A further three months passed and, after the ritual following of instructions whilst simultaneously pressing buttons on the mobile phone, *M* finally got through and repeated the tiresome explanation of who we were and why we didn't have an address. The spokesperson confirmed that our application had expired again; M had to re-apply again!

Her Italian was by now very polished, not just in pure language, but how to handle people using the proper words with the correct inflection. My Italian had hardly changed and could be described as worse. I was spending life with my Vichese friends and they only spoke Vicaiolo and always insisted on speaking to me in the dialect. After all, they reasoned, we were now immersed in Puglia, living in Vico del Gargano. "What use was Italian here?"

~~~

Our olives, we considered, had been an outright catastrophe. The whole season had been plagued with bad weather, the olive fly and other pests and diseases. Our seasoned neighbours had thrown everything at their trees and warned us of the consequences of not following suit. We pleaded organic and they shook their heads.

Just about everybody's crop was a disaster. Their efforts to thwart nature had failed. The price of oil at the mill fell to an all-time low of 2.65 a kilo, less than three Euros a litre. All around in the bars at night the men would mutter about the crop; but then they'd get on with their cards - all smiles and camaraderie. The next day at dawn they would be out pruning and I would be with them, logging and burning.

We left what there was of our olives to fall off the trees. After all, as *mastro* Michele never tired of telling us, 'there would be many *Natale* - Christmases at Villa Oleandro.'

Harvest Festival

The splendid trunk of the Carob tree that collapsed

Cleaning the woods

M on the bedroom vault

Drilling the well

First Water (L to R - electrician Angelo, Antonio the Plumber,
electrician Franco, plumbers mate Pierino

Whisper - walking blindly on the
beach at San Menaio

Bonnie - on the alert

Beautiful Chin-Chin

Pozzo - on the day he arrived

Tish - on an olive root

Tosh - on the scaffolding

Cat pile-up - on top of the boiler

Fizz in her pick-up truck

Michele, Leonardo and Zio Pierino position another column

Installing the Portale half-arches in readiness for the keystone

Portale and front door

Villa Oleandro - recreated by Mastro Michele and his son Leonardo

Villa Oleandro - restored

Approach to Villa Oleandro
(New Year 2004)

9915333R00165

Printed in Great Britain
by Amazon.co.uk, Ltd.,
Marston Gate.